A Guide to the Historical Records of British Banking

A Guide to the Historical Records of British Banking

L.S. Pressnell and John Orbell

with the assistance of
Rosemary Ashbee
John Booker
Kathleen Bryon
Edwin Green
Lesley Millar
Michael Moss
Richard Reed
Veronica Stokes
Audrey Taylor

St. Martin's Press, New York

ISBN 0-312-35303-0

Contents

Acknowledgements

British banks have played a key role in the development of Britain and of many other countries. The appointment of archivists by many banks and the deposit by others of their historical records in record offices demonstrate the banking community's awareness of the value of its historical records. These sentiments are confirmed by the generous financial support which the banking community has provided for the survey work upon which this guide is based. Without this contribution no survey or guide would have been possible.

The compilers of the guide and the Business Archives Council, which has promoted the project, acknowledge with much gratitude the financial assistance they have received, in particular from the Bank of England, Barclays Bank PLC, Lloyds Bank PLC, Midland Bank PLC and National Westminster Bank PLC, but also from Alexanders Discount PLC, The Associated Australian Banks in London, The Australia and New Zealand Banking Group Ltd, Baring Brothers & Co Ltd, The British Overseas and Commonwealth Banks Association, Coutts & Co, The Foreign Banks and Affiliates Association, Gerrard and National PLC, Gillett Brothers Discount Co PLC, Hill Samuel & Co Ltd, C Hoare & Co, The Hongkong & Shanghai Banking Corporation, Kleinwort Benson Ltd, Lloyds Bank International Ltd, Morgan Grenfell & Co Ltd, N M Rothschild & Sons Ltd, J Henry Schroder Wagg & Co Ltd, Seccombe, Marshall & Campion PLC, Smith St Aubyn & Co Ltd, Standard Chartered Bank PLC, Union Discount Co of London PLC, Williams & Glyn's Bank PLC and the Yorkshire Bank PLC. In addition the Houblon-Norman Fund of the Bank of England and the University of Kent have provided financial support for the preparation of the guide for publication.

Financial support has been essential, but no survey would have been possible without the co-operation of the banking community in allowing access to historical records for listing purposes or, alternatively, by providing lists of historical records drawn up by its own archivists. The compilers of this guide are grateful to numerous chairmen, managing directors and company secretaries for the help they have provided and for the trouble they have taken. A heavy workload has fallen upon the shoulders of bank archivists and the compilers are particularly grateful to Miss R A Ashbee, formerly Archivist of

Williams & Glyn's Bank PLC, Mr J F F Blandford, Archivist of Barclays Bank International Ltd, Mr J Booker and Mr M D Roberts, Archivists of Lloyds Bank PLC, Miss K Bryon, formerly Archivist of Barclays Bank PLC, Mr D Corble, Archivist of Hill Samuel & Co Ltd, Dr G Knight, Archivist of N M Rothschild & Sons Ltd, Mr R M Reed, Archivist of National Westminster Bank PLC, and Miss V Stokes, Archivist of Coutts & Co. The Council and authors are particularly thankful for help received from the late Miss Margaret Campbell, formerly Archivist of National Westminster Bank PLC and from the late Mr E M Kelly, formerly Curator, Historical Research Dept, Bank of England.

Space is insufficient to mention the names of all the many other individuals who have co-operated in the production of this guide. The guide's compilers wish, however, to acknowledge their great appreciation of the invaluable help received from county archivists and archivists and curators in museums, libraries, and universities. Special thanks are due to Mrs Rita Hemphill, Miss Clare Findlay and Miss Clare Cahill for having typed and retyped a difficult manuscript; to Mr S H G Twining, Chairman, Business Archives Council, Major T L Ingram, Deputy Chairman and Professor J Wadsworth, formerly Deputy Chairman, for their ready help and wise counsel on so many occasions; to Mr E Green, Archivist of Midland Bank PLC, for his much valued advice on a wide range of matters and for providing details of his bank's archives; to Mr M S Moss for his indispensable help in making arrangements for the printing of the guide; and to Miss A Taylor, formerly Research Assistant, for her work in the early stages of the survey of bank records upon which this guide is based.

Use of the Guide

The guide is arranged alphabetically and the records are described according to the bank to which they relate. In all cases the bank title at the head of each list is the final title under which the bank operated. Thus, for example, the records of the hundreds of private and joint stock banks, out of which the present day clearing banks emerged, are each described separately under their final titles before merger. Each list comprises four sections: geographical location, an outline of the bank's history, list(s) of its historical records and location(s) of its records.

Geographical location indicates the town or village where the bank was based or, in those cases of banks with branches, where its head office was located. Where a bank changed location then more than one address is given. The present day county or metropolitan county is noted and in the case of London, street or district names are given when known. Overseas banks are all shown with their head offices in London, the countries in which they operated frequently being obvious from the names under which they traded.

A brief history of each bank provides dates of establishment or closure and describes the fate of the bank, for example whether it failed or merged with others. The name(s) of the bank(s) with which it merged and the name of the new bank thus formed are also given. This section also records changes in the name under which a bank operated or, in those cases of private banks which changed name frequently, just the names under which they operated for the longest periods. This information is largely taken from the list of amalgamations published in *The Bankers' Almanac and Year Book* but further details can be obtained from S L Grant *The Standard Catalogue of Provincial Banks and Banknotes* (Spinks & Son Ltd, London, 1977) and James Douglas *Scottish Banknotes* (Stanley Gibbons Publications Ltd, London, 1975). A comprehensive index of all bank titles appearing in the history section, or at the head of each list, is provided at the end of the volume.

Records are listed in date order and are not classified by function. When known, the bulk of the records is indicated, by the number of volumes, bundles, items, etc. When a series is incomplete the abbreviation 'inc' follows the dates. Branch records are listed against branch name.

The location of records section provides the postal address at which the records are stored or, in a few cases, where advice for access to them can be obtained. This is an important distinction as some clearing bank records are not always located in the central archives of banks but remain at the branch where they were originally created. Those wishing access to records of the constituent banks of the Bank of Scotland and Royal Bank of Scotland should write in the first instance, to the Scottish Record Office which has been responsible for drawing up the lists of records from which the summaries in this guide have been made. For the sake of brevity the postal addresses of the clearing banks are not given in the text. These are as follows:

The Archives,
Barclays Bank PLC,
Head Office,
54 Lombard Street,
London EC3P 3AH

The Archives,
Midland Bank PLC,
Head Office,
Poultry,
London EC2P 2BX

The Archives,
Williams & Glyn's Bank PLC,
Head Office,
67 Lombard Street,
London EC3P 3DL
(The title of this Bank is to be changed to Royal Bank of Scotland)

The Archives,
Lloyds Bank PLC,
Head Office,
71 Lombard Street,
London EC3P 3BS

The Archives,
National Westminster Bank PLC,
Head Office,
41 Lothbury,
London EC2P 2BP

(The old style of Ltd is used in the text in place of PLC.)

IMPORTANT

It should be noted that the co-operation of the banks with the Survey should not be taken to imply that the banks will allow access to their historical records. Access can only be granted when records are not deemed to be confidential and when facilities exist to allow assistance to be given to researchers.

Archive Resources of the British Banking Community

This guide describes the historical records of old established banks in England, Scotland and Wales. These include the Bank of England, the London and Scottish clearing banks which have been formed by merger of scores of private and joint stock banks, British owned overseas banks, merchant banks and discount companies. The guide's terms of reference exclude savings banks and finance houses. All the clearing banks and overseas banks have co-operated with the survey of records upon which this guide is based, so the description of their historical records is comprehensive. A very small number of merchant banks and discount houses have preferred not to allow their records to be surveyed so the guide cannot claim to be as comprehensive in this area.

Unlike most sectors of business the banking community has tended to retain direct control over its historical records and has not deposited them in record offices in significant quantities. On the one hand this reflects caution over protecting the confidentiality of customers' affairs, while on the other it signifies a recognition that historical records play an important role in the mainstream of a bank's current business activity — for management information, public relations and so on. Thus most of the clearing banks and some merchant and overseas banks have appointed full-time archivists: Barclays, Barings, Coutts, Lloyds, Midland, National Westminster, Rothschilds, Standard Chartered. Many others have archivists who work on a part-time basis sometimes linking this with one or more other functions within the bank. Barclays Bank International, Hill Samuel, Hoares, Morgan Grenfell, Williams & Glyn's and Royal Bank of Scotland have made such appointments.

The historical records of clearing banks consist not only of records created by banks in their present form but also of records of the hundreds of banks they absorbed as nationwide branch networks were developed between the mid-nineteenth and early twentieth centuries. Lloyds Bank expanded between 1865 and 1923 alone by taking over about 200 private and joint stock banks throughout the country, and National Westminster Bank encompasses even more. At least some historical records have survived for many of these banks and so where centralisation of records is advanced a clearing bank's archive contains material covering banking in almost all parts of the country. Such collections are very extensive. For example National Westminster Bank's archives include 3400 ledgers and registers, 5700 dossiers, 6000 photographs, etc.

The degree of centralisation of the English clearing banks' archives varies greatly from bank to bank although it is the policy of all to concentrate their historical records at head office in London. This has important implications for availability and use by researchers, quite apart from effecting the survival of records when they are uncatalogued and outside the archivist's control. National Westminster and Midland have made great strides in centralising and then cataloguing their archives. Lloyds, while it has had a central archive for many years, has recently embarked upon a vigorous policy of centralising the very considerable volume of records remaining in its branches but much work remains to be done. Barclays, and to a smaller extent Williams & Glyn's, still hold a great deal of material at their branches. Barclays continues to house at Liverpool the archives of the constituent banks of Martins Bank (which it absorbed in 1969) apart from those of the original Martins Bank which are held in London. Considerable concentration of branch and constituent bank records of the Bank of Scotland and Royal Bank of Scotland has been achieved.

With only a few exceptions, present day merchant banks and discount houses have been created by the merger of perhaps two or three older concerns, so their archives may contain material relating to their constituents. The same applies to overseas banks which have often been formed by mergers of larger numbers of banks; for example Barclays DCO (Dominion, Colonial and Overseas), now known as Barclays Bank International, was formed in 1925 through the merger of the much older Colonial Bank, Anglo-Egyptian Bank and National Bank of

South Africa, while some of these were already the results of mergers of other concerns. The archives of such banks mostly consist of records created at head office, as it has not yet become general policy to gather overseas branch records into the London archive. The only substantial deposits of overseas bank records are of the Ionian Bank at the London School of Economics and of the constituent banks of the Bank of London & South America at University College, London.

Merchant banks and discount houses have been the most enthusiastic depositors of historical records in record offices, perhaps because their generally small size has not allowed them to make effective in-house provision for keeping such records and making them available to researchers. As most old established merchant banks and discount houses are located in the City of London, the Guildhall Library has become the major centre in Britain for deposited banking records. It holds historical records of Baring Brothers, Brown Shipley, Antony Gibbs, Hambros, Kleinwort Benson and other merchant banks, as well as those of discount houses such as Cater Allen, Gerrard and National, Gilletts and Smith St Aubyn. The records of the defunct merchant bank of Huths are largely held at University College, London while those of Brandts are at the London School of Economics and the University of Nottingham.

A few private bank and joint stock bank records have been deposited in local authority record offices by clearing banks, often before the establishment of a Head Office archive. However most deposited private and joint stock bank records consist of partnership papers and papers circulated to shareholders and have been placed on deposit by private individuals. Some useful, and remarkably extensive, collections of bank records are held in the Public Record Office; these were submitted as exhibits in legal actions, but were not subsequently reclaimed.

The guide excludes some classes of records. While it describes the major series such as partnership and corporate records relating to ownership and administration, records relating to customers, and accounting, investment, premises and staff records, it does not include reference to bank notes, cheques, share certificates, premises deeds, photographs of staff and premises or customers' passbooks except where they have a special significance. Such records exist in large numbers both in bank archives and in record offices and their description would consume an undue amount of space. It should also be stressed that this guide provides a description of historical records at one point in time. Hitherto unidentified records are continuously being located and the absence of references in the lists to relevant material must not discourage a researcher from getting in touch with banks.

The guide does not always describe the post-1914 records of banks. This is particularly the case with clearing bank records. Such records have sometimes not yet come under the direct control of the archivist although he may have access to them, while access to twentieth century customers' records cannot be given freely at present. Notwithstanding this, researchers requiring access to later material should not be in the least discouraged from applying to the banks for help. There are many instances of banks opening up twentieth century records to researchers. Moreover twentieth-century bank records appear to have a much higher survival rate than earlier records, reflecting more careful record keeping and the major reorganisation in British banking in the thirty years to 1918 which undoubtedly reduced the prospects for the survival of older records.

Access to banking records has become steadily easier over the past decade, and there is a genuine desire by banks to encourage the use of their records by historians. The attitudes of banks inevitably vary however, especially when access to customer records is required. Most banks will ask researchers for letters of introduction from, say, a supervisor or similar authority and they will ask to read, and perhaps to approve, what is written based on information extracted from their archives, before publication. Where a researcher wishes access to relatively recent customer records, then a bank might endeavour to obtain the permission of the customers' successor before making any records available. In the first instance the researcher should make written application for access to bank records. Applications should be addressed to the Archivist, when one exists, otherwise to the Company Secretary.

Functions and Structure of British Banking

An understanding of the uses to which historical records can be put demands some knowledge of the different functions of the organisation creating the records. Traditionally the principal functions of British banking have been distinguished according to those of the five main types of financial institutions: clearing banks, merchant banks, discount houses and British overseas banks, with the Bank of England at their head.

When describing the work of banks in the eighteenth and nineteenth centuries, an explanation of a crucial instrument used in the finance of industry and trade, the bill of exchange, is in place. In effect, it represented an undertaking to make payment of a stated sum at a future date (most often three or six months) for goods received in the present. It provided a merchant, say, with credit for the period between purchasing goods and selling them to the retailer or consumer. Whilst, however, this eased the merchant's management of his cash flows it did not directly assist the manufacturer who might need funds immediately to purchase raw materials or to pay wages. The problem was overcome by discounting the bill. The manufacturer found a third party with surplus funds to whom he 'sold' or discounted the bill for an amount slightly less than its face value; the difference represented a charge for interest and for commission, the latter sometimes being separately distinguished. When the bill matured it was presented to the merchant, or his agent or bank, for payment.

This explains the mechanism in its simplest form. In practice it was a good deal more elaborate. There were two particular problems: what happened if there were not regular facilities for financial intermediation by discounting, and what happened if the merchant could not make payment when the bill matured?

A mechanism developed during the eighteenth and nineteenth centuries for discounting bills originating in regions which were relatively short of capital. Country banks were active discounters, but, should they have insufficient resources to discount all the bills coming forward, or if they needed to realise bills in order to replenish their liquidity, they might send them to the London money market for re-discount. They sent these bills either indirectly, through their London bank agents, or — increasingly from the period of the Napoleonic wars — directly to bill-brokers, who put those wishing to dispose of bills in touch with others who had surplus funds for discounting. Later the bill-brokers evolved into discount houses, which borrowed money in order to discount on their own account.

The problem of ensuring that there would be sufficient confidence in the ability of the merchant to provide funds for the settlement of the bill on maturity was substantially resolved when banks or merchant banks 'accepted' bills drawn on them by their customers. In this manner banks guaranteed, in return for a small commission, that the bill would be paid.

The Bank of England

Since the end of the seventeenth century the Bank has been at the centre of British banking, although in the eighteenth century its activities were largely restricted to London. It was, in effect, the Bank of London. Formed by merchants and financiers in 1694 it soon obtained a monopoly in England of joint stock banking. From the outset it was the Government's bank, frequently making interest free loans in return for a renewal of its statutes, and also holding government balances, handling the Government's foreign payments, issuing and receiving subscriptions for government stocks and Exchequer bills, purchasing gold and silver for the mint and government, and so on.

From its earliest days the Bank also acted as a commercial bank, although this is now a comparatively minor aspect of its business. It originally held accounts of London based chartered trading companies, merchant houses and later manufacturing companies, discounting their bills of exchange, making short-term loans and undertaking other general banking business.

An increasingly important function carried on alongside its role as government and private banker was the issue of bank notes which initially passed into circulation through loans made to the Government and credit extended in the money market. These notes were literally promises to pay and thus had to be backed by substantial bullion reserves. By 1770 the Bank had a virtual monopoly of note issue in London, having displaced the notes of London private bankers. The 1844 Bank Charter Act was designed to secure the ultimate concentration of note issue in England in the hands of the Bank by restricting private issues, within prescribed limits, to those already existing at the time of the Act. The issue of Bank of England notes in the provinces was stimulated by the establishment of branches in a number of major cities, beginning in the 1820s with those at Manchester and Liverpool and shortly afterwards at Leeds, Birmingham, Newcastle and elsewhere.

Confidence in the Bank, and confidence in the notes it issued, led to its emergence as lender of last resort and its central role in the money market. Merchants who could not find accommodation from their private bankers sought discounts from the Bank and eventually it came to act in the same way for private banks that had run short of cash. London private banks, and later country and joint stock banks, began to hold some of their reserves with the Bank. In the 1820s the Bank was also becoming lender of last resort to the emerging discount houses (q.v.), providing the vital mechanism of allowing the immediate repayment of short-term loans made to those houses by private and joint stock banks.

In the present century the Bank has maintained its roles of government banker, private banker, note issuer and lender of last resort. On the way it has assumed a number of other diverse functions to be expected of a central bank: management of the Exchange Equalisation Account, supervision of the money market, operating in the foreign exchange market in order to protect the pound sterling, concern with industrial reorganisation and with the affairs of specific companies when national or banking interests were at stake, regulation of the banking community to preserve good order and early warning of banks in difficulties, and, most importantly, general control over the money market through its influence upon interest rates.

The Clearing Banks
The origins of the clearing banks lie largely in two distinct yet ultimately closely linked groups of banks — the London private banks and the country private banks. Each group derived capital from partnerships limited to six individuals, although the principle of multi-partnered banks was well established in Scotland in the eighteenth century.

The oldest London private banks were established about a century before the Bank of England. In the early seventeenth century scriveners and goldsmiths provided banking services. They issued notes, made short-term advances, discounted bills of exchange, dealt in bullion and foreign exchange and held customers' funds in current and deposit accounts. They had already widened the use of cheques and promissory notes. By 1677 their number is thought to have exceeded forty.

By the eighteenth century London private banks, highly respected and conservative institutions, fell into two groups. The West End bankers, which included such famous names as Hoares, Coutts, Drummonds and Childs, catered for the needs of the aristocracy, gentry and wealthy gentlemen. They made transfers and collected payments, made advances which often turned into long-term commitments secured by mortgage on landed property, invested customers' surplus funds in government and other stocks, and provided other banking services.

The second group was based in the City where customers were merchants, manufacturers and country banks. Their main business was the discount of customers' bills, or bills sent from the country by banks for re-discount. Again they kept current and deposit accounts, made collections, payments and transfers, invested funds, made short-term loans especially to brokers, but did not undertake much long-term lending. An important and lucrative function was agency work for country banks. These needed clearing facilities for the notes of other issues, transfer and payment facilities for their own customers, supplies of gold and silver and later Bank of England notes, overdrafts in times of difficulty, investment of their own and customers' funds in stock or bills, and especially the rediscount of bills.

The London private banks were restricted by inadequate communications and capital as well as by the legal constraint on the size of firms, in the extension of their business beyond London. As economic activity quickened in the provinces during the eighteenth century, so local banks were established based on local capital. Some of these established their own London banks, and some others had partners jointly with London banks. By mid-century there were about a dozen country banks, but by 1784 numbers had reached about 120, and then 290 by 1797, 370 by 1800 and 650 by 1810. Most were formed by local merchants, manufacturers, brewers, drapers, millers and lawyers, and in their earliest form might consist of just a counter in a general office, although most soon became entirely independent businesses. They discounted bills, made short-term loans and usually issued their own notes. The confidence they attracted resulted in current and deposit accounts being opened in their ledgers.

Concern with the stability of the financial structure in the deflationary period after the Napoleonic Wars, and experience of banking difficulties during the financial crisis of 1825, led to measures to protect the currency and to strengthen the banking system. In addition to the formal establishment of the gold standard in 1816, these included the restriction of private note issues to denominations of £5 and above in 1826, the authorisation of the Bank of England branches outside London, and, above all, the legalisation of joint stock banking in an attempt to strengthen the commercial banking system. In 1826 the establishment of banking co-partnerships, with any number of shareholders and with right of note issue, was permitted outside a radius of sixty-five miles of London. The first joint stock bank opened in 1826; by 1833 there were almost fifty in England and Wales and one hundred three years later. In 1833 the first joint stock bank was formed in London although note issue was not permitted. Restrictions, such as the inability to handle bills of less than six months date, severely curtailed the number of formations so that by 1844 only five were operating.

Joint stock banks proved successful, notwithstanding some unsatisfactory formations, both in the provinces and in London. Their wide capital base gave customers much greater confidence in their standing, especially in the industrial districts. Many country banks sold their businesses to joint stock banks or simply closed down when joint stock banks were quick to fill this gap by establishing branches. Between 1825-26 and 1841-42 the number of country banks fell from 554 to 311 while 118 joint stock banks were operating by the latter date. Moreover they were extending the number and range of their customers and were slowly extending their branch network as communications improved. Many private country banks, however, survived with no serious fear of absorption or disappearance until the low interest rates in the last decade of the nineteenth century, and the greater preference for stronger banks after the 1890 crisis, made their continued survival increasingly improbable.

By the 1880s the number of private banks had fallen greatly despite attempts to establish their own branch banks. The number of joint stock banks had not grown but they had trebled the number of their branch offices, expanded the number of customers at a higher rate, and in the process absorbed many private banks. Most, however, remained regional banks, although a handful were operating both in the provinces and the capital. In the 1880s and 1890s the large clearing banks with head offices in London and nationwide networks, began to take shape. Lloyds Bank in 1884, and the Midland Bank in 1891 (then known as the Birmingham & Midland Bank), acquired existing London banks. Barclays was formed, unusually, by the amalgamation of thirteen private banks in 1896. The small country banks were now fast disappearing with just thirty-five in business in 1904. National banks were firmly established by 1900, although it was not until 1918 that the so-called 'Big Five' were recognisable, with banking resources equal to nearly two-thirds of the total for the whole country. By then the term clearing bank, denoting membership of the London Clearing House for the settlement of payments to each other, had come into general use to denote the major banks.

Several decades before this, loans and overdrafts had already eclipsed the inland bill as the means of financing business and, with the increasingly complex needs of customers, a much wider range of services began to develop. In 1905 the Midland Bank opened a special foreign exchange department, for example, and shortly afterwards the larger banks began to act for customers as trustees and executors.

Merchant Banks

These banks have diverse histories, but have evolved by specialisation in at least one of three functions — trading in goods, accepting bills of exchange and issuing securities. An important feature is the international nature of these activities with many customers being located abroad, although in the present century domestically-based activities have become more important.

More often than not, trading was the first activity on which merchant banks were founded. This involved the purchase of goods, either at home for export or abroad for import, on their own or on joint account with other merchant houses. This led to London houses acting as agents for overseas merchants, fulfilling a wide range of functions, but mainly receiving consignments of goods for sale, arranging insurance, and purchasing goods for account of the customer.

Inevitably a banking function developed as agents came to collect bills of exchange for customers, make and receive payments, deal in exchange, hold or invest balances, etc. Those merchant houses which established a generally recognised high standing developed an accepting business or, in other words, they provided their merchant customers with 'commercial credits' under which they guaranteed to pay bills of exchange at maturity, the customer placing the house in funds immediately before maturity of bills and their presentation for payment. Such a guarantee, or acceptance, by reputable houses, of bills drawn by merchants in remote parts of the globe and whose credit standing might well be unknown in London, much facilitated the discount of their bills. The 'Bill on London' became the major instrument for financing world trade in the nineteenth and early twentieth centuries and this trade might not necessarily touch Britain's shores. Moreover, bills did not always finance trade. Merchant banks agreed 'financial credits' with foreign governments, banks and business organisations in order to provide short-term finance. In return for accepting bills, merchant banks received a commission income which, in most cases, soon replaced trading as the principal income source. Other banking business was undertaken such as the making of advances, but to a much lesser extent.

Many merchant banks also had private customers and provided them with general banking services and a degree of informal investment management. Such clients were invariably connected with the business or government customers of the bank or were related to the bank's owners.

Merchant banks participated fully in the development of London as a major international market in which to raise long-term capital. This greatly increased during the nineteenth century and merchant banks, with their widespread network of overseas clients and correspondents, were uniquely suited to issue on to the London market the securities of overseas governments, provinces, municipalities, railway companies and, later, of other business organisations. Indeed, their high reputations, which had led to the development of accepting business, reassured investors who might have little knowledge of the standing of the organisations for which the securities were issued. Later in the nineteenth century merchant banks also issued securities of British based companies; in the present century they have combined this with arranging mergers, participating in industrial reconstructions and offering general financial advice to corporate organisations. Most merchant banks remained as partnerships well into the twentieth century. Since 1945 there have been numerous mergers, particularly amongst smaller houses.

Discount Houses
These institutions are unique to the London money market. They carry on business as principals, purchasing and selling short or slightly longer-term assets such as bills of exchange and certificates of deposit, deriving their profit from narrow margins between selling and buying prices. Their portfolios are financed by borrowing very short-term, largely from banks and a range of financial intermediaries. They provide a mechanism in the London money market whereby banks and other financial institutions regulate their financial position on a daily basis.

Present day discount houses were formed in the last century either as partnerships or, in the second half of the century, as joint stock companies. The origins of discount houses were as bill brokers towards the end of the eighteenth century. By the end of the Napoleonic Wars there were possibly a score of them; their numbers subsequently increased slightly, but there were also failures. As bill brokers they supplemented the facilities of London agents of country banks in providing mechanisms whereby country banks with a surplus of deposits found bills of exchange in which to invest, while banks with limited deposits found opportunities for re-discounting bills. The historic role of the bill broker was to facilitate the movement of bills from areas where industry was developing rapidly, and which consequently were short of cash, to agricultural areas which had a large surplus of savings.

Bill brokers were transformed into bill dealers after the Napoleonic Wars when a general fall in interest rates led London private banks to put out at least part of their liquid reserves at rates sufficiently below the yield on bills. This transformation was eventually facilitated by the Bank of England's willingness, from the late 1820s, to provide dealers with re-discount facilities in time of need. This enabled the bill brokers to borrow such funds in order to finance a portfolio of bills. The function of bill broking might otherwise have declined with the advent of joint stock banks with national branch networks.

In the second half of the nineteenth century the importance of discounting inland bills began to decline as other forms of domestic trade finance — the cheque and the overdraft — became common. At the same time discount houses were becoming increasingly involved in the finance of foreign trade which was then beginning to grow rapidly, by discounting international bills accepted by London merchant banks. Such bills were predominantly for the finance of trade but by the end of the century the volume of finance bills drawn in connection with movements of short-term funds was growing in importance.

The outbreak of war in 1914 much reduced the volume of foreign trade and discounting of foreign bills. At the same time it caused a massive increase in government expenditure and discount houses began to hold substantial proportions of their assets in short-term government debt, especially Treasury Bills.

Overseas Banks

The presence of many 'overseas banks', closely connected with the UK, yet with their principal banking activities elsewhere, has long characterised the London money market. The establishment of many of these banks, from the second quarter of the nineteenth century, reflected in particular the close links between the economic and financial systems of the British Empire with those of Great Britain. Some of these banks were concerned predominantly with banking in a given territory; a distinctive group comprised the 'exchange banks', which specialised in the short-term finance of international trade, by providing bill finance and overseas currencies. Numerous banks were also established, with head offices in London, to trade predominantly with and in *non*-Empire countries, such as those of Latin America, for which the pound sterling was the principal currency used in their overseas trade and London their major source of external long-term capital. During the second half of the nineteenth century, there was not only a notable expansion in the formation of various types of overseas banks but also an increase in the numbers of foreign-based banks which found it advantageous to be represented in London.

Recession in world trade during the 1920s and 1930s, the constraints on trade and payments during the war of 1939-45, decolonisation accompanied by new controls by new states on banks, and the end of the old Sterling Area by the early 1970s: these brought the disappearance, often by merger, of many institutions, whilst others shifted their head offices from London, although continuing to maintain offices and active trading there.

In contrast to this reduction in the numbers of overseas banks there has been striking growth in the range and scale of their business. Many have become major international banks, providing a range of international services in many countries. Moreover, the greatly increased importance of the overseas operations of the British clearing banks has encouraged integration between domestic banking and the operations of formerly specialised subsidiaries or affiliates. Doubtless this growth, diversification and integration owe something to external pressures, but they owe much more to the opportunities that the 'euro-currency' markets have offered since the early 1960s for short-term and long-term international financing on a scale and of a compexity hitherto unknown. Further, the relaxation in some countries of previous constraints, contrasting sharply with trends elsewhere, has permitted the establishment of new overseas branches, whilst in the UK the old barriers between different types of banking, and between banking and other financial activities, have been disappearing since the early 1970s. Indeed, broadly the same influences have fostered the greatly increased representation of foreign banks both in London and elsewhere in the UK, so that American banks in particular play a considerable part in the finance of British trade and industry.

Use of Historical Records of Banks
Bank records break down into two basic groups, the first covering a bank's internal affairs and the second covering the activities of customers. The former will generally be similar for all banks while the latter will tend to vary with the different types of business undertaken. It is essential to realise, moreover, that information available in bank archives will extend well beyond the boundaries of banking and monetary history.

Ownership: Partnership records
These are made up mostly of partnership agreements which provide names, addresses and perhaps the other occupations of partners, their capital contributions and their shares of profits. They record the constitution of partnerships and the terms under which they were formed or could be dissolved. Partnership or private ledgers may contain balance sheets and profit

and loss accounts, and perhaps other general accounts, but they will almost certainly contain capital contribution and profit distribution accounts. Minutes of partners' meetings were seldom kept, doubtless because the close working environment of the 'partners' room' made a formal record of decision-taking unnecessary. Partnership records will also include papers and accounts relating to partners' private investments, and other work undertaken and public offices held.

Ownership: Corporate Records
Joint stock banks will have more diverse and much more voluminous ownership records than partnerships. The most bulky may be share registers recording names of shareholders, perhaps their addresses and occupations, the size of their holding and the dates of acquisition and sale of shares. Dividend books and sheets record profit allocation to shareholders.

The 'constitution' of early joint stock banks was embodied in a deed of settlement, otherwise known as a deed of constitution or deed of co- partnership or co-partnery. It laid down the conditions under which the bank operated and was signed by all shareholders, an important undertaking in early joint stock banks that did not benefit from limited liability.

Annual and extraordinary meetings of shareholders were minuted and recorded in general or shareholders' minute books. Sometimes proceedings were recorded verbatim. The names of shareholders attending AGMs were either recorded with minutes or noted in attendance books.

Matters considered at AGMs largely concerned ownership, such as changes in share or loan capital or election or dismissal of directors but they also provide useful reviews of the local economy and of local events in the previous year. AGMs of early banks formed the sole means by which directors advised shareholders of performance in the previous year. Eventually annual reports were issued which in their earliest form seldom extended beyond a profit and loss account, the interpretation of which is always in some doubt in view of a desire to indicate favourable performance and to avert a loss of confidence by shareholders and customers.

A most useful group of records concerns amalgamations of banks. Sometimes these might not extend beyond an amalgamation agreement between two banks, but frequently supporting papers have survived which record the performance of the bank over, perhaps, the prevous decade. They provide key financial information on the bank being taken over; profit and loss accounts and balance sheets of previous years, lists of current clients with balances, lists of bad and doubtful debts, details of staff and pension fund commitments, valuations of buildings, and so on.

The day-to-day affairs of a bank were under the supervision of a board of directors responsible for monitoring performance and making key decisions. The proceedings of boards were summarised in board minutes, and this was often done in great detail. Rough minutes, recording duplicate information, may also have survived.

Minutes will include details of decisions covering a wide range of subjects — expansion of the business through, say, the acquisition of other banks or the establishment of more branches, changes in the type of business undertaken, the expansion of share capital, changes in the distribution of a bank's assets, the establishment of links with corresponding banks, the rebuilding of premises, the appointment of senior staff, and so on. They will also contain much useful information about customers, as board sanctions were required for particularly large customer facilities, while there would also be discussion on particularly large bad debts. Reports on the performance of the bank might be summarised in the minutes or kept separately as 'board papers'.

As banks grew in size so committees subordinated to the board would be formed, each dealing with a different area of the business. In some cases 'regional' committees were formed to handle various aspects of the bank's business on a geographical basis.

Internal Accounting Records

These will include the usual range of account books kept by any business organisation — cash books or waste books giving details of daily transactions, journals which summarise these, and general ledgers to which information in the journals was posted. The general ledgers, otherwise known as 'impersonal' or 'nominal' ledgers are the most useful source by providing the basic income and expenditure accounts of the bank which, after analysis, will provide a basic scaffolding from which to deduce the bank's performance. Sometimes summary books containing the balances of general accounts were kept.

Income accounts will show, for example, interest received from funds placed at call with discount houses, commission received from discounting, charges received from the operation of customer accounts or sales and purchases of investments for customer account, commissions received from accepting, underwriting or issuing, and profits made through transactions in securities. Expenditure accounts will include office expenses, salaries, pension contributions, premises costs, etc., as well as other 'cost' accounts such as bad debts written off. Such accounts go to form the general profit and loss account which might be kept in general or private ledgers, or in special profit and loss account books.

General ledgers will also contain the information underlying the bank's balance sheet, which shows the composition of its assets and liabilities at a particular time. On the one side will be the bank's liabilities — shareholders' funds, reserves, customers' monies lodged, etc.; on the asset side will be money at call, bills discounted, investments, advances, buildings, etc. The striking of a balance of total customer funds in the bank was a time-consuming exercise and special books recording the balance of each customer's account, whether struck quarterly, half yearly or annually, were sometimes kept. In the absence of customer account ledgers (q.v.) they provide useful lists of customers and the relative size of their accounts, albeit at a single point in time.

Other accounting records include head office ledgers, in the case of banks with branches. These show transactions between branch and head office and perhaps between branches. They are important in showing the relative importance of each branch, especially through their contribution to turnover.

Where banks issued notes, note registers were kept recording number and value of notes in circulation, to whom they were issued, and when they were cancelled and destroyed.

Staff Records

Salary books are perhaps the most commonly surviving class of staff records and are particularly useful in identifying individual staff and showing total numbers employed, promotion prospects, lengths of service, different salary grades, and so on. Other records include pension contribution ledgers and papers such as minutes and accounts concerning pension fund administration. There are various other records of differing degrees of usefulness; appearance (i.e. attendance) books, clerk apprenticeship agreements, declarations of secrecy books, papers concerning social clubs, rules for the guidance of managers and clerks, and so on.

Premises Records

As premises became larger and more elaborate, so premises records became more important. They will include plans, drawings and photographs and perhaps correspondence with architects and minutes of committees supervising particularly large building schemes such as head offices. Deeds are the most frequently surviving records but they are often held outside the bank's historical archive.

Correspondence

The survival rate of letters sent to a bank, or of copies of those dispatched, is generally low, and especially so if they are not bound into letter books or kept in organised bundles.

The volume of correspondence sent and received will tend to vary with the distance of a bank from its customers or agents. Thus a local country bank probably corresponded with customers relatively infrequently, with business being conducted at intervals and with decisions and notes being recorded in memoranda or interview books. For banks based in the country, the most frequently surviving correspondence is with their London agent and for banks based in the capital it is correspondence with their country customers.

Given the distance of merchant and overseas banks from their customers, correspondents or branches, extremely extensive correspondence was created and, *relatively speaking,* much has survived. It will cover a much wider range of subjects than that covered in the letters of domestic banks. Whereas correspondence with customers will have fairly narrow terms of reference, that with correspondents or agents will not only cover the affairs of customers but will report on a wide range of matters, such as the local business community as a whole, local projects seeking finance, the political climate, the state of crops or output of raw materials such as minerals, and prices current.

With the increasing volume of correspondence conducted by the business community towards the end of the nineteenth century, more organised methods of letter-keeping began to emerge. Subject files organised into registry systems replaced general letterbooks and bundles. Certainly, from the First World War many banks had such systems in operation and much of this material has survived although, generally speaking, it is not covered by this guide.

Directors'/Partners' Private Papers

Senior managers tended to keep their own private records relating to key business affairs and where these survive they are of the greatest value. Such records may include diaries, journals, memoranda books and correspondence. Their papers may also cover private and public appointments, such as their membership of government or Bank of England committees, their directorships of industrial companies, and their connections with charitable organisations.

Customer Records

These form the most bulky, diverse and, in many ways, most valuable source of information for the general historian. However, their bulkiness has meant that survival of comprehensive series of records is poor.

This is most frequently so of customer ledgers which record daily transactions of customer accounts. In the early days of banking, especially in the country, there was often no clear distinction between current and deposit accounts, although by the mid-nineteenth century it was common for the latter to be kept in separate 'deposit receipt ledgers' or registers. This distinction had been made by London bankers much earlier. Customer accounts will identify the bank's customers and perhaps their addresses, but will also indicate sources of income and types of expenditure. However, the key to understanding the latter will be the narrative written against each transaction, and this is not always easy to interpret. Because of bulk, often just one or two ledgers from an entire series will have survived, but this is not so of many of the old London banks such as Hoares, Coutts and Drummonds and of merchant banks such as Barings, Brandts, Kleinworts and Rothschilds where large series have been retained.

Should a customer not keep his surplus capital in an interest-bearing deposit account he might invest it in securities. Certainly banks held securities for clients, mostly as collateral for loans but sometimes for the efficient collection of dividends or for safe custody at a time when securities were often in the form of bearer stock. The book in which clients' securities were recorded was generally known as a security register; such a register will again help to show the identity of customers, the nature of their investments, the periods for which they held a given stock, and so on. Sometimes securities held for safe custody were recorded in a safe custody register, when other items of valuable property — wills, trust deeds, jewellery, plate, etc. — might be listed.

Other customer records will include character reference books providing details of an individual's resources and credit rating, as collected for the bank's own use or for use by its correspondents. There will also be memoranda books, interview books and information books covering much the same ground as character books, but extending mostly to the facilities granted by a bank to its customer.

Signature books, perhaps the most commonly surviving bank record, preserve specimen signatures of customers and may also give addresses and the dates covering the operation of their accounts.

Customer Records Particular to Merchant Banks
Merchant banks will have created the same type of customer records as are listed above, but for the nineteenth century at least, they will have created records relating to issuing and accepting that are much less likely to be found in archives of other types of bank.

Records concerning issues of securities will include correspondence with the borrower and with other banks involved in the issue, the loan agreement, the issue prospectus, specimen copies of the bearer bond or share certificate issued, and perhaps loan books giving the names of those subscribing to the loan. There might also be accounts showing the financial position of the borrower and technical reports on the projects to be financed. Records relating to accepting might include account books showing the operation of credits and commercial credit agreements stipulating the terms under which a credit is granted and the procedures to be adopted for its operation.

Records Particular to Discount Houses
Discount houses' records will consist of ledgers and registers showing the funds placed with them at call by other financial institutions, and their holdings of bills of exchange and other short-term assets. Diaries or memoranda books will show the daily position of the company and provide details of factors affecting the money market such as interest rates.

List of Records

1 ABERDEEN BANK

Location: Aberdeen, Grampian

History: est 1767; failed 1849 & business acquired by the Union Bank of Scotland

Records 1: ledger 1770–71, letter book 1767–69

Records' 1 Enquiries: National Register of Archives (Scotland), H M General Register House, P O Box 36, Edinburgh EH1 3YY
Ref: list 1110

Records 2: cash books 1837–47, deposit receipts 1839–49, ledger 1844–47

Records' 2 Enquiries: National Register of Archives (Scotland), HM General Register House, PO Box 36, Edinburgh EH1 3YY
Ref: list 945

Records 3: extracts from letter books 1767–94, extracts from board minutes 1769–76, extracts from agenda books 1776–99

Records' 3 Location: Scottish Banking Collection, University of Glasgow Archives, The University, Glasgow G12 8QQ

2 ABERGAVENNY FINANCIAL CO LTD

Location: Abergavenny, Gwent

History: est 1885; liquidated 1890 & business taken over by the Birmingham, District & Counties Banking Co

Records: liquidation papers 1890

Records' Location: Barclays Bank Ltd

3 SAMUEL ADAMS & CO

Location: Hertford, Herts

History: est 1813; failed 1856

Records: liquidation papers 1843—60, agreements for clerk's service 1849 1851

Records' Location: Hertfordshire Record Office, County Hall, Hertford SG13 8DE
Ref: D/EL B338–355

4 ADELPHI BANK LTD

Location: Liverpool, Merseyside

History: est 1862; amlg with Lancashire & Yorkshire Bank Ltd 1899

Records: articles of association 1861

Records' Location: Barclays Bank Ltd

5 AFRICAN BANKING CORPORATION LTD

Location: London

History: overseas bank; est 1890; amlg with Standard Bank of South Africa 1920

Records: board minutes (10) 1890–1915 1918–1920, prospectus 1890, articles of association 1890, annual reports 1890–1920, registers of directors etc (2) 1890–1920, seal registers (2) 1891–1930, registers of members (15), share application register 1891, share transfer register 1891–1905, instalments register 1891, powers of attorney registers (3) 1891–1906, current account ledgers (20) 1891–1916, general accounts balance books (15) 1892–1908, dividend sheets (14) 1893–1920, general ledgers (12) 1894–1918, audited balance sheets 1895–1919, profit & loss ledgers (10) 1895–1906, stock ledgers (3) 1895–1935, investment ledgers (2) 1898–1920, foreign staff book c1898, branch drafts payable (16) 1901–15, branch analysis managers & staff 1901–18, 'branches & present staff book' c1903, New York agency account books (3) 1909–18, journals (17) 1910–25, balances with banks (4) 1909–21, bill registers (3) 1909–14, head office accounts (2) 1916–18, bills of exchange purchased by branches registers (7) 1918–20, liquidation papers 1920–44

Records' Location: Standard Chartered Bank Ltd, Head Office, 10 Clements Lane, London EC4 7AB
At the time of publishing this guide very limited access to the records can be given to researchers

6 ALEXANDERS & CO

Location: Ipswich, Suffolk

History: est 1744; known as Gurneys Alexanders & Co from 1878 & later as Gurneys, Alexanders, Birkbeck, Barclay, Buxton & Kerrison (Ipswich); incorporated with Barclay & Co Ltd 1896

Records: current account ledgers (c100) fl776, deposit ledger 1800–01, stock accounts 1807, licences (2) 1819 1895, opinions on banking matters (4) 1822–59, confidence declaration 1825, letters re

banking matters 1840s, partner's will 1845, letters re Overend Gurney crisis 1866, letters re silver currency 1873, partnership deed 1878, clerk's agreement 1880, private letter books 1872–96, liquidation papers 1896
Needham Market: balance books (15) 1807–74, account with Ipswich office 1835–37
Sudbury: papers re settlements and trusts 19 cent
Records' Location: Barclays Bank Ltd

7 ALEXANDERS DISCOUNT CO LTD

Location: London

History: discount house; est as A & G W Alexander; name changed to Alexanders, Cunliffes & Co in 1862 & to Alexanders & Co in 1877; known as above 1891

Records: customer ledgers (2) 1810–15 1864–71, private ledgers (3) 1810 1868–90, partners' wills (2) & re papers 1811–1901, premises leases 1812–1954, customer balances extract 1819–23 1836, clerk agreements 1836–66, papers re G W Alexander c1840–1920, reports on firms etc (7 + cards) c1850–1920, partnership deeds 1856–64, private day books (2) 1865–99, analysis of expenses c1877–1900, balance sheets & profit & loss accounts c1877–1900, stock register 1882–94, board minutes f1891, daily balances of bill transactions 1910–14, prospectus 1910, register of members f1910, annual reports f1913

Records' Location: Alexanders Discount Co Ltd, 1 St Swithin's Lane, London EC4N 8DN

8 ALLEN, HARVEY & ROSS LTD

Location: London

History: discount house; est 1888 as Allen Hellings & Co; known as above c1905

Records: general ledgers (17) 1892–93 1895–96 1911–45, scrap book 1890–1940s, ledger of accounts at banks 1905–46, investment ledgers (4) 1909–46, 'journals' (3) 1913–56, sold bills ledger 1914, diaries (2) 1914, private ledgers (4) 1920–46, directors' minutes f1934, partnership accounts (2) 1934–46

Records' Location: Carter Allen Ltd, 1 King William Street, London EC4

9 ALLIANCE BANK

Location: Manchester, Gt Manchester

History: est 1836; absorbed by Bank of Manchester 1842

Records 1 deeds of settlement 1839 1842, lists of shareholders 1841

Records' 1 Location: National Westminster Bank Ltd

Records 2: annual report 1841

Records' 2 Location: Kent Archives Office, County Hall, Maidstone ME14 1XH
Ref: U1287 C32

10 ALLIANCE BANK LTD

Location: Liverpool & London

History: est 1862 as the Alliance Bank of London & Liverpool Ltd; title changed to Alliance Bank Ltd in 1865; Southwark branch amlg with London Joint Stock Bank 1870; Liverpool business absorbed by National Bank of Liverpool in 1871; amlg with Parr's Banking Co Ltd to form Parr's Banking Co & the Alliance Bank Ltd in 1892

Records 1: prospectus 1862, articles of association 1862, correspondence with firm of merchants 1859–65, security register 1862–65, annual reports f1863, sub-committee minutes 1865–86, list of shareholders 1863, miscellaneous notices & instructions 1866–92, papers re reconstruction 1868–71, London committee minutes 1869–78, board minutes (3) 1871–92, agm minutes 1871–92, branch committee minutes (2) 1886–92, amlg papers 1892

Records' 1 Location: National Westminster Bank Ltd

Records 2: Southwark: signature book 1862–84

Records' 2 Location: Midland Bank Ltd

11 ALNWICK & COUNTY BANK

Location: Alnwick, Northumberland

History: est 1858; amlg with the North Eastern Banking Co Ltd 1875

Records: Bellingham: bills discounted book 1872–1918

Records' Location: Barclays Bank Ltd

12   ANGLO-AUSTRIAN BANK LTD

Location: London

History: overseas bank; est 1863; amlg with British Trade Corporation to form Anglo-International Bank Ltd 1926

Records: papers re reconstruction 1922–26

Records' Location: Public Record Office, Ruskin Ave, Kew, Richmond, Surrey TW9 4DU

Ref: T160/3277

13   ANGLO-EGYPTIAN BANK LTD

Location: London

History: overseas bank; est 1864; amlg in 1925 with Colonial Bank Ltd & National Bank of South Africa Ltd to form Barclays Bank (Dominion, Colonial & Overseas) Ltd

Records 1: board minutes (16) 1864–1929, agm minutes 1865–1925, staff provident fund ledgers (5) 1890–1928, chairman's miscellaneous correspondence 1900–27, private letters from Cairo 1912–22, general ledger 1919–22, analysis of head office expenses 1922–26, special committee minutes 1923–27, secretary's correspondence 1921–27

Records' 1 Location: Barclays Bank International Ltd, Head Office, 54 Lombard St, London EC3P 3AH

Records 2: papers re amlg 1925

Records' 2 Location: Lloyds Bank Ltd

14   ANGLO SOUTH AMERICAN BANK LTD

Location: London

History: overseas bank; est 1888 as Bank of Tarapaca & London Ltd; amlg with Anglo-Argentina Bank Ltd to form Bank of Tarapaca & Argentina Ltd 1888; name changed to Anglo-South American Bank Ltd 1907; business acquired by Bank of London & South America Ltd 1936

Records 1: letter book & files (3) Iquique to/from Valparaiso & elsewhere 1888–89 1922–29, letter books, (7) Santiago to/from London 1895–1907 letter books (10) Punta Arenas to London & branches 1904–34, letter books (37) Valparaiso to/from London & branches 1906–36, letter books (39) Santiago to/from London & branches 1907–37, letter books (5) Coquimbo to/from branches 1911–12 1923–29 1932–33, letter books (2) Montevideo to/from various 1912–13 1931–32, letter book Barranquilla to/from various 1921–22 1927–28 1933–34, letter books (3) Buenos Aires to/from London Santiago & branches 1924–25 1929–33, letter books (3) Cartagena to Bogota & branches 1925–34, letter books (23) Bogota to London & branches 1926–36, letter books (2) Santa Marta to London & branches 1927–28 1932–34

Records' 1 Location: DMS Watson Library, University College, Gower St, London WCIE 6BT

Records 2: annual reports 1889–1934

Records' 2 Location: Lloyds Bank International Ltd, Head Office, 40 Queen Victoria St, London EC4P 4EL

15   ARKWRIGHT & CO

Location: Wirksworth, Derbys

History: est 1780 as John Toplis; known as Arkwright, Toplis & Co 1804; known as above 1829; amlg with Moore & Robinson's Nottinghamshire Banking Co Ltd 1875

Records: customer ledgers (6) 1804–67 mostly inc, security books (2) 1857–1900, probate register 1869–1924, profit & loss ledger 1870–1901, amlg papers 1875

Records' Location: Lloyds Bank Ltd

16   THOMAS ASHBY & CO

Location: Staines, Middlesex

History: est 1796; amlg with Barclay & Co Ltd 1904

Records: Chertsey: security register 1870s, current account ledger 1895–1901 Woking: customer balance book f1890, security register f1899

Records' Location: Barclays Bank Ltd

17   ASHTON, STALYBRIDGE, HYDE & GLOSSOP BANK LTD

Location: Ashton-Under-Lyne, Gt Manchester

History: est 1836; amlg with Parr's Bank Ltd 1900

Records: deeds of settlement (3) 1836–82, board minutes (4) 1836–1902, stock register 1836–1900, staff secrecy pledges 1836–1900, managers' memorandum book 1875–80, half yearly general balance books 1880–

1900, lists of shareholders 1895–99, articles of association 1898, amlg agreement 1900

Records' Location: National Westminster Bank Ltd

18 ATHERLEY, FALL & ATHERLEY

Location: Southampton, Hants

History: est 1812; amlg 1869 with Maddison & Co to form Maddison Atherley, Hankinson & Darwin

Records: general ledgers 1797–1803 1827–30

Records' Location: Lloyds Bank Ltd

19 ATKINSON, CRAIG & CO

Location: Penrith, Cumbria

History: est 1815; failed 1840

Records: estate, personal & business papers of M Atkinson c1796–1833

Records' Location: Cambridge University Archives, West Rd, Cambridge CB3 9DR

Ref: Joslin papers

20 ATTWOODS, SPOONER & CO

Location: Birmingham, W Midlands

History: est 1790; failed 1866 & premises acquired by Birmingham Joint Bank Co Ltd

Records: private ledger 1861–76

Records' Location: Lloyds Bank Ltd

21 JOHN AYLWARD

Location: Chichester, W Sussex

History: unknown

Records: papers of J Aylward 1672–1717

Records' Location: Arundel Castle, Sussex. See F W Steer, The Arundel Castle Archives, 1, 1968

22 JONATHAN BACKHOUSE & CO

Location: Darlington, Co Durham

History: est 1774 as James & Jonathan Backhouse & Co; name changed to above 1798; incorporated with Barclay & Co Ltd 1896

Records: apprenticeship agreements 1761–98, partners' wills 1762–1850, papers re Backhouse estates 1763–1869, safe custody register 1791–1842, old debts & outstanding accounts 1797–1895, private ledgers (8) 1800–1900, customer account balance books (10) 1807–93, valuation of premises 1802–

05, banker's licences 1809–29, partnership agreements 1812–57, declarations of confidence 1816–25, general balances 1816–27, letters with Barclay & Co 1816–24, salary books (4) 1829–33 1882–1905, note register 1833–40, memoranda book re advances 1838–44, charges book 1840–44, list of bad & doubtful debts 1858–59, papers re pension fund 1864–1900, private ledger (J H Backhouse) 1866–72, cash books (2) 1870–1913, general ledgers (2) 1874–1902, cancelled note register 1881–96, balance sheets 1883–95, amlg papers 1896

Barnard Castle: current account ledgers with profit & loss accounts (2) 1838 1847, deposit account ledger 1844

Durham: ledger 1815–23

Middlesbrough: current accounts ledger 1850s, memoranda book 19 cent

Newcastle: correspondence (9 bdls) 1830–46, balance sheets 1833–38

Sunderland: balance sheets 1818–29

Records' Location: Barclays Bank Ltd

23 EDWARD BACKWELL

Location: London

Records: customer ledgers (4) 1668–72, 'Dunkirk' ledger 1659–78

Records' Location: Williams & Glyn's Bank Ltd

24 BACON, COBBOLD & CO

Location: Ipswich, Suffolk

History: est 1786 as Crickitt, Truelove & Kerridge; later known as Crickitt, Bacon & Co 1822; as Crickitt, Bacon, Duningham & Co 1825; as Bacon, Duningham & Co 1825; as Bacon, Cobbold, Rodwell, Duningham & Cobbold 1826; later as above; amlg with Capital & Counties Bank Ltd 1905

Records: security register 1868–78, day book 1882–88, memoranda book 1886–93, private ledger 1892–1908, balance sheets 1893–1904, letters to Harwich branch 1897–98, signature book 1900–08, Cobbold family papers c1900, general ledger 1903–04, amlg agreement 1904–06

Woodbridge: general memoranda & letter book 1880s, safe custody register f1895, security register f1901

Records' Location: Lloyds Bank Ltd

25 H, H J & D BADCOCK

Location: Taunton, Somerset

History: est 1777; amlg with Stuckey's Banking Co 1873

Records 1: partnership agreements (5) 1844–72, letters of advice from customers 1858, private ledger 1868–78, suspense account 1872–93, amlg papers 1872, private papers of H J Badcock 1877–1926

Records' 1 Location: National Westminster Bank Ltd

Records 2: correspondence 1801–31

Records' 2 Location: Somerset Record Office, Obridge Rd, Taunton, Somerset TA2 7PU
Ref: DD/X/HRG4

26 BAGGE & BACON

Location: King's Lynn, Norfolk

History: est 1764; known as Everards & Co from 1827; acquired by Gurneys & Co 1861

Records: partnership agreements 18–19 cent, Everard family papers & accounts 1761–1845, account with London correspondent 1769–78, cash books (3) 1809–26, letter books (5) 1826–58, customer accounts not taken over by Gurneys 1861–85

Records' Location: Norfolk Record Office, Central Library, Norwich NR2 1NJ
Ref: Bradfer-Lawrence Records

27 BAKER, SHAFTO, ORMSTON, CUTHBERT & LAMB

Location: Newcastle, Tyne & Wear

History: est 1777; known as Loraine & Co 1800; declined business 1816; otherwise known as Tyne Bank

Records 1: partner's notebook 1783–94, papers re closure 1816–33

Records' 1 Location: Durham University (Dept of Palaeography), The Prior's Kitchen, The College, Durham DH1 3EQ
Ref: Baker Baker Papers

Records 2: papers re closure (3 letters) 1816

Records' 2 Location: Northumberland Record Office, Melton Park, North Gosforth, Newcastle upon Tyne NE3 5QX
Ref: ZALC 9

28 BALA BANKING CO LTD

Location: Bala, Gwynedd; Corwen, Clwyd; Dolgellau, Gwynedd

History: est 1864; liquidated & business acquired by North & South Wales Bank 1877

Records: liquidation papers 1877

Records' Location: Midland Bank Ltd

29 BANK OF AFRICA LTD

Location: London

History: overseas bank; est 1879; absorbed by National Bank of South Africa Ltd 1912

Records: board minute books (5) 1879–1912, circulars 1889–1912

Records' Location: Barclays Bank International Ltd

30 BANK OF ASIA

Location: London

History: overseas bank; applied for charter 1840

Records: papers re charter 1840

Records' Location: Public Record Office, Ruskin Av, Kew, Richmond, Surrey TW9 4DU
Ref: T1/3471

31 BANK OF BIRMINGHAM

Location: Birmingham, W Midlands

History: est 1832; absorbed by Birmingham Banking Co 1837

Records 1: deed of settlement 1832, directors' report with list of shareholders 1833

Records' 1 Location: Birmingham Reference Library, Central Libraries, Birmingham B3 3HQ

Records 2: deed of settlement 1832

Records' 2 Location: Midland Bank Ltd

32 BANK OF BOLTON

Location: Bolton, Gt Manchester

History: est 1836; reconstructed 1880 to form Bank of Bolton Ltd; amlg with Manchester & County Bank Ltd 1896

Records: deed of settlement 1836, prospectus 1836, board minutes 1836–97, customer ledgers (2) 1839–43 1893–95, probate register 1839–1900, shareholder registers (2) 1879–95, directors' attendance book

1879–97, annual reports 1880–96, manager's letter book 1888–1900, board agenda books (3) 1888–97, loan minute books (2) 1890–98, customer reference book 1891–1912

Farnworth: private memoranda books (3) 1864–1903

Tyldesley: private memoranda book 1886–97, salary book 1892–1935

Records' Location: National Westminster Bank Ltd

33 BANK OF ENGLAND

Location: London

History: Founded by Act of Parliament 1694, the Bank was the first public bank in the British Isles. In 1708 it gained the monopoly of joint stock banking, a privilege which was given up in the development of banking in the 19th cent. In 1946 it was taken into public ownership & today, as Central Bank of the United Kingdom, has two main functions: to act as the Government's bank & as the bankers' bank.

Business: For the Government, in addition to normal banking & advisory services, the Bank provides the following specific services:

a. since 1694, the management of the larger portion of the National Debt

b. since 1844, the Note Issue, of which the Bank has had complete monopoly in England & Wales since the early years of this century

c. arranging short-term finance by way of Treasury Bill issues

d. since 1932, management of the Exchange Equalisation Account, & since 1939 the administration of Exchange Control Regulations

As banker to the bankers, the Bank holds part of the liquid reserves of UK banks & certain financial institutions & maintains close relations with them & financial organisations & markets on matters of policy; the Bank also keeps close contacts with other Central Banks, holding accounts for many of them

Records: The main series of records cover the functions described above & can be classified as follows:

Corporate Records: charters & statutes; capital of the Bank – subscription books, ledgers; general courts of proprietors – minutes, papers; court of directors – minutes, papers; committee of treasury – minutes; general ledgers covering the Bank's own business.

Banking Records: drawing & securities account ledgers (government, central bankers, bankers, private customers accounts, including accounts at branches)

Monetary Policy Records

Stock Management Records: terms of issue, subscription lists, account ledgers

Note Issue Records

Exchange Equalisation Account Records

Exchange Control Records

Economic/Overseas Affairs Records

Staff & Premises Records

Industrial Rationalisation Records

Enquiries: Ordinarily, access is not given to records which are less than 30 years old but, subject to the availability of staff, consideration may be given to specific enquiries within the period. Access to older records is restricted to historians & research workers, who are known to the Bank or suitably sponsored, engaged in approved academic projects.

Applications should be addressed to the Secretary & approval is conditional on the Bank seeing before publication the use to which their records have been put.

Many of the records over 30 years old have not yet been assessed for sensitivity nor formally transferred to the Bank's archives; applicants may, therefore, experience considerable delays before particular records become available.

Location: The Bank of England, Threadneedle St, London EC2R 8AH

34 BANK OF INDIA

Records 1: papers re establishment 1833–36

Records' 1 Location: University of London Library, Senate House, Malet St, London WC1E 7HU Ref: ULL MS 172

Records 2: prospectus & papers re establishment

Records' 2 Location: Public Record Office, Ruskin Av, Kew, Richmond, Surrey TW9 4DU

Ref: T1/3471

35 BANK OF LEEDS LTD

Location: Leeds, W Yorks

History: est 1844; amlg with National Provincial Bank of England Ltd 1878

Records: information book (customers, salaries, interest rates etc) 1865–80

Records' Location: National Westminster Bank Ltd

36 BANK OF LIVERPOOL LTD

Location: Liverpool, Merseyside

History: est 1831; amlg 1918 with Martin's Bank Ltd to form Bank of Liverpool & Martins Ltd

Records 1: share application book 1830–31, resolution books 1830–1927, deeds of settlement 1831–83, board minutes 1831–1918, annual reports 1831–1918, reports to agms 1831–38, board minutes memoranda 1831–1903, character books (2) 1831–35 1857, customer ledgers (c12) 1831–41, private ledger 1831–36, petty cash book 1831–56, general (?) ledgers 1832–35 1862–73, half year statements 1832–34, correspondence re clerks' salaries 1853, notebooks re staff, premises, etc 1870–93, amlg papers 1883–1914, private minute book 1886–1904, investment & contingency accounts 1887–1910, estate committee minutes 1889–1905, directors' & managers' register 1901–48, articles of association 1907 1914, shareholder list 1908, amlg papers 1911

Ambleside: probate register f1895
Kendal: probate register 1895–1919
Keswick: draft register f1894, security register f1894, probate register f1898
Lancaster: status enquiry book 1894–1913, probate register 1895–1954, weekly statistics book f1907
Liverpool, Church St: security register 1892–1908
Liverpool, Mossley Hill: drafts book f1898
Liverpool, Old Swan: security register 1894–1919, probate register 1897–1949
Liverpool, Victoria St: staff reports f1881
Newcastle, Quayside: head office instruction book 1892–1905

Records' 1 Location: Barclays Bank Ltd

Records 2: papers re dealing in stocks, shareholdings & sub-manager's appointment 1835–51

Records' 2 Location: Kent Archives Office, County Hall, Maidstone ME14 1XH
Ref: U1287/C10, 18, 28, 29, 36–39, 73

37 BANK OF LONDON

Location: London; Threadneedle St

History: est 1855; failed 1866; amlg with Consolidated Bank but soon rescinded

Records: staff rules book 1865, amlg agreement 1866, creditors' agreement 1867

Records' Location: National Westminster Bank Ltd

38 BANK OF LONDON & SOUTH AMERICA LTD

Location: London

History: overseas bank; est 1862 as London, Buenos Aires & River Plate Bank Ltd; known as London & River Plate Bank Ltd 1865; known as above 1923; acquired London & Brazilian Bank Ltd 1923; acquired assets of Anglo-South American Bank Ltd 1936; acquired by Lloyds Bank International Ltd 1971

Records 1: board minutes f1862, agm minutes f1863, journal 1862, balance sheets & profit & loss accounts (4) 1863–1907, general ledgers (30) 1860s 1938–58, letter books (2) 1865–66 1887–90, annual reports f1863, inspection reports 1886–1920, agm reports 1882–1925, daily committee minute books (4) 1890–99, profit & loss statements 1896–1925, analysis of profit & loss accounts 1921–36, summary profit & loss accounts 1921–36, branch capital & loans ledgers (2) 1923–59, amlg profit & loss ledgers 1923–53, head office profit & loss ledgers 1923–31, amlg balance sheets 1923–31, private ledger 1924–53, head office statistics 1926–48, agenda books (35) & supporting papers 1926–71, branch comparative statements 1930–60, profit & loss summary books 1936–65, head office circular books (30) 1936–65

Records' 1 Location: Lloyds Bank International Ltd, Head Office, 40 Queen Victoria St, London EC4P 4EL

Records 2: secretary's letter books (2) 1863–1923, letter packets (4) branches to Montevideo 1865–67 1870–73, letter books (33) London to Buenos Aires 1865–1923, letter books (28) & boxes (7) Buenos Aires

to London Paris & branches 1869–1925,
letter books (28) Montevideo to London
Paris Buenos Aires & branches 1869–1922,
letter books (11) branches to Buenos Aires
1870–1931, letter books (10) London to
Montevideo 1872–1920, letter books (6)
Rosario to Buenos Aires & London 1872–86
1890–1921, letter books (57) & packets (2)
Rio de Janiero to/from London & branches
1891–1930, letter books (4) Paysandu to
various 1892–1919, letter books (4) Paris to
Buenos Aires 1893–1908, letter books (2)
Para to various 1894–1901, letter books (7)
Mendoza to Buenos Aires 1896–1922, letter
books (4) Bahia to Buenos Aires 1898–1922,
letters Santos to Rio 1899–1901, letter books
(3) Sao Paulo to various 1899–1900 1914–
23, letters Pernambuco to/from Rio &
branches 1901–02 1923, letter books (2)
Salto to various 1905–17 1931–50, letter
books (16) Valparaiso to London Buenos
Aires & Santiago 1906–31, letter books (2)
Bahia to London 1913–21, letter books (21)
Santiago to London Buenos Aires &
Valparaiso 1913–31 1937–38, letter books
(11) Santiago to London Valparaiso &
Buenos Aires 1914–23, letters Brazilian
branches to/from London 1919–22, letter
book Rosario to various 1918–23, letter book
Montevideo 1919–24, letter books (3) Sao
Paulo to Rio London & branches 1919–30,
letter books (66) Para to London Rio &
branches 1919–37, letter books (2) Bogota
to London & elsewhere 1920–30, letter book
London to Valparaiso 1921–26, letter book
Rio Grande to London 1923–30, letter books
(15) Antofagasta to London & branches
1921–31, letters from Paysandu 1922–37,
letter books (15) Rio to London & elsewhere
1922–33, letter books (9) Buenos Aires
to/from London & branches 1922–37, letter
books (11) Brazilian branches to/from
London 1923–33, letter book Pôrto Alegre to
Rio 1923–30, letter book Bogota to various
1924–30, letter books (21) Valparaiso to/
from London Buenos Aires & branches
1924–32 1937–39, letter books (3) Bahia to
Rio & London 1926–35, letter books (2)
Barranquilla to London & branches (2)
1925–30, letter books (3) Chilean branches
to/from London 1926–27 1932–34, letter
books (2) Asuncion to Buenos Aires (2)
1928–30 1933–34, reports Peletas to London
1929, letters Victoria to London 1931–33

Records' 2 Location: DMS Watson Library,
University College, Gower St, London
WC1E 6BT
Records 3: amlg papers 1908–23
Records' 3 Location: Lloyd Bank Ltd

39   BANK OF MANCHESTER
Location: Manchester, Gt Manchester
History: est 1829; amlg 1863 with Heywood,
Kennard & Co to form Consolidated Bank
Records: deed of settlement 1829,
shareholder list 1836, annual report 1842,
board minutes 1853–63, daily minutes/
diaries 1856–63
Records' Location: National Westminster
Bank Ltd

40   BANK OF NIGERIA LTD
Location: London
History: overseas bank; est 1899; amlg with
Bank of British West Africa Ltd 1912
Records: articles of association & amlg
papers 1911–12
Records' Location: Standard Chartered Bank
Ltd, Head Office, 10 Clements Lane,
London EC4 7AB
At the time of publishing this guide,
researchers can be given very limited access
to the records

41   BANK OF PRESTON
Location: Preston, Lancs
History: promoted 1836 but not formed
Records: papers re promotion 1836
Records' Location: Lancashire Record Office,
Bow Lane, Preston PR1 8ND
Ref: DDT 33

42   BANK OF SCOTLAND
Location: Edinburgh, Lothian
History: est 1695
Records 1: records at Glasgow Chief Office:
ledgers (3) 1803–22, deposit receipt register
1810–19, customer report books (3) 1837–
54, bond books (3), 1844–1903, manager's
cash account proposals 1852–94, closing
entry book 1853–55, books of annual reports
of Scottish banks (3) 1853–1917, minute
books (2) 1855–64, casual proposals & order
book 1860–80, manager's private letter
books (5) 1862–71 1877–78 1893, private

letter books (27) 1862–1900 1927, official letter books (6) 1867–73, business statistics books (2) 1868–1913, special Edinburgh & London office in-letter books (17) 1874–98, failure book 1875–1907, security registers for bills overdrafts etc (7) 1874–1936, opinion books (2) 1873–75 'progressive view of overdrafts & deposits' 1879–88, procedure books (3) 1879–98, discount account proposals book 1887–1903, cash credit proposals book 1883–94, letters from Edinburgh office (9 bdls) 1888–96, 'results & analysis of expenditure book' 1896–97, securities letter book 1904

Anderston: branch ledgers (10) 1882–92
Cathcart: branch ledgers (21) 1878–96
Dennistoun: branch ledgers (8) 1887–92
East Park: branch ledgers (10) 1881–91
Gorballs: branch ledgers (10) 1879–86
Hillhead: branch ledgers (8) 1874–82
Kinning Park: branch ledgers (10) 1883–93
St George's Cross: branch ledgers (14) 1875–88
Stockwell Rd: branch ledgers (10) 1876–85
Whitevale: branch ledgers (10) 1874–83

Records' 1 Enquiries: National Register of Archives (Scotland), HM General Register House, PO Box 36, Edinburgh EH1 3YY
Ref: list 1110

Records 2: list of proprietors 1697–1861, record of minutes' 1696–1936, record of minutes of proprietors in England 1697–1702, ledgers, journals, allotment records, transfer ledgers re bank stock & investment (extensive) 1696–20 cent inc, general journals 1696–1809, teller's book 1696–1701, cash books 1696–1737, bank note registers 1696–20 cent, ledgers, lists, receipts etc re dividends paid 1698–20 cent, general ledgers 1703–1964, 'adventurers' journals' 1706–69, 'record of minutes of committee of directors' 1711–1805, salary lists 1730–1823, 'adventurers' ledgers' 1731–49, letter books to British correspondent banks 1751–1923, promissory notes 1764–1809, 'directors' daily sheets or order books' 1793–1803, letters to 'private parties' 1801–20 cent, private, confidential & secret letter books 1803–1970, directors' standing order book 1809–23, directors' duty rosters 1809–64, correspondents' department in letters from private parties 1809–1968, register & other

papers re bad debts c1809–20 cent, deposit receipt registers 1812–20 cent, cash, deposit, consignment, parish savings bank accounts balance books 1819–32, customer signature books 1820–1935, investment ledgers 1828–71, customer credit opinions 1830–84, 'states of deposits, loans, investments & circulation' 1832–20 cent, law department records c1833–20 cent, London office abstracts & balances 1834–1959, 'records of minutes & meetings of proprietors' 1834–1971, circular letters 1834–94, accounts with British correspondents 1834–98, government account ledger 1837–63, directors' administrative order book 1837–57, government account cash books 1838–75, register of annuities falling due 1840–94, safe custody registers 1846–20 cent, 'state of profits' apportioned among branches 1846–62, 'bills of exchange issued' 1854–1938, 'credits established for customers' 1854–1942, salary books 1855–1945, fidelity books 1857–20 cent, 'annual records' ie balance sheets & profit & loss accounts 1856–1946, arrangements, accounts, letters re foreign correspondents 1860–70, correspondents' commission on accounts etc 1864–67, half yearly balance books 1865–1960, security registers 1870–20 cent, bank property reports c1870–1935, bank surveyor's letter books 1875–1929, benefit/pension fund accounts f1880, clerk of work's letter books 1882–1931, specifications for work at bank premises 1884–1935, review of current accounts 1885–1902, 'state of the books' ie balances of ledgers 1886–1961, accountants' office circular letters 1903–24

Branch Records (with covering dates): Aberdeen, George St 1878–1943, Aberdeen 40 Union St 1780–1923, Aberdeen 355 Union St 1932–58, Aberfeldy 1857–1924, Aberfoyle 1923–61, Airdrie 1836–56, Alexandra 1906–34, Alloa 1832–1956, Alva 1955–58, Alyth 1864–89, Annan 1864–1928, Arbroath 1855–1927, Ardgay 1906–07, Ardrossan 1839–1905, Auchterarder 1834–1946, Auchtermuchty 1833–1957, Avoch 1895–1953, Ayr 1776–1934, Ayr (Burns Statue Sq) 1922–51, Ballater c1883–1912, Banff & Macduff 1878–1951, Barrhead 1857–1942, Bathgate 1848–84, Bearsden 1891–1925, Beauly 1864–1910, Bellshill 1874–1928, Blackwaterfoot 1924–30, Blackford 1868–1951, Blairgowrie (High St)

1839–1943, Blairgowrie (Wellmeadows) 1865–1934, Bonar Bridge 1857–61, Bo'ness 1898–c1961, Bonnyrigg & Lasswade 1874–1950, Bothwell 1923–32, Braemar 1873–1957, Brechin 1872–1959, Broadford 1911–59, Brodick 1922–28, Buckie 1876–1934, Bucklyvie 1876–78, Burghead 1866–1904, Callander 1842–58, Camelon 1924–52, Campbeltown 1884–1930, Carnoustie 1874–1936, Castle Douglas 1840–64, Coatbridge 1900–21, Coldstream 1855–1930, Coupar Angus 1853–1956, Crieff 1818–1971, Cromarty 1839–46, Cullen & Portknockie 1837–1955, Cupar 1955–58, Denny 1874–78, Dingwall 1839–1959, Dornoch 1839–1938, Doune 1840–1956, Dumbarton 1879–1958, Dunblane 1843–1958, Dundee 1872–1954, Dunfermline 1783–1939, Dunkeld 1834–1903, Dunning 1856–1967, Dysart 1854–1928, Edinburgh (29 branches) c1854–1969, Edzell 1945–55, Elgin 1839–1930, Eskbank 1896–1953, Falkirk 1826–69, Fochabers 1804–44, Forfar 1865–1933, Forres 1839–1938, Fort Augustus 1883–1944, Fortrose 1864–1926, Fort William 1874–51, Fraserburgh 1835–1958, Galashiels 1857–1953, Garmouth 1841–1968, Gatehouse of Fleet 1856–1924, Glasgow (12 branches) c1855–1938, Glenlivet 1875–79, Glenrothes 1954–55, Glenurquhart 1877–84, Gorebridge c1925–50, Grahamston 1922–25, Grangemouth 1874–1927, Grantown-on-Spey 1839–1940, Greenock (2 branches) 1836–1926, Gullane c1922–42, Haddington c1783–1947, Halkirk 1883–1940, Hamilton 1857–81, Hawick 1904–31, Helensburgh 1869–1949, Hillfoot 1933–38, Hopeman c1907–52, Huntly c1887–1951, Inverleithen 1863–1956, Inverness 1775–1937, Inverurie 1834–1958, Jedburgh 1864–1928, Kelso 1774–1859, Killin 1853–1957, Kilmarnock 1838–1926, Kincardine 1832–1907, Kinghorn 1932–69, Kingussie 1846–1925, Kirkcaldy 1785–1959, Kirkcudbright 1790–1957, Kirkwall 1878–80, Kirriemuir 1876–1968, Kyle of Lochalsh c1906–26, Lairg 1865–1958, Lamlash 1879–1913, Lauder 1839–1947, Leith 1829–1910, Lerwick 1838–1958, Leslie 1865–1957, Lochgelly 1856–1955, Lochmaddy 1875–84, Lockerbie 1877–1939, Lossiemouth 1865–1954, Macduff 1875–1955, Mallaig 1835–1950, Milngavie 1886–1926, Moffat 1857–1946, Montrose 1835–

1930, Motherwell 1865–1926, Nairn 1842–1958, New Cumnock 1838–1933, New Pitsligo 1852–58, Oban 1865–1927, Paisley 1836–1938, Peebles 1857–1930, Perth 1784–1930, Pitlochry 1835–1958, Polmont c1914–70, Port Glasgow 1883–1925, Portsoy 1846–1949, Partick 1911–51, Rothes 1855–1928, Rothesay 1879–1928, St Andrews 1792–1935, Saltcoats 1878–1925, Sandyford 1894–95, Scone 1930–68, Shawlands 1908–11, Slamannan 1878–81, Stevenston 1912–17, Stirling 1788–1927, Stonehaven 1825–1953, Stornoway 1874–1907, Strathaven 1837–74, Tain 1879–1960, Tarbert 1947–53, Tarland 1857–1965, Thurso Halkirk 1840–1942, Tillicoultry c1854–1957, Troon 1937–44, Turriff 1881–1957, Uddingston 1868–72, Ullapool 1865–74, Walkerburn 1937–42, West Linton 1857–1960, Wick 1878–1958, Wishaw 1921–25

Records' 2 Enquiries: National Register of Archives (Scotland), HM General Register House, PO Box 36, Edinburgh EH1 3YY
Ref: list 945

Records 3: extracts from minutes 1696–1918, copy memoranda & correspondence re proposed merger 1845–50, balance sheets & relating papers 1866–1907 inc

Records' 3 Location: Scottish Banking Collection, The Archives, University of Glasgow, Glasgow G12 8QQ

43   BANK OF STOCKPORT

Location: Stockport, Gt Manchester

History: est 1836; absorbed by Manchester & County Bank Ltd 1872

Records: deed of settlement 1836, directors' & managers' register 1836–83, fortnightly balances 1836–71, managers' notebook 1858–84, letters re customer accounts 1858–81, list of shareholders eligible for directorships 1865–72, agm minutes 1869–71

Records' Location: National Westminster Bank Ltd

44   BANK OF WALES

Location: Swansea, Glamorgan

History: est 1863; amlg with Provincial Banking Corp 1865

Records: preliminary committee minutes 1862–63, general purpose committee

minutes 1863, signature book 1863–69
Neath: customer ledger 1863
Records' Location: Barclays Bank Ltd

45 BANK OF WEST AFRICA LTD

Location: London

History: overseas bank; est 1894 as Bank of British West Africa Ltd; name changed to Bank of West Africa Ltd 1957; known as Standard Bank of West Africa Ltd 1964

Records: board minutes f1894, agm minutes f1894, registers of members (19) f1894, articles of association f1894, seal & document registers (19) f1894, annual reports f1894, balance sheet books (2) 1894–1959, private ledgers (8) 1894–1960, agreements with colonial governments 1894–1902, share application & allotment books 1896-1919, chief accountants' papers (3 boxes) 1902–56, London committee minute books (3) 1902–27, coast staff signature book 1904–24, share transfer registers (21) 1906–60, dormant balance register 1904–22, signature books (3) 1906–12, powers of attorney register 1908–56, premises ledgers (2) 1910–27, Liverpool committee minute books (2) 1910–18, analysis of charges books (2) 1911–59, profit & loss account books (2) 1911–63, Liverpool building committee minutes 1912–13, London finance committee minute books (18) 1912–42, Liverpool finance committee minute books (3) 1912–30, building committee minutes 1913–23, Manchester finance committee minute books (2) 1917–30, circulars (2 boxes) 1917–53, London foreign finance committee minutes 1918–21, premises correspondence (c34 boxes) 1920–50s, staff committee minute books (5) 1922–54, premises plans, correspondence, specifications, contracts 1920s-70s, general balance books (8) 1928–59, management committee minutes 1936–42, foreign exchange ledgers (4) f1939

Records' Location: Standard Chartered Bank Ltd, Head Office, 10 Clements Lane, London EC4N 7AB

At the time of publishing this guide very limited access to the records can be given to researchers

46 BANK OF WESTMORLAND

Location: Kendal, Cumbria

History: est 1833; acquired by Midland Bank 1893

Records 1: list of shareholders 1833, head office elevation plans 1833, shareholders' minutes 1834–93, shareholders' ledger 1834–90, out-letter book 1833–34, board minute books (4) 1857–93, balance sheets 1878–92, auditors' reports 1878 1884, annual reports 1888–93, valuation of investments 1888–90, amlg papers 1893

Records' 1 Location: Midland Bank Ltd

Records 2: deed of settlement 1834, regulations 1888, manager's personal letter book 1849–72, liquidation papers (2 boxes) c1890–95

Records' 2 Location: Cumbria Record Office, County Offices, Kendal LA9 4RQ
Refs: WDX/64; WD/MM 155–156; WDB/54

47 BANK OF WHITEHAVEN LTD

Location: Whitehaven, Cumbria

History: est 1837; amlg with Manchester & Liverpool District Banking Co Ltd 1916

Records: board minute books (7) 1838–1916, deed of settlement 1859, security registers (3) 1861–1916, general letter books (9) 1865–1916, salary book 1865–1917, shareholders' registers 1866–1903, share transfer register 1866–1913, agm minutes 1867–1916, dividend registers (6) 1870–1915, monthly balance sheets (5) 1871–1915, managers' diaries (33) 1873–1916, half yearly returns on unstamped notes & bills in circulation 1873–1919, branch statistics book 1875–82, summary of shareholder books (2) 1883–97, general ledger 1884–94, security register 1886–1913, half yearly summaries of notes & bills 1893–1916, head office ledger of branch deposits f1896, half yearly reports 1899–1911, directors' register 1901–08, deposit ledger 1902–47, note register f1910, amlg papers 1916
Aspatria: deposit ledger 1884–1913

Records' Location: National Westminster Bank Ltd

48   BARCLAYS, BEVAN, TRITTON & CO

Location: London

History: est 1694; known as Barclay, Tritton & Bevan 1797; Barclay, Tritton, Bevan & Co 1810; Barclay, Bevan, Tritton & Co 1834; amlg with Spooner, Attwood & Twells to form Barclay, Bevan, Tritton, Twells & Co 1865; known as Barclay, Bevan, Tritton & Co 1880; amlg with Ransom, Bouverie & Co 1888 to form Barclay, Bevan, Tritton, Ransom, Bouverie & Co 1888; amlg with 13 banks to form Barclays & Co Ltd 1896

Records: customer balance books 1733–47, half yearly general balances f1748, partnership deeds (23) 1783–1894, discount ledgers with private & personal accounts (c167) 1768–1895, private ledgers (c10) f1784, balance sheets 1783–1895, loan book 1798–1826, bad & doubtful debt register f1798 out-letters to bankers 1812–16, private letter book 1817–19, abstract of customer accounts 1817 1857, character book 1820–40, in-letters (22 pkts) 1836–98, current account ledgers (25) 1846–51, correspondence re Overend Gurney & Co 1864–66, weekly returns to Bank of England 1874–1904, interview book 1882–97, overseas letter book 1884–1903, papers re partnership 1888, clerks' guarantee fund rules 1889, amlg papers 1896

Records' Location: Barclays Bank Ltd

49   BARCLAYS BANK INTERNATIONAL LTD

Location: London

History: overseas bank; est as Colonial Bank 1836; absorbed National Bank of South Africa Ltd & Anglo-Egyptian Bank Ltd 1925 & name changed to Barclays Bank (Dominion, Colonial & Overseas); name changed to Barclays Bank DCO 1954 & to above 1971

Records: board minutes f1925, local board minutes 1925–31, committee minutes 1925–59, seal books 1925–44, bank ledger 1925–39, branches ledger 1925–36, head office ledgers (7) 1925–38, premises ledgers (6) 1925–44, staff provident fund ledgers (2) 1925–40, balance sheets 1926–35, daily report books (53) 1926–48, investment

ledger balance books (2) 1926–34, papers re agms 1928–44, general manager's register 1929–33, inspection report comments 1930–35, furniture & fittings ledger 1921–37, central board registers (28) 1932–37, staff provident fund balance sheets 1935–48, liquidity book 1938–41, half yearly agenda (15) 1939–46, branch statistics 1944–47, investment valuations 1939–48, papers re Egyptian Financial Agreement 1947–52

Records' Location: Barclays Bank International Ltd, Head Office, 54 Lombard St, London EC3P 3AH

50   BARCLAYS BANK LTD

Location: London, Lombard St

History: est 1896 as Barclay & Co Ltd; known as above 1917

Records: articles of association f1896, board minutes f1896, amlg papers 1896, board agenda books f1896, registers of members f1896, dividend registers f1899, allotment registers f1905
Aldeburgh: character book f1899
Alnwick: salary book 1897–1933
Birmingham local head office: board attendance books 1916–23, advance control books (2) 1920–29, legal opinion books 1920–40, bad & doubtful debt books (2) 1921–25, seal registers (4) 1925–40
Darlington: monthly balances 1898–1902
Ely: information book f1903
Halesworth: out-letter book 1896–1921
King's Lynn: status enquiry book f1899
London, Brompton Rd: security register 1915–19
Northampton: information book 1911–22
Norwich: security registers (2) 1920–49
York local head office: minute book 1902–07, monthly balance sheets 1902–38, branch statistics 1932–40

Records' Location: Barclays Bank Ltd

51   BARING BROTHERS & CO LTD

Location: London, Bishopsgate

History: merchant bank; est 1762 as John & Francis Baring & Co; known as Sir Francis Baring & Co 1801; as Baring Brothers & Co 1807

Records 1: general ledgers (c220) f1766, journals (205) f1766–1910, English /European current account ledgers (372)

f1777, American current account ledgers (230) f1800, legal documents (extensive) f1804, French current account ledgers (128) f1814, statistics of trade (extensive) f1815, reports on business houses (extensive) f1816, staff correspondence f1816, N American correspondence (extensive) f1817, English correspondence (extensive) f1817, European correspondence (extensive) f1820, S American correspondence (extensive) f1821, partners' private & personal correspondence (extensive) f1821, proposals for commercial credits & other business (extensive) f1823, private out-letter books (c90) f1831, Spanish current account legers (50) f1831, security registers (c220) f1834, issues prospectus books (2) f1850, premises papers f1853, ships' papers (extensive) f1863, Far Eastern & Indian current account ledgers (13) 1868–1905, American clients accounts supplementary ledgers (59) f1871, foreign exchange ledgers (c50) f1878, specimen issue papers f1882, Spanish clients accounts supplementary ledgers (c60) f1888, European clients accounts supplementary ledgers (c200) f1890, salary accounts f1890, stock brokers accounts (35) f1903, French clients accounts supplementary ledgers (77) f1916

Records' 1 Location: Baring Brothers & Co Ltd, 8 Bishopsgate, London EC2N 4AE

Records 2: papers re Baring family 19 cent

Records' 2 Location: Lewisham Archives & Local History Dept, The Manor House, Old Road, Lee, London SE1 5SY

52 BARINGS & CO

Location: Exeter, Devon

History: est c1783; wound up 1811; otherwise known as Devonshire Bank

Records: partnership deeds 1788–1803

Records' 1 Location: Devon Record Office, Castle St, Exeter EX4 3PQ

Ref: 1926B/BX116

53 THOMAS BARNARD & CO

Location: Bedford, Beds

History: est 1799; amlg with Parr's Bank Ltd 1915

Records: correspondence, some re note issue dispute 1798–1833, partnership agreements & relating papers 1801–1912, balance sheets

1801–1914, profit & loss accounts 1801–90, correspondence re swindle 1809–15, correspondence re run on bank 1809–10, papers re staff inc fidelity bonds 1823–1910, indemnifications for lost bank notes 1813–81, T Barnard's pass book & accounts 1806–53, security register 1841–83, amlg papers re public appointments of T Barnard 1863–1901, papers re partners' income tax 1859–1916, cash book of account with London agents 1866–76, safe custody ledgers 1869–83, partners' ledgers (2) 1872–95, profit & loss statements 1872–1915, papers re securities 1884–1904, papers re sale of business 1902–15

Records' Location: Bedfordshire Record Office, County Hall, Bedford MK42 9AP

Ref: BD

54 BARNETTS, MOORE, HANBURY & LLOYD

Location: London; Lombard St

History: est 1664 as Bland, Barnett & Co; known as Bland, Barnett & Bland 1762; Bland & Barnett 1765; Bland, Barnett & Moore 1772; Moore, Mill & Barnett 1800; Moore, Barnett, Moore & Co 1807; Barnett, Moore & Co 1826; absorbed Hanbury, Lloyds & Co 1864 to form Barnetts, Moores, Hanbury & Lloyd; amlg with Lloyds Banking Co & Bosanquet, Salt & Co to form Lloyds, Barnetts & Bosanquets Bank Ltd 1884

Records: discounted bills registers (2) 1774–75, loan book 1788–1911, general ledgers (32) 1789–1833, customer balance books (88) 1798–1883, partnership agreements 1806–84, day book 1809–62, stock ledgers 1821–52, private letter books (3) 1840–84, interest account book 1849–69, day book & profit & loss ledger 1859–64, clerks' application book 1863–84, fidelity bonds 1864–76, clerks' agreement book 1868, papers re Widows' Fund 1880s, partners' letter books (2) 1881–84, letter book 1882–86, amlg papers 1884

Records' Location: Lloyds Bank Ltd

55 BARNSLEY BANKING CO LTD

Location: Barnsley, S Yorks

History: est 1832; acquired by York City & County Bank 1896

Records: prospectus 1831, board minute books (2) 1831–96, share registers (3) 1831–96, deed of settlement 1832, share certificates & transfers (5 bdls) 1832–96, fidelity bonds (2) 1832, analysis of balance sheets 1832–58, annual reports 1833–96, memoranda books re bills & advances (2) 1841–60, estimates for building head office (1 bdl) 1857–60, security book 1882–97, security rental accounts (1 bdl) 1882–95, securities valuations (1 bdl) 1883–93

Records' Location: Midland Bank Ltd

56   BARTLETT & CO

Location: Buckingham, Bucks

History: est 1785; merged with T R Cobb & Son to form Bucks & Oxon Bank Ltd 1853

Records: partnership agreement 1845, waste books (2) 1854–55

Records' Location: Lloyds Bank Ltd

57   BASSETT SON & HARRIS

Location: Leighton Buzzard, Beds

History: est 1812 as Bassett & Grant; known as Bassett, Son & Harris 1854; incorporated with Barclay & Co Ltd 1896

Records: partnership agreements 1810–53, general ledger 1821–29, partners' minutes 1823–26, account of bad debts 1827, papers re partnership matters 1835–42, signature book 1846–91 with character reports 1846–60, probate register 1861–95, balance sheets 1889–96, amlg papers 1896

Records' Location: Barclays Bank Ltd

58   BATE & ROBINS

Location: Stourbridge, Here & Worc

History: est c1770; failed 1851; known also as Stourbridge Old Bank

Records 1: comparative statement properties at Blaenavon, Plymouth & Rhymney 1836, memoranda of agreement with schedule of accounts & securities 1851

Records' 1 Location: Midland Bank Ltd

Records 2: report re failure 1851–52

Records' 2 Location: Hereford & Worcester Record Office, Shire Hall, Worcester WR1 1TR

Ref: 6705:260 BA 4000/820

59   BECK & CO

Location: Shrewsbury, Salop, & Welshpool, Powys

History: est 1800; taken over by Lloyds Banking Co Ltd 1880; also known as Shrewsbury & Welspool Old Bank

Records: letter & memoranda book 1836–42, private ledger 1840–50, letter book 1852–57, amlg papers 1880

Records' Location: Lloyds Bank Ltd

60   BECKETT & CLARKE & CO

Location: Barnsley, S Yorks

History: est 1796; absorbed by Wakefield Banking Co 1840; otherwise known as Beckett, Birks & Co

Records: partnership agreements (3) 1796–1833

Records' Location: Barclays Bank Ltd

61   BECKETT & CO (LEEDS BANK)

Location: Leeds, W Yorks

History: est c1759; amlg with London, County, Westminster & Parr's Bank Ltd 1921

Records: partnership deeds f1776, statistics & balance books (2) 1782–1892, signature books (3) 1785–1840, ledger balance books (4) 1797–1822 inc, customer account ledgers (10) 1813–25, list of foreign bills credited to accounts 1815–16, security register 1820s, correspondence with Bank of England 1832, miscellaneous partners' private letters 1840–69, staff registers (4) 1840–1920 inc, memoranda books (2) 1840–92, security receipt books (2) 1841–79, bad & doubtful debt registers (3) 1847–91, private ledgers (5) 1857–1920, outstanding balances 1872–1920, customer interview books (4) 1864–70, sundry attendance book 1859–1911, customer balance sheets 1877–91, private journal 1880–1921, balance sheets & consolidated accounts 1891–1920, branch earnings & expenses 1896–1920, partners' minutes 1902–23, bill register 1904–14, information book 1910, investment ledgers (3) 1910–20, letters to East Riding Bank 1895–1906, premises register 19 cent, branch balance sheets 1912–13, working papers 1915–17, staff list 1920, amlg papers 1920

Retford: customer average balance book 1886–94, information book 1886–94
Worksop: customer average balance book 1888–90,
Doncaster: customer average balance book 1889–90
Records' Location: National Westminster Bank Ltd

62   BECKETT & CO (YORK & EAST RIDING BANK)

Location: York, N Yorks
History: formed by union of Bower Hall & Co, Beverley with Beckett & Co, Leeds; amlg with London, County, Westminster & Parr's Bank 1921
Records: private ledgers (4) 1875–1920, branch statistics book 1876–86, monthly balance sheets 1877–79, branch balance sheets 1875–84 inc, partners' minutes 1904–15
Beverley & Malton: information books 1880
Driffield: information book 1883–92, customer average balance book 1888–90
York: information book 1886–91
Records' Location: National Westminster Bank Ltd

63   BEECHING & CO

Location: Tunbridge Wells, Kent
History: est 1815; amlg with Lloyds Bank Ltd 1890
Records 1: amlg papers 1890
Records' 1 Location: Lloyds Bank Ltd
Records 2: agreements for loans to bank 1789–1808
Records' 2 Location: Kent Archives Office, County Hall, Maidstone ME14 1XH
Ref: U642 T38

64   BELLAIRS, SONS & CO

Location: Stamford, Lincs; Derby, Derbys
History: est c1783; failed 1814
Records: papers re failure 1808–14
Records' Location: Nottingham University Manuscripts Dept, University Library, University Park, Nottingham NG7 2RD
Ref: Dr E 89–92

65   ROBERT BENSON, LONSDALE & CO LTD

Location: London
History: merchant bank; est 1852 as Robert Benson & Co; known as above 1947; merged with Kleinwort, Sons & Co Ltd to form Kleinwort, Benson Ltd 1961
Records: general ledgers (31) 1825–1928, private ledgers (6) 1888–1926, balance sheets & profit & loss accounts 1888–1962, investment ledgers 1888–1928, stock ledgers (3) 1897–1905 1908–43, papers re Mexican Cotton Estates of Talahvalilo Ltd (c20 pcls) 19 cent, general expenses analysis book 1930–44
Records' Location: Kleinwort Benson Ltd, 20 Fenchurch St, London EC3P 3DB

66   BENTLEY & BUXTON

Location: Leicester, Leics
History: est c1783; ceased 1803
Records: notices (2) re payment of interest on liabilities 1807
Records' Location: Leicestershire Record Office, 57 New Walk, Leicester LE1 7JB
Ref: 8D39/9611 a & b

67   WILLIAM & JOHN BIGGERSTAFFE

Location: London, Smithfields
History: est 1790; taken over by National Provincial & Union Bank of England Ltd
Records: amlg papers 1919
Records' Location: National Westminster Bank Ltd

68   BIRCH, PITT, POWELL, TRIPP & BRICE

Location: Bristol, Avon
History: est 1808; known as Pitt & Co 1820; failed 1826
Records: partnership deed 1808
Records' Location: National Westminster Bank Ltd

69   BIRKBECK BANK

Location: London, Chancery Lane
History: est 1851; liquidated & business taken over by London, County & Westminster Bank Ltd 1911

Records 1: ledger of mortgaged accounts 1851–58, deposit ledger 1852–58

Records' 1 Location: National Westminster Bank Ltd

Records 2: correspondence re failure

Records' 2 Location: Bodleian Library, Dept of Western Manuscripts, Oxford OX1 3BG

Ref: Asquith MSS 24f21

70   BIRMINGHAM JOINT STOCK BANK LTD

Location: Birmingham, W Midlands

History: est 1861; absorbed by Worcester City & County Banking Co Ltd 1889

Records: prospectus 1861, board minute books (3) 1861–67 1875–89, rough minute books (2) 1862–69, annual reports 1862–89, books with details of debts of Attwoods, Spooner & Co (2) 1865, signature book 1865–91, salary report 1864, amlg papers 1889

Records' Location: Lloyds Bank Ltd

71   BODENHAM, GARRETT & SON

Location: Hereford, Hereford & Worcester

History: est c1800; failed 1826; known otherwise as Hereford City & County Bank

Records: in-correspondence c1822–25

Records' Location: Public Record Office, Chancery Lane, London WC2A 1LR

Ref: C110/96–97

72   BOROUGH OF ST MARYLEBONE BANK

Location: London, St Marylebone

History: est 1837; failed 1841

Records 1: papers & letter book re failure 1837–47

Records' 1 Location: City of Westminster Archives Dept, Marylebone Library, Marylebone Rd, London NW1 5PS

Records 2: papers re director's resignation 1838

Records' 2 Location: Public Record Office, Ruskin Av, Kew, Richmond, Surrey TW9 4DU

Ref: J90.821

73   BOROUGH OF TYNEMOUTH TRADING BANK LTD

Location: N Shields, Tyne & Wear

History: est 1885; acquired by York City & County Bank 1897

Records: current account ledgers (2) 1888–97, deposit account ledger 1888–1910, general ledger 1892–98

Records' Location: Midland Bank Ltd

74   BOSANQUET, SALT, WHATMAN, HARMAN, SALT & BOSANQUET

Location: London; Lombard St

History: est 1780 as Bosanquet, Beachcroft & Reeves 1780–1809; known as Bosanquet, Beachcroft, Pitt & Anderson 1809; known as Bosanquet, Pitt, Anderson & Franks 1816; amlg with Stevenson, Salt & Co to form Bosanquet, Salt, Whatman, Harman, Salt & Bosanquet 1867; amlg with Lloyds Banking Co Ltd to form Lloyds, Barnetts & Bosanquets Bank Ltd 1884

Records: partnership agreements 1867–71, amlg agreement 1884

Records' Location: Lloyds Bank Ltd

75   BOURNE, RHODES & CO

Location: Alford, Lincs

History: est 1844; acquired by Stamford, Spalding & Boston Banking Co 1861

Records: balance book 1861; amlg papers 1861

Records' Location: Barclays Bank Ltd

76   BOUVERIE, MURDOCH, BOUVERIE & JAMES

Location: London

History: est 1812 as Bouverie & Co; known as Bouverie Lefevre 1826; as Bouverie, Murdoch & Bouverie 1850; amlg with Ransom & Co to form Ransom, Bouverie & Co 1856

Records: general ledgers (4) 1800–12, letter announcing amlg 1855

Records' Location: Barclays Bank Ltd

77 BOWES, HODGSON, FALCON, KEY & CO

Location: Workington, Cumbria

History: est before 1800; failed 1813

Records: till books 1800–13

Records' Location: Cumbria County Record Office, The Castle, Carlisle CA3 8UR

Ref: Allison MSS

78 BOWER HALL & CO

Location: Beverley, Humberside

History: est c1790; otherwise known as Bower, Dewsbury & Co & Bower, Hutton & Co; amlg with Beckett & Co to form Beckett & Co, East Riding Bank, 1875

Records 1: papers re securities 1831–80, partnership deeds 1849 1862, private ledger 1867–75, papers re admission of partner 1870–81, balance sheet 1874, papers re financial position 1874, amlg agreement 1875

Records' 1 Location: National Westminster Bank Ltd

Records 2: 'Hull account' 1793, valuation of securities 1794–98, stock accounts 1794–99, balances of accounts 1795–99, 'list of our friends at Hull' nd

Records' 2 Location: Brynmor Jones Library, University of Hull, Cottingham Road, Hull HU5 7RX

Ref: DDSY/79/3

79 BOWLES, OGDEN & WYNDHAM

Location: Salisbury, Wilts

History: est 1790; otherwise known as Salisbury & Shaftesbury Bank; failed 1810

Records: papers re failure 1810

Records' Location: Wiltshire County Record Office, County Hall, Trowbridge, BA14 8JG

Ref: 776

80 BRADFORD BANKING CO LTD

Location: Bradford, W Yorks

History: est 1827; acquired by Midland Bank 1910

Records 1: formation papers 1825–27, deed of constitution 1827, board minute books (24) 1827–1910, private ledgers 1827–30, security registers (7) 1827–1909, shareholders' minute books (3) 1828–1910, profit & loss statement 1828, abstract of shareholders' wills books (2) 1845–97, safe custody register 1855–82, annual reports 1864–96, balance sheets 1868–1908, income tax returns 1870–1909, salary book 1871–91, certificates of incorporation & list of shareholders 1875, staff register c1890, amlg papers 1909–10

Records' 1 Location: Midland Bank Ltd

Records 2: deed of constitution 1827

Records' 2 Location: Bradford Central Library, Archives Dept, Prince's Way, Bradford BD1 1NN

Ref: B942 PAM

81 BRADFORD COMMERCIAL JOINT STOCK BANKING CO LTD

Location: Bradford, W Yorks

History: est 1833; acquired by Bradford District Bank Ltd 1904

Records: note register 1833–34, agm minutes 1834–77, annual report 1904, amlg agreement 1904

Records' Location: National Westminster Bank Ltd

82 BRADFORD DISTRICT BANK LTD

Location: Bradford, W Yorks

History: est 1862; absorbed by the National Provincial Bank of England Ltd 1919

Records: board minute books (12) 1862–1919, declaration of secrecy register 1862–1912, salary books 1870–1918, half yearly reports 1863–1917, annual reports 1891–1917 inc, signature book 1899–1914, private minutes 1910–19, balance sheets 1910–19, comparative statistics of branches 1910–20, private ledgers (2) 1913–19, interview book 1911–21, shareholders' register 1916–18, amlg papers 1918–26

Records' Location: National Westminster Bank Ltd

83 BRADFORD OLD BANK LTD

Location: Bradford, W Yorks

History: est 1864; amlg with Birmingham, District & Counties Bank to form United Counties Bank Ltd 1907

Records: prospectus 1864, articles of association 1864, half yearly reports 1864–1907, half yearly profit & loss accounts & bad debt balances 1864–1907, declarations of secrecy 1865–1906, board minute book 1893–1907, shareholders' minute books 1893–1907, amlg papers 1904–07
Tadcaster: deposit ledger 1882–1907
Records' Location: Barclays Bank Ltd

84   BRETT & NICHOLS AND BRETT, NICHOLLS & HIGGS

Location: Stone & Cheadle, Staffs
History: Brett & Nichols est 1802 as Brett & Gilbert; failed 1816; Brett, Nichols & Higgs est 1806 as Brett, Gilbert & Higgs; failed 1816
Records: counsel's opinion on liabilities of executors of deceased partners 1825
Records' Location: William Salt Library, Eastgate St, Stafford
Ref: 93/24/41

85   M & J BRICKDALE

Location: Taunton, Somerset
History: est c1793; failed 1816
Records: papers re business & failure 1775–1853, partnership agreements (2) 1776–85
Records' Location: Somerset Record Office, Obridge Rd, Taunton TA2 7PU
Ref: DD/DP 6–7; D/B/ta 31/5/12; DD/SAS TN 19

86   BRIDGES, GODFREY & COX

Location: Harwich, Essex
History: est 1807; taken over by Cox & Co 1815
Records: partnership agreement 1812
Records' Location: Lloyds Bank Ltd

87   BRIGHTWEN & CO

Location: London
History: discount house; est 1860; absorbed by Cater & Co Ltd 1939
Records: general ledgers (3) 1867–91, partnership agreements 1869–98, analysis of profits 1876–1916, signed receipts for quarterly salaries 1861–82
Records' Location: Guildhall Library, Aldermanbury, London EC2P 2EJ

88   BRISTOL & WEST OF ENGLAND BANK LTD

History: est 1879; amlg with Lloyds Bank Ltd 1892
Records: amlg paper 1892
Records' Location: Lloyds Bank Ltd

89   BRITISH BANK OF MIDDLE EAST LTD

Location: London
History: overseas bank; est 1889 as Imperial Bank of Persia; known as Imperial Bank of Iran 1935; as British Bank of Iran & the Middle East Ltd 1949; as British Bank of the Middle East Ltd 1952; acquired by Hongkong & Shanghai Banking Corp 1960
Records 1: board minutes f1889, annual reports f1889, shareholders' records f1889, investment ledger c1889–1913, special staff & semi-official letter books from Tehran (c22) c1889–1917, reports on office in Persia c1890–1906, powers of attorney books (4) c1890–1911, private ledgers c1890–95, note registers (5) c1890–1933, special letter books to chief office & branches in Persia (c20) c1890–1937, letter books to Persian minister & Foreign Office (c10) c1900–08, staff report books (14) f1889, special staff & semi-official letter books to Tehran (c11) 1891–1917, letter books to staff officers in Persia (10) 1891–1921, general ledgers (27) 1892–1940, progress reports (5 boxes) 1893–1936, deposit account ledgers (53) 1893–1929, security registers (11) 1898–1943, charges ledgers (10) 1899–1945, letter books re branches & inspections (5) 1900–15, photograph albums of premises (7) fc1900, press cutting books (3) fc1900, interest & commission account ledgers (8) 1902–27, papers re officers' provident fund (10) 1905–44, premises account book 1908–25, premises memoranda book 1909–14, confidential in-letters books (73) 1917–53, staff out-letter books (15) 1919–35, telegram copy books (31) 1920–50, register of loans granted 1922–40, confidential out-letter books (29) 1925–53, branch balance sheets (5) 1928–36
Records' 1 Location: British Bank of the Middle East Ltd, 99 Bishopsgate, London EC2P 2LA

Records 2: press cutting books (3) 1890–1906, letter books Tehran to London (6) 1917–24

Records' 2 Location: Centre of Middle East Studies, St Antony's College, Oxford OX2 6JF

90   BRITISH BANK OF NORTHERN COMMERCE LTD

Location: London

History: overseas bank; est 1912; amlg with C J Hambro & Son to form Hambros Bank of Northern Commerce Ltd

Records: general ledgers (5) 1912–27, annual reports 1913–20

Records' Location: The Guildhall Library, Aldermanbury, London EC2P 2EJ

91   BRITISH BANK OF SOUTH AMERICA LTD

Location: London

History: overseas bank; est 1863 as Brazilian & Portuguese Bank Ltd; known as the English Bank of Rio de Janeiro Ltd 1868; known as British Bank of South America Ltd 1891; wound up 1936

Records 1: letter books (14) Sao Paulo to London, Rio & branches 1886–1927, letters London & branches to Sao Paulo 1892–1913, letter books (5) London to Montevideo 1912–13

Records' 1 Location: DMS Watson Library, University College, Gower St, London WC1E 6BT

Records 2: annual reports 1863–1936, general ledgers 1863, journal 1863, summary private ledgers (2) 1924–36

Records' 2 Location: Lloyds Bank International Ltd, Head Office, 40 Queen Victoria St, London EC4P 4EL

92   BRITISH GUIANA BANK

Records: papers re establishment 1836–40

Records' Location: Public Record Office, Ruskin Av, Kew, Richmond, Surrey TW9 4DU

Ref: TI/3474

93   BRITISH LINEN BANK

Location: Edinburgh, Lothian

History: est 1746 by royal charter as British Linen Co; known as British Linen Bank 1906; acquired by Bank of Scotland 1969

Records 1: charters 1746–1955, proprietors' meetings minutes 1746–1803, directors' meetings minutes 1746–1965, stock journals 1746–1817, stock ledgers 1846–1971, daily transactions journals 1746–69, day books 1764–65, cash books 1746–1844, dividend books 1747–1810, share transfer records 1748–1972, current account ledgers 1748–99, main series letter books 1748–1800, English & foreign letter books 1748–63, 'Scotch' letter books 1749–61, daily transactions ledgers 1750–1800, 'ledgers' 1751–73, waste book 1751–52, letter book 1760–64, letters to Tod & Anderson (London) 1758–63, court minute books 1761–1878, register of demand & optional notes 1761–65, register of cash credits 1765–97, register of confirmations 1766–85, governors' & directors' obligations 1782–91, concurrent interest ledgers 1784–1801, directors' letter books 1785–1848, branch cash accounts 1786–1928, inspector's dept letter books 1789–1900, branches interest ledgers 1796–1803, interest ledgers (counter cash accounts) 1798–1800, directors' attendance book 1800–1971, circular books 1832–1918, stock (investment) ledgers 1819–1950, register of lodgements for safe keeping 1847–1950, salary books etc 1849–68, memorandum of treasurer re fluctuations of booking profits since 1814 & measures to be taken to increase profits 1840, 'general & particular register of sasines' 1863–65, officers' guarantee fund minute book 1877–1955, directors' committee minutes 1879–1971, secretary's letter books 1880–1971, head office instructions manuals 1883–1950, note registers 1896–1962, London office letter book 1900, 'book note balances' 1908–64, bye laws 1914, register of notes given out for signature 1916–47, 'account of unstamped notes in circulation' 1935–64

Records' 1 Enquiries: National Register of Archives (Scotland), HM General Register House, Edinburgh EH1 3YY

Ref: list 945

Records 2: extracts of court minutes (2) 1746–1920, letter book copy 1748–50, balance sheets & profit & loss accounts 1865–1908 inc, annual reports 1869–1927 inc

Records' 2 Location: Scottish Banking Collection, The Archives, University of Glasgow, Glasgow G12 8QQ

94   BRITISH MUTUAL BANK LTD

Location: London

History: est 1857 as British Mutual Banking
Co Ltd; name changed to above 1945; amlg
with Martins Bank Ltd 1951

Records: impersonal ledgers (2) 1896–1930s,
deposit account ledgers (33) 1906–43 inc,
current account ledgers (47) 1910–43 inc,
discount ledgers (4) 1913–32, balance sheets
1915–50, board minute books (4) 1923–50,
general ledgers (3) 1940–51, guard book
containing prospectus, annual reports, press
cuttings, shareholders' circulars, etc 19–
20cent

Records' Location: Barclays Bank Ltd

95   BRITISH OVERSEAS BANK LTD

Location: London

History: overseas bank; est 1919; current
banking business transfered to Glyn Mills &
Co 1944

Records 1: papers re transfer of business
1940s

Records' 1 Location: Williams & Glyn's Bank
Ltd

Records 2: papers re formation 1919

Records' 2 Location: Public Record Office,
Ruskin Av, Kew, Richmond, Surrey TW9
4DU
Ref: TI/12342/26605

96   BROMAGE & CO

Location: Monmouth, Gwent

History: est 1819; otherwise known as
Monmouth Old Bank; taken over by Lloyds
Bank Ltd 1894

Records: amlg papers 1893–95

Records' Location: Lloyds Bank Ltd

97   BROOKE, RICHES & COLLETT

Location: Woodbridge, Suffolk

History: est 1797; known as Riches & Co
1801; absorbed by Alexanders & Co 1806

Records: customer & general ledger 1805–07,
letters with Hoare & Co re note issue 1809

Records' Location: Barclays Bank Ltd

98   BROOKS & CO

Location: London, Lombard St

History: est 1864; amlg with Lloyds Bank
Ltd 1900

Records: amlg papers 1900

Records' Location: Lloyds Bank Ltd

99   J BROOKS

Location: Woodstock, Oxon

History: ceased 1807; otherwise known as the
Woodstock Bank

Records: private papers of Joseph Brooks,
some re banking, 1785–1836

Records' Location: Berkshire Record Office,
Shire Hall, Reading RG1 3EE
Ref: D/ESV(M) B6–22

100   BROOKSBY & CO

Location: Newark, Notts

Records: partnership agreement 1785

Records' Location: Nottinghamshire Record
Office, County House, High Pavement,
Nottingham NG1 1HR
Ref: DDT 126/4

101   BROTHERS SWAINE & CO

Location: Bradford, W Yorks

History: est 1801; failed & assets purchased
by Rawson, Rhodes & Briggs 1807

Records: papers re securities 1802–07, papers
re failure 1807

Records' Location: Barclays Bank Ltd

102   W W BROWN & CO

Location: Leeds, W Yorks

History: est 1813; amlg with Lloyds Bank
Ltd 1900

Records: profit & loss ledgers 1844–57, amlg
papers 1900

Records' Location: Lloyds Bank Ltd

103   BROWN JANSON & CO

Location: London; Abchurch Lane

History: est 1823; amlg with Lloyds Bank
Ltd 1900

Records: partnership agreements (2) 1814
1891, private ledgers (2) 1844–56 1890–
1900, salary books (2) 1873–1898, amlg
papers 1900

Records' Location: Lloyds Bank Ltd

104   BROWN, SHIPLEY & CO LTD

Location: London

History: merchant bank; est 1810

Records 1: commission & other accounts ledger & accounts of American firms 1860–66, private out-letter book to Liverpool 1864–65, current account ledger 1864–67, private out-letter books (4) 1864–1920 inc, finance out-letter books (12) inc 1864–77, private out-letter books to New York (16) 1864–1914 inc, travellers' ledger 1864–65, miscellaneous private in-letters (7 bdls) 1868–88 inc, commercial current account ledgers (2) 1871–75 1887, private in-letter book from Liverpool 1877–88, comparative weekly returns of business done at Liverpool (1 bdl) 1884, minute books of statements submitted to board 1884–86, 'term slips' being details of new client accounts opened (4) 1889–1901, correspondence re exchange business between New York & S Africa 1895–1921, 'partnership files inwards' being private & confidential letters from N America (10) 1895–1937, current account ledgers individual, institutional & commercial (5) 1895–1934 inc, letters of introduction given 1896–1901, applications for current accounts (15) 1896–1928 inc, partnership agreements & relating papers (5 bdls) 1900–17, private & confidential in-letter books (2) 1901–04, current account ledgers (5) 1902–35 inc, plan & papers re London premises (1 portfolio) 1903–65, book keepers' memoranda book 1903–43, extension & doubtful debt ledger balance book 1904–16, private out-letter books (10) 1908–30 inc, investment ledger 1909–12, monthly statements of deployment of capital & deposits (1 bdl) 1911–1912, annual reports of bills payable department (1 bdl) 1911–27, comparative & condensed profit & loss accounts for New York & Philadelphia houses (5 bdls) 1911–17, deposit receipt advices 1911–1921, private & confidential memoranda books (3) 1911–68, short loans ledger (discount houses) 1912–26, quarterly analysis of charges, commissions etc of New York, Boston & Philadelphia houses (1 bdl) 1912, American accounts being summaries of operating expenses, income accounts, investment & profit & loss accounts (5 bdls) 1913–17, register of sundry charges payable 1914–23, applications for commercial credits (10) 1920–38, weekly financial & percentage statements of balances of assets & liabilities New York, Philadelphia & Boston houses (6 bdls) 1912–17, copy letters to New York (2 files) 1921–39, banks' accounts ledger 1922–35, scrapbook of letters re securities, income tax etc 1921–31, registers of credits opened (2) 1925–55, in & out-letters between London & US partners (1 file) 1926–32, correspondence with banks & companies in Germany (7 files) 1926–39, commercial customer cash accounts (3) 1928–35 inc, London dollar exchange ledger 1934–36, foreign exchange ledger 1935–36 London, Pall Mall: current account ledger 1902–03, applications for current accounts (24) 1904–38, current account ledgers (3) 1919–26 inc

Records' 1 Location: Guildhall Library, Aldermanbury, London EC2P 2EJ

Records 2: memoirs & diaries of G A Brown 1803–61, customer ledgers (2) 1836–45, apprenticeship indenture 1842, letter book 1851–59

Records' 2 Location: Liverpool Record Office, City Libraries, William Brown St, Liverpool L3 8EW

105   BUCKLE & PROCTOR

Location: Chepstow, Gwent

History: est 1804; failed 1829; otherwise known as Buckle, Thompson & Co

Records: partnership agreements 1791–1820, account book 1811–17

Records' Location: Gwent County Record Office, County Hall, Cwmbran NP4 2XH
Ref: D25.0378, 0379, 0730, 1022–3, 1032, 1145

106   BUCKLEY, ROBERTS & CO

Location: Saddleworth, Huddersfield & Ashton-under-Lyne, Yorks

History: est 1806; formed Saddleworth Banking Co 1833

Records: Ashton-under-Lyne: deposit account ledger 1825–31
Dobcross: customer ledgers (2) 1806–13, deposit account ledgers (2) 1824–59, stock book 1831–32

Records' Location: National Westminster Bank Ltd

107   BUCKS & OXON UNION BANK

Location: Buckingham, Bucks

History: est 1853; amlg with Lloyds Bank Ltd 1902

Records: agreements to establish bank 1852, board minutes 1853–1902, draft minutes 1853–1902, directors' attendance book 1853–59, agm minutes 1853–64, monthly balance sheets 1853–74, branch returns 1857–66, annual reports 1866–77, balance sheets & profit & loss accounts 1876–1902, investment ledger 1878–1902, superannuation fund minutes 1887–1902, superannuation fund ledger 1887–1902, private ledger 1893–96, staff book 1902, amlg papers 1902
Aylesbury: signature book 1896–1902
Brackley: safe custody register 1898–1902, security receipt book 1899–1902
Stony Stratford: miscellaneous papers & correspondence 1860–1902
Watford: assets & liabilities book 1887–1902, limits & cash book 1867–1902

Records' Location: Lloyds Bank Ltd

108   BULPETT & HALL

Location: Winchester, Hants

History: est 1789; amlg with Prescott, Dimsdale, Cave, Tugwell & Co Ltd 1892

Records: amlg papers 1892

Records' Location: National Westminster Bank Ltd

109   BURDON, FORSTER & CO

Location: Newcastle, Tyne & Wear

History: est 1784 as Forster, Burrell, Rankin & Harris; known as Burdon, Forster, Burrell, Rankin & Harris 1786; known as above 1788; failed 1793; known otherwise as Commercial Bank

Records: partnership agreement 1791, prospectus 1793

Records' Location: Northumberland Record Office, Melton Park, North Gosforth, Newcastle NE3 5QX
Ref: ZCK 10

110   FREDERICK BURT & CO

Location: London; Cornhill

History: est 1872; amlg with London & County Banking Co Ltd 1907

Records: status reports on firms 1887–1902

Records' Location: National Westminster Bank Ltd

111   JOHN & ANDREW BURT

Location: E Grinstead, Sussex

History: est 1807; failed 1816

Records: papers re liabilities 1806–21, partnership agreement 1806, inventory of fixtures 1818

Records' Location: Barclays Bank Ltd

112   BURTON UNION BANK LTD

Location: Burton on Trent, Derbys

History: est 1839 as Burton, Uttoxeter & Ashbourne Union Bank; name changed 1893; amlg with Lloyds Bank Ltd 1899

Records: deed of settlement 1839, profit & loss book 1839–1884, annual reports 1840–67, letter book 1841–44, balance sheets 1841–99, amlg papers 1899

Records' Location: Lloyds Bank Ltd

113   BURY BANKING CO

Location: Bury, Gt Manchester

History: est 1836; amlg with Lancashire & Yorkshire Bank 1888

Records: deeds of settlement (2) 1836–82, list of shareholders 1854, bad debt ledger 1878–88, income tax records 1880–84, profit & loss accounts 1880–83, amlg papers 1888–91

Records' Location: Barclays Bank Ltd

114   THOMAS BUTCHER & SONS

Location: Tring, Herts

History: est 1836; amlg with Prescott, Dimsdale, Cave, Tugwell & Co Ltd 1900; otherwise known as Tring Old Bank

Records: note registers (3) 1836–99, amlg papers 1900
Chesham: note register 1840–58

Records' Location: National Westminster Bank Ltd

115   A BUTLIN & SON

Location: Rugby, Warws

History: est 1791; taken over by Lloyds Bank Ltd 1868

Records: amlg papers 1869

Records' Location: Lloyds Bank Ltd

116 CAERNARVON OLD BANK

Location: Caernarvon, Gwynedd

Records: letter book 1852–72

Records' Location: Gwynedd Archives Service, County Offices, Shirehall St, Caernarvon LL55 1SH

Ref: M923

117 CALEDONIAN BANKING CO LTD

Location: Inverness, Highlands

History: est 1838; amlg with Bank of Scotland 1907

Records 1: minute book 1838–1907, ledgers etc 1840–1911, branch records 1838–1907, miscellaneous papers 1838–1907, architectural drawings 1850–94, letter books 1851–1924, annual balances 1880–1907, records of notes issued, circulating & retired 1887–1907, reports & returns 1901–06, stock & shareholding records 1905–12

Records' 1 Enquiries: National Register of Archives (Scotland), HM General Register House, Edinburgh EH1 3YY Ref: list 945

Records 2: balance sheets 1865–1970 inc, annual reports 1901–06

Records' 2 Location: Scottish Banking Collection, University of Glasgow Archives, The University, Glasgow G12 8QQ

118 CALL MARTEN & CO

Location: London

History: est 1773 as Sir W P Call, Bart., Arnold & Marten; known as above 1829; amlg with Herries, Farquhar & Co 1865

Records: signature books 1810–84

Records' Location: Lloyds Bank Ltd

119 CAPITAL & COUNTIES BANK LTD

Location: Southampton, Hants, & London

History: est 1877 as Hampshire & North Wilts Banking Co, following a merger of Hampshire Banking Co with North Wilts Banking Co; known as above 1878; amlg with Lloyds Bank Ltd 1918

Records: private minute books (2) 1876–1924, deed of settlement 1877, annual reports 1877–1918, general memoranda book 1878–1918, chairman's agenda book 1889–1917, head office circular books (5)

1877–1917, premises ledgers (2) 1880–1902, private letter books (5) 1891–1918, register of directors 1900–18, memoranda & instruction book 1905, articles of association 1908–18, bad & doubtful debt book 1916–17, instructions to branch managers 1908

Aldershot: security register 1890s

Basingstoke: security registers (2) 1883–1918

Brighton, Western Rd: security registers (2) f1873

Gloucester: authority book f1872, security register 1889–1920, character book f1897

Haslemere: security ledgers f1900, profit & loss account 1918

Hastings: memoranda book 1880s–90s

King's Lynn: correspondence (1 bdl) 1902–09

Llandeilo: coupon register 1898–1918, security register 1900–20

London, Piccadilly: letter books (5) 1890–1916

Luton: security registers 1898–1918

Northampton: minute book 1892

Ryde: security registers (3) 1890–1921

Skegness: security registers (2) 1890–1920

Southampton: security registers (6) 1887–1921, private ledger f1897, staff book 1909–18

Stow on the Wold: security register 1886–1902

Sudbury: circular book 1877–90

Ventnor: security ledgers (2) 1904–18

Westcliff on Sea: security registers (2) 1901–20

Wirksworth: security register 1901–22

Woking: security registers (4) 1893–1920, branch record books (2) 1907–17, security ledger 1908–20

Woolwich: deposit account ledger 1876–1916, signature books (2) 1880–1918, security registers (5) 1891–1918, security ledger 1894–1905, monthly balance book 1915–17

Wootton Bassett: letter book 1890–1926

Worcester: letter books (2) 1906–20

Records' Location: Lloyds Bank Ltd

120 CARLISLE CITY & DISTRICT BANKING CO LTD

Location: Carlisle, Cumbria

History: est 1837; acquired by Midland Bank 1896

Records: deed of settlement 1837, balance sheets 1837–80 1896, fidelity bonds (5) 1837–81, board minutes 1879–80, shareholders' minutes 1880, articles of association 1881, board agenda books (2) 1885–96, amlg papers 1896

Records' Location: Midland Bank Ltd

121   CARLISLE & CUMBERLAND BANKING CO LTD

Location: Carlisle, Cumbria

History: est 1836; amlg with Bank of Liverpool 1911

Records: board minutes 1836–1911, note register 1836–38, balance sheets 1837–82, deed of settlement 1837, annual reports 1837–1910, papers re a director 1841–49, deposit ledger f1858, signature books 1886–1911, interview records 1891–1925, papers re proposed amlg 1903, amlg papers 1911

Records' Location: Barclays Bank Ltd

122   CASSON & CO

Location: Portmadoc, Pwllheli, Ffestiniog; Gwynedd

History: est 1847; acquired by North & South Wales Bank 1875

Records: private ledgers (2) 1848–74, purchase agreement papers 1875, general ledger 1870s

Records' Location: Midland Bank Ltd

123   CATTLE TRADE BANK LTD

Location: Liverpool, Merseyside

History: est 1920; absorbed by Bank of Liverpool & Martins Ltd 1923

Records: amlg agreement 1923

Records' Location: Barclays Bank Ltd

124   CENTRAL BANK OF LONDON LTD

Location: London

History: est 1863 as East London Bank Ltd; renamed Central Bank of London Ltd 1869; amlg with Birmingham & Midland Bank to form London & Midland Bank Ltd 1891

Records: articles of association 1863, board minute books (6) 1863–91, committee minue books (5) 1863–91, resolutions & orders 1863–91, directions for branch

managers 1863, annual reports 1864–91, shareholders' minute books (2) 1864–91, balance sheets 1864–88, balance books (2) 1864–94, general ledgers (4) 1868–89, security registers (3) 1868–1904, record of proceedings in bankruptcies 1872–93, branch ledgers (9) 1873–89, branch balance sheets (2) 1878–91, salary registers (2) 1880–91, amlg papers 1891

Records' Location: Midland Bank Ltd

125   CENTRAL BANK OF SCOTLAND

Location: Perth, Tayside

History: est 1834; amlg with Bank of Scotland 1868

Records 1: stock ledgers 1834–80, minute book 1835–80, balances of notes in circulation 1837–55, deposit books 1843–68, amlg papers 1850–80, accounts of notes issued 1858–60, register of members 1862–69, signature book c1865–1912

Records' 1 Enquiries: National Register of Archives (Scotland), HM General Register House, Edinburgh EH1 3YY Ref: list 945

Records 2: balance sheets 1865–68

Records' 2 Location: Scottish Banking Collection, The Archives, University of Glasgow, Glasgow G12 8QQ

126   CHANNEL ISLANDS BANK LTD

Location: Jersey, Channel Islands

History: est 1858; acquired by Midland Bank 1897

Records: board & committee minute books (4) 1874–1907, auditors' reports 1879–97, articles of association 1887, reports & balance sheets 1887–97, securities list with valuations 1887–96, draft agreement with Channel Islands Bank liquidator 1897

Records' Location: Midland Bank Ltd

127   CHAPLIN, MILNE, GRENFELL & CO LTD

Location: London

History: est 1899; failed 1914

Records: press cuttings re failure 1914

Records' Location: Alexanders Discount Co Ltd, 1 St Swithin's Lane, London EC4N 8DN

128   THE CHARTERED BANK

Location: London

History: overseas bank; est 1853 as Chartered Bank of India, Australia & China; name changed to The Chartered Bank 1956; 1970 capital was acquired by a holding company Standard Chartered Banking Group Ltd

Records: board minutes f1852, general ledgers f1852, annual reports f1853, charters f1854, call books 1854 1863, registers of members f1854, registers of transfers f1854, papers re establishment of business in India 1854–89, agm minutes f1855, executive committee minutes 1858–1912, deed of settlement 1857, branch balance sheets f1858, half yearly balance sheets f1858, 'posterity files' being legal papers, reports & correspondence etc f1858, statistics book re deposit notes, profit comparisons, profit & loss, deposits, half yearly schedules of office establishments f1862, half yearly returns of London & head offices f1859, powers of attorney registers f1867, premises account book 1867–1907, branch adjusting account books (3) f1887, court minutes 1890–1938, note issue correspondence 1890–1950, government security ledgers f1891, papers re applications for employment f1900, head office circulars f1900, shareholders' address book 1900s-30s, customer signature books 20 cent, staff provident fund papers & accounts f1906, office furniture ledger 1909–12, half yearly journals f1914

Records' Location: Standard Chartered Bank Ltd, Head Office, 10 Clements Lane, London EC4N 7AB
At the time of preparing this guide researchers can be given very limited access to the records

129   CHASEMORE, ROBINSON & SONS

Location: London; Croydon

History: est 1838; taken over by Union Bank of London Ltd 1891; known also as Union Bank of Croydon

Records: partnership agreements (2) 1863 1873

Records' Location: National Westminster Bank Ltd

130   CHEQUE BANK LTD

History: est 1873; liquidated 1901

Records: prospectus 1876

Records' Enquiries: National Register of Archives (Scotland), P.O. Box 36, HM General Register House, Edinburgh EH1 3YY

Ref: list 349

131   CHESTERFIELD & NORTH DERBYSHIRE BANKING CO

Location: Chesterfield, Derbys

History: est 1833; absorbed by Crompton & Evans's Union Bank Ltd 1878

Records: annual report 1859, board minutes 1876–78, liquidator's report & accounts 1879–85

Records' Location: National Westminster Bank Ltd

132   CHILD & CO

Location: London

History: est c1584; absorbed by Glyn, Mills, Currie, Holt & Co 1924

Records 1: customer ledgers (15) 1663–1755, loan ledgers (8) 1667–1740, balance books (5) 1686–1923, record of Goldsmith's notes issued 1691–1712, private accounts of Child family 1694–1760, staff Christmas box book 1728–1896, signature books (4) 1732–1909, letters of credit books (3) 1735–1854, postage record book 1737–40, profit & loss account books (27) 1756–1935, letter book 1762–1835, office expenses books (7) 1785–1916, scrapbooks of documents, notes, letters, etc 17 & 18 cents, letter books re partnership matters (3) 1839–49, Child family papers 19 cent

Records' 1 Location: Williams & Glyn's Bank Ltd

Records 2: correspondence with a Yorkshire customer (3 bdls) 1781–1820

Records' 2 Location: Yorkshire Archaeological Society, Claremont, Clarendon Rd, Leeds LS2 9NZ

Ref: DD56 M10

133   CITY BANK LTD

Location: London

History: est 1855; amlg with London & Midland Bank to form London City & Midland Bank 1898

Records: board minute books (6) 1854–98, deeds of settlement (5) 1855–81, staff appointment list 1855–58, annual reports 1865–98, shareholders' minute books (2) 1856–98, committee minute books (3) 1856–98, balance sheet books (3) 1855–98, foreign banks' arrangement book 1862–98, rules for branch managers 1874, accountants' reports 1884–91, security book 1888–1901, amlg papers 1898
London, Holborn: security registers (4) 1879–99
London, Old Street: deposit receipt book 1894–98
London, Paddington: journal, cash book, letter book 1873–1903
Records' Location: Midland Bank Ltd

134   CITY OF BIRMINGHAM BANK LTD

Location: Birmingham, W Midlands
History: est 1897; acquired by Midland Bank 1899
Records: articles of association 1897, board minute books (2) 1897–99, share registers (2) 1897–98, share transfer registers (2) 1897–98, annual returns & summary book 1897–98, investment list 1897
Records' Location: Midland Bank Ltd

135   CITY OF GLASGOW BANK

Location: Glasgow, Strathclyde
History: est 1839; failed 1878
Records 1: balance sheet 1878, press cuttings 1878, investigator's report 1878
Records' 1 Enquiries: National Register of Archives (Scotland), PO Box 36, HM General Register House, Edinburgh EH1 3YY
Ref: list 349
Records 2: balance sheets & re papers 1857–78, extracts of private ledgers & other accounts 1872–78, list of branches & partners 1874, list of shareholders 1878, papers re liquidation 1878–79
Records' 2 Location: Scottish Banking Collection, University of Glasgow Archives, The University, Glasgow G12 8QQ
Records 3: circulars 1872–83, list of creditors 1878, deposit receipt register 1878–80, tellers' cash books (2) 1878–79, secretary's letter book 1878–87, ledger 1878–82, special

accountant's cash book 1879–80, bills discounted book 1879–85, press cuttings re liquidation 1880–82
Records' 3 Enquiries: National Register of Archives (Scotland), HM General Register House, Edinburgh EH1 3YY
Ref: list 1110
Records 4: contract of co-partnership 1839, list of partners 1844, instructions to agents & accountants 1873, customer's pass book 1877, press cuttings 1878, claims lodged through North of Scotland Bank 1878, report of trial of managers & directors 1879
Records' 4 Location: Clydesdale Bank Ltd, Head Office, 30 St Vincent Place, Glasgow G1 2HL
Records 5: deposit receipts, claims, etc 1878–82
Records' 5 Enquiries: National Register of Archives (Scotland), PO Box 36, HM General Register House, Edinburgh EH1 3YY
Ref: list 945
Records 6: papers re collapse & liquidation 1871–88
Records' 6 Location: Strathclyde Regional Archives, PO Box 27, City Chambers, Glasgow G2 1DU Ref: TD48, 300, 311, 482/3; TBK 162/54, 174–9; THB23, 126–7; THL148
Records 7: papers re liquidation 1840–82
Records' 7 Location: University of Glasgow Archives, The University, Glasgow G12 8QQ
Ref: UGD 108

136   CLARKE, MITCHELL & PHILIPS

Location: Leicester, Leics
History: est 1819; failed 1843; otherwise known as Leicester & Leicestershire Bank
Records: commissions of bankruptcy against customers 1830–40, statement of distribution of assets received under bankruptcy of bank c1843
Records' Location: Leicestershire Record Office, 57 New Walk, Leicester LE1 7JB
Ref: 109 30/13

137   CLAYTON MORRIS & CO

Location: London
History: merchant bankers, scriveners & estate agents; est as Robert Abbott &

succeeded in business by Clayton Morris & Co

Records: current account ledgers (5) 1645–52 1669–80, sundry papers with letters & memoranda 1639–1789

Records' Location: Guildhall Library, Aldermanbury, London EC2P 2EJ

138 CLEMENT ROYDS & CO
Location: Rochdale, Gt Manchester

History: est 1819; absorbed by Manchester & Salford Bank Ltd 1882

Records: customer ledgers (15) f1826, rent book 1830–55, press cutting book 1809–86

Records' Location: Williams & Glyn's Bank Ltd

139 CLIVE DISCOUNT CO LTD
Location: London

History: discount house; est 1946

Records: board minutes f1946, annual reports f1946, shareholders' records f1946

Records' Location: Clive Discount Co Ltd, 1 Royal Exchange Av, London EC3V 3LU

140 CLYDESDALE BANK LTD
Location: Glasgow, Strathclyde

History: est 1838; acquired by London Joint City & Midland Bank Ltd 1920; merged with North of Scotland Bank Ltd to form Clydesdale & North of Scotland Bank 1950; known as above 1963

Records 1: board minute books (18) f1838, contract of co-partnership 1838, press cuttings re general meetings etc 1838–1949, branch letter book 1851–61, instructions to agents 1859 1890, correspondence 1864–67, general manager's office memoranda & documents 1864–91, notes on banking practice 1873, general manager's office memoranda books (5) 1877–1910, statement of debt books (12) 1878–86 1896–1968, list of shareholders 1881–1919, directors' meetings general manager's books (52) 1909–47 1952–58, general manager's letter books (9) 1911–38, accountants' memoranda book f1911, list of correspondents 1922, instruction book 1927 Carnoustie: letter book 1878 Portobello: charges account 1873–99

Records' 1 Location: Clydesdale Bank Ltd,

Head Office, 30 St Vincent Place, Glasgow G1 2HL

Records 2: extracts from directors' minutes 1838–1917, balance sheets & profit & loss accounts 1865–1901 inc, annual reports 1890–1926

Records' 2 Location: Scottish Banking Collection, The Archives, University of Glasgow, Glasgow G12 8QQ

141 COBB & CO
Location: Margate, Kent

History: est 1785; amlg with Lloyds Bank Ltd 1891

Records 1: customer ledgers 1793–1887 inc, day book 1782–89, partnership ledger (3) 1841–1901, petty cash book 1811, agency account ledger 1821–33, partners' cash book 1841–48, security register 1865–89, cash book 1871–83, list of standing orders 1874–91, list of securities held 1878–91 Westgate on Sea: signature book 1879–81

Records' 1 Location: Lloyds Bank Ltd

Records 2: paid cheques 1775–1876, correspondence mainly from clients 1771–1881, note registers 1789–1871, 'miscellaneous early account books' 1781–1834, correspondence with other banks 1794–1869, waste books 1800–61, cash books c1803–80, ledgers 1808–55, partnership agreements 1842–92, amlg papers 1891–93, papers re brewing and shipping (extensive) c1761–1962

Records' 2 Location: Kent Archives Office, County Hall, Maidstone, Kent ME14 1XH

142 COCKS, BIDDULPH & CO
Location: London; Whitehall

History: est as Cocks, Cocks & Biddulph & Co 1775; known as Biddulph, Cocks, Eliot & Praed 1776; Biddulph, Cocks & Co 1782; Biddulph, Cocks & Ridge 1792; Cocks, Cocks, Ridge & Biddulph 1820; Cocks & Biddulph 1827; Cocks, Biddulph & Co 1845; Biddulph, Cocks & Co 1860; as above 1865; amlg with Bank of Liverpool & Martins Bank Ltd 1919

Records 1: customer ledgers (12)1759–1909 mostly inc, country bank ledgers (8) 1775–1801, private cash books (4) 1759–72 1882–1919, private ledgers (2) 1759–68 1892–

1919, long standing balance books (3) 1783–
1856 1869–1918, half yearly balances 1786–
98, letters of specific historical interest
1800–1920, signature books 1805–21 1841–
1912, stock books (2) 1808–17 1838–64, safe
custody registers (4) 1811–89, memoranda
book re history of bank 1817–64, security
ledgers (3) 1822–1907, note & loan registers
(4) 1856–1919, powers of attorney 1864–80,
private letter book 1871–1918, memoranda
book re staff 1899–1919, balance sheet 1919

Records' 1 Location: Barclays Bank Ltd

Records 2: private papers of J Biddulph
1812–40

Records' 2 Location: Hereford Record Office,
The Old Barracks, Harold St, Hereford
HR1 2QX

143   COGGAN, MORRIS &CO

Location: Staines, Middlesex

History: est 1810; failed 1813

Records: partnership agreement 1810

Records' Location: Greater London Record
Office, 40 Northampton Road, London EC1
0HB

Ref: Acc 27/6

144   COLE, HOLROYD & CO

Location: Exeter, Devon

History: est 1807; amlg with National
Provincial Bank of England 1842; otherwise
known as Devon County Bank

Records: partnership agreements (3) 1807–
33, private ledgers (2) 1808–64, licences to
issue notes 1810–41, information book
1817–41, balance sheet books (2) 1817–42,
monthly balances of private accounts (3)
1817–64, private journals (2) 1817–64, stock
balance books (2) 1818–42, statements of
transactions in treasury bills 1826–35,
papers re partnership matters 1834–42, list
of customers 1842, amlg papers 1842

Records' Location: National Westminster
Bank Ltd

145   COLONIAL BANK

Location: London

History: overseas bank; est 1836; amlg with
Anglo-Egyptian Bank Ltd & National Bank
of South Africa to form Barclays Bank
(Dominion, Colonial & Overseas) 1925

Records 1: charter with amendments 1836–

1917, court minute books (25) 1836–1925,
agm minutes 1836–1925, committee minute
books (7) 1836–1923, treasury minute books
(2) 1837–1925, profit & loss account book
1837–1917, note register 1837, annual
reports 1838–1925, stock ledgers (10) 1840–
1912, general ledgers (20) 1845–1926,
statements of general superintendents (2)
1846–66, general information books (2)
1877–1914, remittances unaccepted &
unpaid books (2) 1889–1922, investment
loan ledgers (4) 1894–1916, investment
register 1889–1914, circulars 1897–1927 inc,
pension fund regulations 1881, balance
sheet books (5) 1899–1925, bad & doubtful
debts book 1899–1925, dividend book 1908–
15, share transfer register 1911–18, court
agenda books (3) 1913–26, establishment &
special committee minutes 1915–18,
customer ledgers (9) 1913–26, bills
purchased ledger 1905–12, general
managers' memoranda books 1916–25,
share allotment book 1918, office expenses
analysis book 1926–27, amlg papers 1926
Antigua: general ledgers 1837, letter books
(2) 1879–82
Berbice, Demerara & St Lucia: letter books
(2) 1837–43

Records' 1 Location: Barclays Bank
International Ltd, Head Office, 54
Lombard St, London EC3P 3AH

Records 2: papers re note issue

Records' 2 Location: Public Record Office,
Ruskin Av, Kew, Richmond, Surrey TW9
4DU
Ref: T1/12592/23410

Records 3: papers re charter 1837, petition
against bank 1839

Records' 3 Location: Public Record Office, as
above
Ref: T1/3473

146   COLONIAL BANK OF NEW ZEALAND

Location: London

History: overseas bank; est 1874; business
transferred to Bank of New Zealand 1896

Records: prospectus 1874, papers re
liquidation 1896

Records' Location: Southampton City Record
Office, Civic Centre, Southampton SO9
4XL

44

147 COMMERCIAL BANK OF LONDON

Location: London, Lothbury

History: est 1840; failed & business acquired by London & Westminster Bank 1861

Records: list of customers 1861

Records' Location: National Westminster Bank Ltd

148 COMMERCIAL BANK OF MANCHESTER

Location: Manchester, Gt Manchester

History: unknown

Records: prospectus 1827

Records' Location: Leicestershire Record Office, 57 New Walk, Leicester LE1 7AB
Ref: 3D42/3/13–24

149 COMMERCIAL BANK OF SCOTLAND LTD

Location: Edinburgh, Lothian

History: est 1810; amlg with National Bank of Scotland Ltd to form National Commercial Bank of Scotland Ltd 1959

Records 1: articles of co-partnery 1810, minute books 1810–1954, general abstract 1810–11, cash book 1810–11, London account current book 1810–12, discount progressive ledger 1810–11, stock journals (2) 1810–34 1879–81, property & furniture books (3) 1810–33 1888–1918, private letter books (2) 1810–38, stock registers f1810, statements of profits & losses 1811–73 1887–95, branch statements f1811, agency statements books (2) 1812–1912, branch inspection reports & memos 1812–22, staff attendance book 1814–15, private ledger 1818–34, private letter books (2) 1824–35, statements of profitability of branches 1823–56, branch ledger 1825–30, branch cash book 1825–27, record of losses at agencies 1825–1933, widows' and orphans' fund minutes 1826, branch committee reports 1826–77, agm reports 1827–82 inc, abstract ledgers (3) 1831–58, bank charter and supplements 1831–1925, branch committee reports (2) 1831–1920, accountants' report on branches c1833–36, papers re stage coach robbery 1831, letters from R Ferguson of Raith 1835–39, papers re commission charges 1840–62, letter book 1842–48,

'tellers' account for fund against losses' 1842–48, salary book 1843–65, jot minute books 1843–59, 'list of bills discounted to North of Scotland Bank' 1847–48, inspectors' letters to head office (1 bdl) 1847–80, papers re special advance to North of Scotland Bank 1847–48, accountants' private ledgers (4) 1851–1910, statement of losses over 10 years 1855, reports of special committee on annual balance statements 1854–97, law agents' letter book 1857–1962, general manager's notes on balance sheets 1858–1900 inc, accountants' abstract ledgers (4) 1858–88, statements re protested bills 1862–72, bad and doubtful debt estimates (6) 1862–63 1871, letters to Melville & Lindsay 1863–1930, statements of profits at branches 1863 1871, annual abstracts of assets & libilities 1868–77, private cash book 1866–99, weekly committee minute books 1879–86, annual balance books (2) 1879–98, salary registers (2) 1881–1919, constitutions 1882 1927, report on Kelso agent 1882, papers re proposed London branch 1883, record of cash accounts 1886–1905, general accounts monthly balance books 1887–1915, agency instructions 1893, copy letter books (16) 1894–1934, sequestration records (3) 1894–1909, general managers' reports to board on balance sheets 1898–1930, whisky ledger 1899–1901, register of directors 1900–59, letters from Skene, Edwards & Garson 1906–07, letters to Mitchells, Johnston & Co 1906–34, letters from Brodies 1907–34, circular books (11) 1908–43

Records' 1 Enquiries: National Register of Archives (Scotland), HM General Register House, PO Box 36, Edinburgh EH1 3YY
Ref: list 349 (drawn up in 1967)

Records 2: extracts from directors' minutes & letter books 1810–1922, annual reports 1878–1926

Records' 2 Location: Scottish Banking Collection, University of Glasgow Archives, The University, Glasgow G12 8QQ

150 COMMERCIAL BANK OF SPANISH AMERICA LTD

Location: London

History: overseas bank; est 1904 by amlg of London Bank of Central America & Enrique Cortes & Co Ltd to form Cortes

Commercial & Banking Co Ltd; known as
Commercial Bank of Spanish America Ltd
1911; incorporated into Anglo-South
American Bank Ltd 1926

Records: letter books (4) Caracas to/from
London & New York 1912–16 inc, letter
book Puerto Cabello 1920–22, letter books
(6) Bogota to/from London, New York &
elsewhere 1920–27, letters Federation of
British Industries to Bogota 1924–27

Records' Location: DMS Watson Library,
University College, Gower St, London
WC1E 6BT

151 COMMERCIAL BANKING CO OF ABERDEEN

Location: Aberdeen, Grampian

History: est 1778; absorbed by National
Bank of Scotland 1833

Records: register of dividends & profits
1794–1817

Records' Enquiries: National Register of
Archives (Scotland), PO Box 36, HM
General Register House, Edinburgh EH1
3YY

Ref: list 349

152 CONSOLIDATED BANK LTD

Location: London & Manchester

History: est 1863; amlg with Parr's Bank Ltd
1896

Records: board minute books (2) 1863–96,
daily minutes 1863–96, circulars & notices
1863–99, half yearly balance sheets, profit &
loss accounts & branch accounts 1863–96,
correspondence with London office 1863–
95, salary books 1864–93, managers' letter
books (2) 1867–97, board agenda books (6)
1873–96, directors' reports 1874–93 inc, list
of shareholders 1880, comparative statistics
with other banks' performances 1885 1890
1893, staff list 1896, amlg papers 1892–96

Records' Location: National Westminster
Bank Ltd

153 COOKE, FOLJAMBE, PARKER & WALKER

Location: Retford, Notts

History: unknown

Records: general ledger 1841–67

Records' Location: National Westminster
Bank Ltd

154 COOKE, YARBOROUGH & CO

Location: Doncaster, S Yorks

History: est 1750; absorbed by Beckett & Co
1868; otherwise known as Cooke, Ellison &
Co, & Ellison, Cooke, Childers & Co

Records 1: papers re Cooke family 1737–
1854, balance sheets 1802–05, private
ledgers (2) 1807–67, letter with London
agents 1807–19, general statement books
1809–48, sundry balances 1826–66, papers
re partnership matters 1838–65, premises
valuations 1842–67, papers re increase in
capital 1846–66, partnership agreements (3)
1848–62, papers re applications for
employment 1852–66, amlg papers 1866–76

Records' 1 Location: National Westminster
Bank Ltd

Records 2: legal cases 1813–51

Records' 2 Location: Sheffield City Libraries
Archives Division, Central Library, Surrey
St, Sheffield S1 1X2

155 COOPER, PURTON & SONS

Location: Bridgnorth & Wenlock, Salop

History: est 1817; acquired by Birmingham
Banking Co 1889

Records: cash & discount ledger 1819–20

Records' Location: Midland Bank Ltd

156 CO-OPERATIVE BANK LTD

Location: Manchester, Gt Manchester

History: est 1872 as Co-operative Wholesale
Society, Loan & Deposit Dept; known as
Co-operative Wholesale Society Banking
Dept 1876; as above 1970

Records: impersonal ledgers (7) 1873–1971,
published quarterly accounts 1878–93, cash
book 1902–14, customer ledger 1905,
summaries of investments (6) 1913–25,
investment register 1915–26, deposit note
registers (50) 1919–47, development bonds
registers (2) 1920–25, staff records f1914,
customers' investment register 1925–66,
cash in transit registers (4) 1929–47, sundry
day books (19) 1932–65, current account
weekly summaries (4) 1933–47, daily
balance books (10) 1932–49, daily cash
summaries (2) 1932–40 inc

Records' Location: Co-operative Bank Ltd,
Century House, Manchester M60 4EP

157 COPEMAN & CO

Location: Aylsham, Norfolk
History: est 1809; amlg with Gurney & Co 1855
Records: amlg agreement 1855
Records' Location: Barclays Bank Ltd

158 CORGAN, PAGET & MATHEWS

Location: Chipping Norton, Oxon
History: est c1790; failed 1816; otherwise known as Chipping Norton Bank
Records: papers re failure c1816–34
Records' Location: Oxfordshire County Record Office, County Hall, New Rd, Oxford OX1 1ND Ref: Stockton, Sons & Fortescue Collections Boxes 1 & 2

159 CORNISH BANK LTD

Location: Truro, Cornwall
History: est 1771 as Sir John Molesworth & Co; known as Praeds & Co 1800; as Tweedy, Williams & Co 1830; as above 1879; amlg with Capital & Counties Bank Ltd 1902
Records: minute book 1774–1830, security ledgers & registers 1873–92, staff agreements 1878–1901, board minute books (10) 1879–1906, rough minute books (5) 1888–1905, annual reports 1879–1901, letter books (4) 1889–1905, cash book 1890–1900, audit books & papers 1894–1901, amlg papers 1902
Records' Location: Lloyds Bank Ltd

160 COUNTY BANK LTD

Location: Manchester, Gt Manchester
History: est 1862 as Manchester & County Bank Ltd; known as above 1934; taken over by District Bank Ltd 1935
Records: prospectus 1862, articles of association 1862, general minutes 1862–1935, branch statistics 1877–1923, list of shareholders 1885, half yearly reports 1895–1920, general memoranda book 1897–1914, book of instructions to staff 1899, annual reports 1914–34, superannuation fund rules 1928, widows' & orphans' fund rules 1929
Accrington: minute book 1891–1918
Blackburn: minute book 1891–1910
Bacup: managers' private letter books (2) 1864–1924 inc

Bolton: out-letter books (9) 1897–1930 inc, staff applications 1897–1915, managers' reference book 1897–1902, minute books (5) 1898–1931, managers' information book 1906–08
Buxton: salaries & expenses book 1873–1900
Chorley: minute book 1903–35
Colne: minute book 1872–1909
Farnworth: minute book 1891–1937
Hollinwood: minute book 1891–1931
Oldham: opinion books (2) 1878–1937, register of cotton securities 1887–1934
Stockport: weekly balance book 1872–94, managers' memoranda book 1883–89, managers' reference book 1891–1920, staff register 1894–1948, out-letters 1910–30
Tyldesley: managers' memoranda book 1896–1923, staff record book 1896–1938
Uppermill: cash balance book 1886–87
Walkden: minute book 1898–1938
W Loughton: sanction letters 1902–38
Wigan: out-letter books (2) 1868–89 inc
Records' Location: National Westminster Bank Ltd

161 COUNTY OF GLOUCESTER BANKING CO

Location: Cheltenham, Gloucs
History: est 1836; amlg with Lloyds Bank Ltd 1897
Records 1: deed of settlement 1836, board minute books (7) 1836–95, agm minute books (2) 1836–1901, private ledger 1836–53, local directors' minute books (2) 1860–79, board agenda book 1892, amlg papers 1897
Burford: circulars f1857
Dursley: private memoranda book 1889–97
Gloucester: signature books 1850–90s, safe custody registers (4) 1884–90s, bill register f1888
Records' 1 Location: Lloyds Bank Ltd
Records 2: deed of settlement 1836, notices to shareholders 1838–41, reports 1866–97, shareholders' resolutions 1878–89, papers re increase in capital 1889
Records' 2 Location: Gloucestershire Collection, Public Library, Brunswick Rd, Gloucester GL1 1HT
Ref: 2155; JV13; JR13

162 COUNTY OF STAFFORD BANK

Location: Bilston, W Midlands

History: est 1836; known as County of
Stafford Bank 1874; amlg with National
Provincial Bank of England Ltd 1899

Records: deed of settlement 1836, board
minute books (3) 1836–1900, agm minutes
1838–73, licence to issue notes with list of
shareholders 1856, deed of assent to increase
capital 1864

Records' Location: National Westminster
Bank Ltd

163 COUTTS & CO

Location: London; Strand

History: est c1692 by John Campbell; 1708
name changed to Campbell & Middleton;
George Middleton sole proprietor 1712;
known as Middleton & Campbell 1727;
Middleton, Campbell & Bruce 1741;
Campbell & Bruce 1747; George Campbell
1751; Campbell & Coutts 1755; James
Coutts 1760; James & Thomas Coutts 1761;
Thomas Coutts & Co 1775; as Coutts & Co
1822

Records: papers of John Campbell c1692–
1712, customer wills & probates c1700–
1920, customer account ledgers (c4000)
f1712, partners' wills & re papers 1712–76,
probate registers 1786–1961, private ledgers
1716–19 f1734, out-letter books c1700–50,
leases, plans, elevations re premises f18
cent, waste books (3) 1719–26, private &
business papers of certain partners 1760–
1900, annual balance books (c160) 1761–
1920, in-letters f1770 (c4000 catalogued),
partners' letter books f1777, partnership
agreements 1777–1827, signature books (22)
1794–1917, customer mandates 1802–1900,
clerks' book 1810–1928, money lent books
1817–1946, salary books f1818, registers of
new accounts 1824–1971, customer address
books (18) 1856–1912, staff address books
1857–1912, managing directors' minutes
f1892, agm minutes f1892, sealing
committee minutes f1914

Records' Location: Coutts & Co, 440 The
Strand, London WC2R 0QS
All applications must be made in writing to
the Archivist

164 COVENTRY UNION BANKING CO

Location: Coventry, Warws

History: est 1836; acquired by Midland Bank
1889

Records: deed of settlement 1836, trustees'
declarations & conveyances 1836–73, board
minute books (4) 1836–80, signature book
1836–86, securities for loans papers (title
deeds, bills of costs, insurance policies,
probates, valuations) 1836–94, note
registers (3) 1836–85, 'board memorandum'
(resolutions) (3) 1852–59, annual reports
1877–88, amlg papers 1888–89

Records' Location: Midland Bank Ltd

165 COVENTRY & WARWICKSHIRE BANKING CO

Location: Coventry, Warws

History: est 1835; absorbed by Lloyds
Banking Co Ltd 1879

Records: deeds of settlement 1835–37, board
minute books (12) 1835–77, agm minutes
1837–68, amlg papers 1879

Records' Location: Lloyds Bank Ltd

166 COX & CO

Location: London; Fleet St

History: est 1758 as Cox & Drummond;
known as Cox & Mair 1772; Cox, Mair &
Cox 1779; Cox, Cox & Greenwood 1783;
Cox & Greenwood 1790; Greenwood & Cox
1803; Greenwood, Cox & Co 1806; as above
f1834; absorbed by Lloyds Bank Ltd 1923

Records: papers re Cox family 1718–1865,
day book 1759–61, regimental account
ledgers (c190) 1760–1830, cash book 1767–
68, profit & loss account ledgers (c24)
1772–1899 inc, household accounts (3)
1792–1803, papers of H Hammersley 1795–
1840, partnership deeds 1805–1905, balance
books (dormant accounts) (2) 1819 1822,
'old corps' letter book 1821, outstanding
accounts ledger 1824, out-letter book 1835–
53, 'public office' letter book 1866, premises
report 1868, widows fund letter book 1871,
balance sheets 1892–1922, memoranda re
average figures for Indian branches 1908–
14, report on foreign dept 1918, report on
US army branch 1919, report on Indian
business 1922, amlg papers 1923–43

Records' Location: Lloyds Bank Ltd

167   COX, COBBOLD & CO

Location: Harwich, Essex

History: est 1807; acquired by Bacon, Cobbold, Tollemache & Co 1893

Records: note registers (3) 1811–91, abstract of general ledger 1815–18, partnership agreement 1817, stock book 1822–80, customer ledger 1838–42, balance book 1839–44, security registers (2) 1855–1908

Records' Location: Lloyds Bank Ltd

168   CRAVEN BANKING CO

Location: Skipton, N Yorks

History: est 1791 as Birkbecks, Alcocks & Co; name changed to Birkbecks, Alcock, Peart & Moffat 1812; to Birkbecks, Alcocks, Birkbeck & Robinson 1833; to Alcocks, Birkbeck, Robinson, Birkbeck & Stansfeld 1844; to Alcocks, Birkbeck & Co 1858; to Birkbeck, Robinson & Co 1873; to Craven Bank Ltd 1880; amlg with Bank of Liverpool Ltd 1906

Records 1: customer ledger 1791–1803, half yearly balances 1816–44, partnership accounts (3) 1825–1911, stock ledger 1806–36, declaration of confidence 1826, customer balances 1827–36, diaries with notes on customers etc (2) 1866–91 inc, prospectus 1880, articles of association 1880, annual reports 1880–1905, list of shareholders 1881, 1892, agm minutes 1906
Barnoldswick: draft book 1898–1909
Clitheroe: security register 1900–20
Colne: security registers 1876–1902
Settle: stock book 1800s, private ledger 1813–30, general balances abstract 1834–1840, note register 1844–70

Records' 1 Location: Barclays Bank Ltd

Records 2: customer ledgers (17) 1802–06, general balances pre 1805, Birkbeck family correspondence (9 items) 1830, partnership agreement 1859

Records' 2 Location: Pig Yard Museum, Castle Hill, Settle, N Yorkshire

Records 3: business letters of William Birkbeck & other papers re bank 1773–1823

Records' 3 Location: Leeds Archives Dept, Chapeltown Rd, Sheepscar, Leeds LS7 3AP
Ref: Birkbeck MSS

169   CREDIT FONCIER ET MOBILIER OF ENGLAND LTD

History: unknown

Records: general papers including reports & share certificates 1866–67

Records' Location: Devon Record Office, Castle St, Exeter EX4 3PQ
Ref: 58/9, 52/7

170   CROMPTON & EVANS'S UNION BANK LTD

Location: Derby, Derbys

History: formed 1877 by amlg of Crompton, Newton & Co & W & S Evans & Co; amlg with Parr's Bank Ltd 1913

Records: prospectus 1877, agm minutes 1877–1913, articles of association 1877, share allotment books (3) 1877–96, list of overdrawn accounts taken over from Chesterfield & N Derbyshire Bank 1878, profit & loss account memoranda book 1877–84, head office instructions to branches 1879–1914, annual reports 1882–1914 inc, staff instructions 1883, general managers' letter book 1884–1917, weekly memoranda book 1886–90, balance sheets 1888–89, clerkship application registers 1891–1913, committee minutes 1895–1914, chairmen's agenda books (7) 1896–1918, salary books (3) 1897–1913, select committee minutes 1905–13, board minute books (2) 1905–13, memoranda re investments & advances 1906–13, rough minute book 1908–13, directors' correspondence 1911–14, amlg papers 1913–14
Bakewell: half yearly returns 1879–1913
Chesterfield: profit & loss account 1880, list of overdrawn accounts 1882, general ledger balances (5) 1896–1913 inc
Hathersage: half yearly returns 1892–93

Records' Location: National Westminster Bank Ltd

171   CROMPTON, NEWTON & CO

Location: Derby, Derbys

History: est 1685; merged with W & S Evans & Co to form Crompton & Evans Union Bank Ltd 1877

Records: memoranda & cash books (3) 1707–79, private account book & papers of S Crompton 1739–68, investment & loan ledger 1755–1877, private cash book of C

Crompton 1806–30, partnership agreements 1808, cash balance books (3) 1808–29, balance sheet 1877, accounts with London agent 1761–66 1777–85
Chesterfield: note registers 1821–25, customer ledger 1808–24, deposit ledger 1808–15
Records' Location: National Westminster Bank Ltd

172 CROMPTON & SON, MORTIMER, EWBANK & SWANN

Location: York, N Yorks
History: est 1771; ceased business 1798
Records: notice of opening 1771
Records' Location: National Westminster Bank Ltd

173 CROXON, JONES & CO

Location: Oswestry, Salop
History: est 1792; amlg with Parr's Banking Co & the Alliance Bank Ltd 1893; otherwise known as Oswestry Old Bank
Records 1: customer ledger 1854, balance sheet 1893, notice of amlg 1894
Records' 1 Location: National Westminster Bank Ltd
Records 2: partnership agreements (3) 1812–47
Records' 2 Location: Salop Record Office, Shire Hall, Abbey Foregate, Shrewsbury SY2 6ND
Ref: 800/Box 69D

174 CUMBERLAND UNION BANKING CO LTD

Location: Workington & Carlisle, Cumbria
History: est 1829; acquired by York City & County Banking Co 1901
Records: deeds of settlement (3) 1829–65, board minute books (9) 1829–1905, shareholders' minute book 1829–1901, current accounts ledger 1829–30, managers' memoranda book 1849–78, general ledgers (4) 1851–75, balance books (6) 1851–1901, note register 1851–97, head office letter books (2) 1851–1905, staff declarations of secrecy 1852–1901, board agenda (6) 1865–1905, annual reports 1865–96, share register 1865–67, customers' balance sheets 1865–66, current account ledger 1866–1902, committee minutes 1867–68, security books

(7) 1868–1901, salary registers (2) 1871–89, branch letter books (8) 1876–91, branch inspection reports 1876–1901, managers' interviews (2) 1879–98, directors' attendance books (4) 1880–1905, enquiry book 1883–87, half yearly balance sheets 1884–1900, register of overdrafts 1885–88
Brampton: deposit account ledgers (4) 1856–1906, general ledger 1877–89
Carlisle: general ledgers (2) 1861–78
Records' Location: Midland Bank Ltd

175 CURTEIS, POMFRET & CO

Location: Rye, Kent
History: est as Curteis & Co 1790; known as above 1866; taken over by Lloyds Bank Ltd 1893
Records: interview books (5) 1887–92
Records' Location: Lloyds Bank Ltd

176 CURRIES & CO

Location: London
History: est 1773 as Currie, James & Yallowley; known as Lefevre, Curries, James & Yallowley 1782; as Lefevre, Curries, Yallowley & Raikes 1788; as Lefevre, Curries, Raikes & Lawford 1806; as Curries, Raikes & Co 1813; as Curries & Co 1826; absorbed Dorriens & Co 1842; amlg with Glyn, Mills & Co to form Glyn, Mills, Currie & Co 1864
Records: partnership agreement 1773, discount ledger 1773–76, balance book 1774–80, customer ledger 1776–77, salary book 1776–1864, sundry balances 1797–1864, abstract of current accounts 1786, letter book 1831–63, loan books (2) 1826–36, half yearly results 1833–63, partners' profits & interest payments 1846–63, cash books (2) 1847–64, petty cash books 1850–63, personal papers of B W Currie 1853–62
Records' Location: Williams & Glyn's Bank Ltd

177 ROGER CUNLIFFE, SONS & CO

Location: London
History: discount house; est 1816; absorbed by Cater, Brightwen & Co Ltd 1941
Records: partnership agreements 1835–83, Roger Cunliffe's will 1864
Records' Location: Guildhall Library, Aldermanbury, London EC2P 2EJ

178 CUNLIFFE, BROOKS & CO

Location: Blackburn, Lancs

History: est 1792; amlg with Lloyds Bank Ltd 1900

Records: profit & loss accounts 1823–1900, staff appearance books 1847–98, list of partners 1851–1900, salary books 1862–1900, bad debt book 1869–97, enquiry reply book 1870s, private correspondence 1872–1901, minute books 1884–1900, amlg papers 1893
Altrincham: profit & loss book 1857–98
Darwen: signature book 1889–1900
Manchester: branch diaries 1833–1900, memoranda re old balances c1840, realisation ledgers (2) 1841–1925, signature books 1851–97, salary book 1870–91, private memoranda books 1885–94, stock books (2) 1885–99, press cuttings 1890s, status book 1895–1900

Records' Location: Lloyds Bank Ltd

179 DALE, YOUNG & CO

Location: Newcastle upon Tyne, Tyne & Wear

History: est 1858; amlg with North Eastern Banking Co Ltd 1892

Records 1: deposit ledger 1872–1913, signature book 1882–97

Records' 1 Location: Barclays Bank Ltd

Records 2: partnership agreements (3) 1858–80, amlg agreement 1892

Records' 2 Location: Durham County Record Office, County Hall, Durham DH1 5UL
Ref: D/X 344/1–5

180 DAVIES, BANKS & CO

Location: Kington & Knighton, Powys

History: est c1808; Knighton business acquired by North & South Wales Bank 1856; Kington business acquired by Metropolitan Bank (of England & Wales) Ltd 1910; known otherwise as Kington & Radnorshire Bank

Records: partnership agreements 1812 1857, bill books (3) 1808–1924, general ledgers (2) 1863–93, 'valuation book' (balance sheets) 1867–99, current account ledger 1868–79, Kington Savings Bank Treasurer's pass book 1873–83, deposit ledgers (3) 1880–1901, 'manager's book' (deposit account journal) 1881–83, balance sheets 1893–1910, security register 1898–1910, drib ledgers (2) 1908–18, partners' private ledger 1901–08, agreement with Metropolitan Bank 1910
Penybont: general ledger 1891–99
Rhayader: general ledgers (4) 1873–1904, deposit ledger 1897–1900, security register 1901

Records' Location: Midland Bank Ltd

181 ROBERT DAVIES & CO

Location: London; Shoreditch

History: est 1841; failed & business taken over by London & County Bank 1860

Records: managers' information book 1853–67, notice of takeover 1860

Records' Location: National Westminster Bank Ltd

182 DAVISON, NOEL, TEMPLER, MIDDLETON & WEDGWOOD

Location: London; Pall Mall

History: est 1793 as Edwards, Smith, Templer, Middleton, Johnson & Wedgwood; known as Davison, Noel, Templer, Middleton, Johnson & Wedgwood 1804; as above 1806; absorbed by Coutts & Co 1816

Records 1: agreement for security put up by new partner 1803

Records' 1 Location: Leicestershire Record Office, 57 New Walk, Leicester LE1 7JB
Ref: 81/30/10

Records 2: papers re partners 1794–1816, list of customers 1816

Records' 2 Location: Coutts & Co, 440 The Strand, London WC2R OQS
All applications must be made in writing to the Archivist

183 DAY, NICHOLSON & DAY

Location: Chatham & Rochester, Kent

History: est 1782; absorbed by Provincial Banking Corp 1864

Records: day book 1791–1843, balance sheet 1793

Records' Location: Barclays Bank Ltd

184   DEANE & CO

Location: Winchester, Hants

History: est 1787; amlg with Prescott, Dimsdale, Cave, Tugwell & Co 1891

Records: press cuttings 1819, balance sheet 1890, amlg agreement 1891

Records' Location: National Westminster Bank Ltd

185   DERBY COMMERCIAL BANK LTD

Location: Derby, Derbys

History: est 1868; acquired by Midland Bank Ltd 1890

Records: prospectus 1868, articles of association 1868, board minute books (4) 1868–86, half yearly balance sheets 1868–89, amlg circular 1889

Records' Location: Midland Bank Ltd

186   DERBY & DERBYSHIRE BANKING CO LTD

Location: Derby, Derbys

History: est 1833; amlg with Parr's Bank Ltd 1898

Records: minutes of provisional committee 1833, deed of settlement 1833, customer ledger 1835, amlg papers 1898

Records' Location: National Westminster Bank Ltd

187   DEVON & CORNWALL BANKING CO

Location: Plymouth, Devon

History: est 1831 as Plymouth & Devonport Banking Co; known as above 1833; amlg with Lloyds Bank Ltd 1906

Records: board minute book 1831–41, annual reports 1861–1905, articles of association 1899, amlg papers 1906

Brixham: draft register 1870s

Exeter: security registers (2) 1862–1906, private memoranda book 1893–1905

Holsworthy: private memoranda books f1899

Lynton: signature book 1888–1906, security registers 1889–c1910, safe custody registers 1890–1906

Tavistock: safe custody registers 1840–1906, security registers 1870–1900, signature books 1880–1906

Tiverton: security registers f1875

Torquay: inspection report book 1855–67

Records' Location: Lloyds Bank Ltd

188   DICKINSON & GREEN

Location: Ware, Herts

History: est 1808; failed 1814

Records: private ledger 1809–14

Records' Location: Hertfordshire Record Office, County Hall, Hertford SG13 8DE

Ref: 79951X

189   DILWORTH, ARTHINGTON & BIRKETT

Location: Lancaster, Lancs

History: est 1793; failed 1826

Records: discharge of partner from bankruptcy, with list of creditors 1826

Records' Location: Lancaster District Library, Local History Dept, Market Sq, Lancaster LA1 1HY

Ref: MS 7339

190   DIMSDALE, FOWLER, BARNARD & DIMSDALE

Location: London; Cornhill

History: est 1760 as Amyand, Staples & Mercer; known as Cornewall, Staples & Watts 1773; Staples, Baron, Dimsdale, Sons & Co 1774; Baron, Dimsdale, Sons, Barnard & Staples 1784; Barnard, Dimsdale & Dimsdale 1812; absorbed Drewett, Fowler & Co to form Dimsdale, Drewett, Fowler & Barnard 1852; known as Dimsdale, Fowler & Barnard 1866; Dimsdale, Fowler, Barnard & Dimsdale 1868; amlg with Prescotts & Co to form Prescott, Dimsdale, Cave, Tugwell & Co Ltd 1891

Records: partnership agreement 1774, customer list 1774, current account ledger 1774–75, balance sheets 1777–91, unpaid bills & drafts 1778–1893, signature books (3) 1783–1891, balances of current, bankers & discount accounts 1795–1800, security ledgers (2) 1862–1906, partnership ledgers 1872–90

Records' Location: National Westminster Bank Ltd

191 DINGLEY, PETHYBRIDGE & CO AND DINGLEY, PEARS & CO

Location: Launceston, Cornwall & Okehampton, Devon

History: est 1855 & 1856 respectively; absorbed by National Provincial & Union Bank of England Ltd 1922

Records: details of staff, premises etc (2) 1871–1922, amlg papers 1922 Stratton: cash journal 1855–57, day books (4) 1907–17

Records' Location: National Westminster Bank Ltd

192 DISTRICT BANK LTD

Location: Manchester, Gt Manchester

History: est 1829 as Manchester & Liverpool District Banking Co; known as above 1924; absorbed into the National Westminster Bank Ltd 1968

Records 1: board minutes books (17) 1829–1968, share ledger 1829–38, list of managers 1829–1916, Liverpool shareholders' minutes 1830, instructions for directors & officers 1831, past due bills register 1830–96, declarations of secrecy f1832, share register 1837–57, deed of settlement 1843, investments memoranda book 1849–56, staff register 1846–66, list of securities held against advances 1849–73, dividends memoranda book 1851–97, bills for acceptance registers (4) 1864–1900, registers of bankruptcies & liquidations (3) 1865–1915, memoranda book re directors 1865–99, draft minute book 1866–67, list of shareholders 1873, annual reports 1874–1969, bank rate memoranda book 1880–93, pension fund rules 1889–1962, pension fund minutes 1889–1918, correspondence re overseas business 1892–1941, directors' committee minute books (10) 1896–1959, security register 1893–95, head office staff register 1897–1914, head office minute books (27) 1897–1923, list of directors 1903–69, overdraft memoranda book 1912–16, balance sheets & profit & loss accounts f1914, foreign department minutes 1917–25, staff register 1918–20 Alderley Edge: branch minutes 1896–97, memoranda book 1896–1935 Ashton: local board minutes 1831–95, customer ledger 1831–84, expenses book

1833–41, signature book 1862–89, managers' opinion book 1867–75, branch minute books (2) 1886–98 Barrow: advances registers (2) 1898–1927, managers' letter books (2) 1899–1911, minute book 1910–25 Bury: local board minutes 1875–95 Cannock: information book 1883–1908 Cheadle: information book 1886–1908, branch minute books (3) 1886–1924, managers' opinion book c1877–1927 Chester: branch minutes 1908–38 Chorley: information book 1907–44, managers' minutes 1911–31 Dukinfield: managers' minutes 1898–1909 Fallowfield: information book 1883–1908, managers' minute books (2) 1889–1925 Fenton: out-letter books (3) 1874–1923, expenses book 1875–99, information book 1883–1908, branch minutes 1885–1919 Hanley: bad debts register 1839–86, information book 1883–91, minute books (12) 1885–1969, half yearly returns 1888–1957 inc, abstract of customers' balances 1907–50 inc, letter books (2) 1911–20, letter book re staff 1919–29 Haslingden: branch minutes 1885–1906 Knutsford: branch minutes 1909–40 Levershulme: branch minutes 1898–1959 Liverpool: bankruptcies register 1834–38, opinion book 1835–42, managers' letter books (63) 1836–1931, minute books (59) 1844–1970, local board minutes (2) 1845–95, analysis book 1880–1908, information book 1891–1908 London Office: statistics 1842–1908 London, Cornhill: branch minutes 1886–1928 Manchester: local board minutes 1831–76, managers' memoranda book 1873–95 Maryport: managers' opinion book 1919–27 Nantwich: letters re routine business 1870–80 Ramsbottom: branch minutes 1908–39 Rochdale: expenses book 1833–46, managers' out-letter book 1839–72 Stafford: balance sheet 1834, expenses book 1839–69, local board minutes 1843–64, manager's diary 1883–85, minute books (2) 1886–94 Stoke-on-Trent: customer ledger 1877, information book 1883–1908 Ulverston: managers' out-letter books (2) 1907–16, branch minutes 1910–24

Warrington: instructions re bad debts 1839
Whitehaven: deposit ledger 1916–59,
manager's diaries (4) 1917–20
Wilmslow: memoranda book 1898–1914
Windermere: out-letter books (4) 1907–28
Records' 1 Location: National Westminster
Bank Ltd
Records 2: 'accounts' 1832–33
Records' 2 Enquiries: National Register of
Archives (Scotland), HM General Register
House, Edinburgh EH1 3YY
Ref: list 945

193   DIXON, DALTON & CO

Location: Dudley, W Midlands
History: est c1790; failed & absorbed by
Birmingham Banking Co 1843; otherwise
known as Dudley Old Bank
Records 1: apprenticeship agreement 1800
Records' 1 Location: Lloyds Bank Ltd
Records 2: assignment of partnership 1844
Records' 2 Location: Staffordshire Record
Office, Eastgate St, Stafford ST16 2LZ
Ref: D 695/4/20/5/4
Records 3: list of E Dalton's creditors &
debtors c1844
Records' 3 Location: Dudley Archives & Local
History Dept, Central Library, St James's
Rd, Dudley DY1 1HR

194   DIXON, WARDELL & CO

Location: Chester, Cheshire
History: est 1813; amlg with Parr's Banking
Co Ltd 1878
Records: general ledger 1813–19, cash
balance book 1849–69, weekly balance book
1849, amlg agreement 1878
Records' Location: National Westminster
Bank Ltd

195   DORRIENS, MAGENS, MELLO & CO

Location: London
History: est as Dorrien, Rucker & Carleton
1770; known as Dorrien, Rucker, Dorrien &
Martin 1775; Dorriens, Mello & Martin
1779; as above 1794; absorbed by Curries &
Co 1841

Records: ledgers (2) 19 cent
Records' Location: Williams & Glyn's Bank
Ltd

196   DORSETT, JOHNSON, WILKINSON & BERNERS

Location: London; Bond St
History: est 1784; ceased 1803
Records: papers re customer's account 1794–
1807
Records' Location: Guildhall Library,
Aldermanbury, London EC2P 2EJ

197   DOUGLAS, HERON & CO

Location: Ayr, Strathclyde
History: est 1769; failed 1772
Records: papers re failure 1773–93
Records' Enquiries: National Register of
Archives (Scotland), PO Box 36, HM
General Register House, Edinburgh EH1
3YY

198   DRUMMOND & CO

Location: London; Charing Cross
History: est 1712 as Andrew Drummond;
known as Andrew Drummond & Co 1753;
John Drummond & Co 1768; Robert
Drummond & Co 1774; known as above
1804; absorbed by Royal Bank of Scotland
1924
Records 1: customer ledgers (c300) f1717,
safe custody registers (4) 1830–51, signature
& address books (2) 1800 1835, address
books (3) c1890s
Records' 1 Location: Drummond's Branch,
Royal Bank of Scotland, 49 Charing Cross,
London SW1A 2OX
Records 2: papers re Drummond family
18–19 cents, partnership agreements (8)
1780–1892, correspondence of Drummond
family re banking & partnership matters
1811–91, deed of settlement 1894
Records' 2 Location: Hampshire Record
Office, 20 Southgate St, Winchester SO23
9EF
Ref: 3M60
Records 3: correspondence with Shropshire
agent 1812–21
Records' 3 Location: Guildhall Library,
Aldermanbury, London EC2P 2EJ

199 DUDLEY & WEST BROMWICH BANKING CO

Location: Dudley, W Midlands

History: est 1833; amlg with Birmingham Town & District Banking Co to form the Birmingham, Dudley & District Banking Co 1874

Records: deed of settlement 1833, customer ledgers (2) 1834–36, private ledger 1834–48, resolutions 1840–75, rules & regulations for clerks 1869, profit & loss accounts 1869–74, amlg papers 1874
Bilston: customer ledger 1866, balance book 1866–76, stock book cash analysis 1866–70

Records' Location: Barclays Bank Ltd

200 DUIGNAN & SON

Location: Walsall, W Midlands

History: est c1840; acquired by Staffordshire Joint Stock Bank 1864

Records 1: agreement for acquisition 1864

Records' 1 Location: Midland Bank Ltd

Records 2: correspondence, memoranda sent to the Bank of Walsall and South Staffordshire re banking business c1837–40

Records' 2 Location: Walsall Library and Museums Services, Central Library, Tichfield St, Walsall WS1 1TR

Ref: 48/1/61

201 DUMBELL'S BANKING CO LTD

Location: Isle of Man

History: est 1853 as Dumbell, Son & Howard; known as above 1874; liquidated & business acquired by Parr's Banking Co Ltd 1900

Records 1: articles of association 1874, salary book 1880s, annual reports 1897–98, papers re failure & take over 1900

Records' 1 Location: National Westminster Bank Ltd

Records 2: papers re formation 1849–61

Records' 2 Location: Manx Museum Library, Kingswood Grove, Douglas, Isle of Man

202 DUNDEE BANKING CO

Location: Dundee, Tayside

History: est 1763; amlg with Royal Bank of Scotland 1864

Records: sederunt book including articles of co-partnership 1763–67, book of conduct of accounts including character reports c1823–64, list of partners 1836

Records' Enquiries: National Register of Archives (Scotland), HM General Register House, Edinburgh EH1 3YY

Ref: list 1964

203 DUNDEE UNION BANK

Location: Dundee, Tayside

History: est 1809; absorbed by Western Bank of Scotland 1844

Records 1: list of partners 1836

Records' 1 Enquiries: National Register of Archives (Scotland), HM General Register House, Edinburgh EH1 3YY

Ref: list 1964

Records 2: deed of accession to the contract of co-partnery 1832

Records' 2 Location: University of Glasgow Archives, The University, Glasgow G12 8QQ

Ref: UGD/85

204 DUNLOP, HOUSTON, GEMMELL & CO

Location: Greenock, Strathclyde

History: est 1785; failed 1842; known otherwise as Greenock Banking Co

Records: cash book 1813–20, state book 1820–28

Records' Enquiries: National Register of Archives (Scotland), PO Box 36, HM General Register House, Edinburgh EH1 3YY

Ref: list 349

205 DUNSFORD & CO

Location: Tiverton, Devon

History: est 1786; amlg with Stuckey's Banking Co Ltd 1883; otherwise known as Tiverton & Devonshire Bank

Records 1: deposit ledger 1789, sundry correspondence & instructions 1880–83

Records' 1 Location: National Westminster Bank Ltd

Records 2: papers re formation 1786–87

Records' 2 Location: Harrowby Manuscripts Trust, Sandon Hall, Stafford Ref: Tiverton MSS vols 5 & 6

206 EAST OF ENGLAND BANK

Location: Norwich, Norfolk

History: est 1836; absorbed by Provincial Banking Co 1864

Records: copy of statutory return with list of partners 1847

Records' Location: Barclays Bank Ltd

207   EASTERN BANK LTD

Location: London

History: overseas bank; est 1909; became a subsidiary of The Chartered Bank 1957

Records: prospectus 1909, board minute books (5) 1909–71, general ledgers (c170) 1909–71, legal & financial documents (8 boxes) 1909–17, list of shareholders 1910, seal registers (3) 1910–55, Bombay committee minute books (3) 1910–17, annual reports 1910–70, head office & branch balance sheets (70 boxes) 1910–71, security ledgers & registers (11) 1910–71, salary book 1910–56, agm attendance register 1914–67, finance committee reports (6) 1918–41, staff records 1923–29, circulars to branches 1925–58, comparative statements branches general charges 1928–60, finance committee minute books (2) 1934–43, general managers' correspondence (10 parcels) f1940

Records' Location: Standard Chartered Bank Ltd, Head Office, 10 Clements Lane, London EC4N 7AB

At the time of preparing this guide only very limited access can be given to the records

208   EASTERN BANK OF SCOTLAND

Location: Dundee, Tayside

History: est 1838; absorbed by Clydesdale Bank 1863

Records 1: list of partners 1838, licences to issue notes (1 bdl) 1838–61, statements of affairs 1840–44, annual reports 1849–61, amlg agreement 1862, statement of assets & liabilities 1863

Records' 1 Location: Clydesdale Bank Ltd, Head Office, 30 St Vincent Place, Glasgow G1 2HL

Records 2: 'bills received, negotiated, etc' 1857–58

Records' 2 Enquiries: National Register of Archives (Scotland), PO Box 36, HM General Register House, Edinburgh EH1 3YY

Ref: list 945

209   EATON, CAYLEY & CO

Location: Stamford, Lincs

History: est 1800 as Eaton & Cayley; known as above 1844; purchased by Stamford, Spalding & Boston Banking Co 1891

Records 1: Uppingham: half yearly balances 1873–91

Records' 1 Location: Barclays Bank Ltd

Records 2: annual partnership balance books, papers etc 1819–34, S Eaton's exors papers 1834–59

Records' 2 Location: Northamptonshire Record Office, Delapre Abbey, Northampton NN4 9AW

Ref: Acc 1982/168

210   EDINBURGH & GLASGOW BANK

History: est 1838 as Edinburgh & Leith Bank; reorganised 1844; absorbed by Clydesdale Bank 1858

Records: general meeting notebook 1840–58, agreement with Glasgow Joint Stock Bank 1844, directors' Glasgow committee minute books (2) 1851–58, trustee committee minutes 1858–60

Records' Location: Clydesdale Bank Ltd, Head Office, 30 St Vincent Place, Glasgow G1 2HL

211   EDINBURGH LINEN CO-PARTNERY

Location: Edinburgh, Lothian

Records: cash book 1745–60, journals 1745–67, general ledger 1745–66, letter book 1745–49, accounts ledger 1745–47

Records' Enquiries: National Register of Archives (Scotland), PO Box 36, HM General Register House, Edinburgh EH1 3YY

Ref: list 945

212   ELAND & ELAND

Location: Thrapston, Northants

History: est 1812; otherwise known as Thrapston & Kettering Bank; failed & business acquired by Stamford, Spalding & Boston Banking Co Ltd 1888

Records: statement of assets & liabilities 188

Records' Location: Barclays Bank Ltd

213   SIR WILLIAM ELFORD, TINGECOMBE & CO

Location: Plymouth, Devon

History: est c1782; failed 1825

Records: papers re failure 1823–63

Records' Location: National Westminster Bank Ltd

214   ELIOT, PEARCE & CO

Location: Weymouth, Dorset

History: est 1791; failed & amlg with Capital & Counties Bank Ltd 1897; otherwise known as Weymouth Old Bank

Records: amlg papers 1897

Records' Location: Lloyds Bank Ltd

215   EQUITABLE BANK LTD

Location: Halifax, W Yorks

History: est 1899 as Halifax Equitable Bank Ltd; name changed to above 1913; amlg with Bank of Liverpool & Martins Ltd 1927

Records: amlg papers 1926–27

Records' Location: Barclays Bank Ltd

216   ERLANGERS LTD

Location: London

History: merchant bank; est as Emile Erlanger & Co 1870; known as Erlangers 1917; as Erlangers Ltd 1928; merged with Philip Hill, Higginson & Co Ltd 1959

Records: agm minutes (locked), balance sheets 1928–59, board minute books (7) (locked), routine ledgers 1940–59, private ledgers 1949–59, committee minutes 1953

Records' Location: Hill, Samuel & Co Ltd, 100 Wood St, London EC2P 2AJ

217   SIR JAMES ESDAILE, ESDAILE, GRENFELL, THOMAS & CO

Location: London

History: est 1780 as Esdaile, Hammett & Esdaile; amlg with Smith, Wright & Co to form Sir James Esdaile, Esdaile, Smith, Wright, Hammett & Co 1792; known as Sir James Esdaile, Esdaile, Hammett, Esdaile & Hammett 1798; known as above 1832; failed 1837

Records: customer ledgers (3) 1820–22 inc, papers re failure (1 box) 1836–37, Hammett family papers 19 cent

Records' Location: Williams & Glyn's Bank Ltd

218   JOHN EWER

Location: London

Records: letter book 1730/31–1733/34

Records' Location: City of Westminster Archives Dept, Victoria Library, Buckingham Palace Rd, London SW1W 9UD

219   EXCHANGE BANK

Location: Bristol, Avon

Records: partnership agreement 1764, papers re partnership matters 1764–96, agreement with cashier 1764

Records' Location: Gloucestershire Collection, Public Library, Brunswick Rd, Gloucester GL1 1HT

Ref: OF6 3(1–63)

220   EXCHANGE & DISCOUNT BANK LTD

Location: Leeds, W Yorks

History: est 1860 as J J Cousins; known as Cousins, Allen & Co 1863; reconstructed as Exchange & Discount Bank Ltd 1866; acquired by Midland Bank Ltd 1890

Records: partnership agreement 1863, board minutes 1865–71, annual reports 1874 1889, security book 1883–89, amlg papers 1890–92

Records' Location: Midland Bank Ltd

221   EYTON, BURTON & CO

Location: Shrewsbury, Salop

History: est 1792 as Rocke, Eyton & Co; amlg with Burton, Lloyd, Salt & How to form Eyton, Burton & Co 1884; amlg with Capital & Counties Bank Ltd 1907

Records 1: partnership agreement 1866, private correspondence 1883–84, amlg papers 1907–10

Records' 1 Location: Lloyds Bank Ltd

Records 2: partnership agreements (3) 1792–1866

Records' 2 Location: Salop Record Office, Shire Hall, Abbey Foregate, Shrewsbury SY2 6ND

Ref: 665/477

222   FARLEY, LAVENDER & CO

Location: Worcester, Hereford & Worcester

History: est 1794; failed 1857; otherwise known as Worcester Bank

Records: papers re law suits 1820–40, partnership agreement 1821, papers re salaries 1829–36, papers re failure 1857

Records' Location: Hereford & Worcester Record Office, Shire Hall, Worcester WR1 1TR

Ref: 705:380 BA 2309/1

223   FARROW'S BANK LTD

Location: London

History: est 1907; suspended payment & business taken over by London, County & Westminster Bank Ltd 1920

Records: papers re failure 1921–25

Records' Location: Public Record Office, Ruskin Av, Kew, Richmond, Surrey TW9 4DU

Ref: T172/1209, 13669

224   FENN ADDISON

Location: Sudbury, Suffolk

History: est 1795; amlg with Oakes, Bevan & Co 1830; otherwise known as Sparrow, Fenn & Co & Sparrow, Brown, Fenn & Co

Records: security registers 1820s, correspondence with Oakes, Bevan & Co 1828

Records' Location: Lloyds Bank Ltd

225   THOMAS FIRTH & SON

Location: Northwich, Cheshire

History: est 1817; amlg with Parr's Bank 1865

Records: amlg agreement 1865

Records' Location: National Westminster Bank Ltd

226   JOHN FORDHAM & CO

Location: Royston, Herts

History: est 1808; known later as Fordham, Gibson & Co; incorporated with Barclay & Co Ltd 1896

Records: partnership agreements 1879–83, licence to issue notes 1887, amlg papers 1896

Records' Location: Barclays Bank Ltd

227   SIR WILLIAM FORBES, JAS HUNTER & CO

Location: Edinburgh, Lothian

History: est 1723; amlg with Glasgow Union Banking Co 1843

Records: 'state of bank notes' 1814–45

Records' Enquiries: National Register of Archives (Scotland), PO Box 36, HM General Register House, Edinburgh 1EH 3YY

Ref: list 945

228   FOSTER & CO

Location: Cambridge, Cambs

History: est 1804; taken over by Capital & Counties Bank Ltd 1904

Records: amlg papers 1903–05
Ely: security registers f1860s

Records' Location: Lloyds Bank Ltd

229   FOX BROTHERS, FOWLER & CO

Location: Wellington, Somerset

History: est 1787 as Fox & Co; known as above 1879; amlg with Lloyds Bank Ltd 1921

Records: note register 1824–1921, security registers (2) 1879–1917, private memoranda book 1886–1906, signature books (3) 1891–1921, amlg papers 1921
Bideford: signature book 1880s
Bridgwater: security registers 1896–1924, private memoranda books (2) 1905–19, safe custody registers 1906–21
High Bridge: salary book f1905
Lynton: security registers (2) 1890–1923, safe custody registers 1895–1920, private memoranda books (2) 1892–1924
Tavistock: letter books (2) 1890–1912
Tiverton: signature books f1891, private memoranda books f1891

Records' Location: Lloyds Bank Ltd

230   R & W F FRYER

Location: Wolverhampton, W Midlans

History: est 1807; taken over by Lloyds Banking Co Ltd 1872; otherwise known as Wolverhampton Old Bank

Records: amlg papers 1872

Records' Location: Lloyds Bank Ltd

231   FRYER, ANDREWS & CO

Location: Wimborne, Dorset

History: est 1790; amlg with National Provincial Bank of England 1840

Records: extracts from W Fryer's letter book 1811–28, circulars re take-over 1841

Records' Location: National Westminster Bank Ltd

232   FULLER BANBURY & CO

Location: London; Lombard St

History: est 1737; amlg with Parr's Banking Co Ltd 1891

Records: papers re loans 1806–57, papers re securities for loans 1834–91, papers re investments 1861–93, papers re G Banbury's account 1862–77, amlg papers 1891

Records' Location: National Westminster Bank Ltd

233   GARFIT, CLAYPON & CO

Location: Boston, Lincs

History: est 1754; amlg with Capital & Counties Bank Ltd 1891

Records 1: private cash books (2) 1791–92, cash book 1791–98, partnership agreement 1814, amlg papers 1891–92

Horncastle: customer ledger 1808–11

Louth: cash book 1791, customer ledger 1809–12

Records' 1 Location: Lloyds Bank Ltd

Records 2: notebook of Spalding agent 1791–93

Records' 2 Location: Spalding Gentlemen's Society, The Museum, Broad Street, Spalding, Lincs PE11 1TB

234   ANTONY GIBBS & SONS LTD

Location: London

History: merchant bank; est 1808

Records: Gibbs family papers (extensive) 1744–1905, London ledgers (3) 1809–14, register of bills payable & receivable 1809–14, London journals (2) 1813–19, general ledgers (61) 1815–1918 inc, extracts from letters re Guano business (3 folders) 1840–

56, out-letter books of H H Gibbs (5) 1845–88, Guano ledgers (5) 1850–66 1882–83, papers re partnership matters 1852–75, in-letter book of W Gibbs 1854–55, information books re clients etc (3) 1859–1905, out-letter books of G L M Gibbs (5) 1863–81, papers re Gibbs' Ceylon estates 1865–96, S American manager's letters re nitrate (4 bdls) 1872–99, out-letter book of A G H Gibbs 1874–1936, scrapbook of deposit letters 1880–1910, papers re Guano cargoes (1 file) 1879–80, special out-letter books (2) 1881–1922, West India ledgers (2) 1882–1909, balance books (2) 1882–1925, private letters to partners' books (5) 1884–1919, out-letter books of F A Keating (5) 1884–1911, general private out-letter books re Greek loans (4) 1888–1901, London private accounts of West coast partners & managers 1889–1910, papers re iodine industry c1890–1954, private journal 1891–1929, scrapbook re issues & company reports 1891–1904, deposit account register 1895–1908, public loans accounts ledger 1896–1914, scrapbook of deposit agreements 1896–1918, correspondence of J I Smail 1896–97, papers re American copper mines 1897–1905, copy out-letter books to S America (3) 1897–1936, papers re sale of warships to Japan & UK 1903–05, commission ledgers (4) 1904–18, dividend dept out-letter book 1907–17, general out-letter books (6) 1907–34, general private out-letter books to S America (4) 1910–19, S American branches powers of attorney (1 bdl) 1910–25, general out-letter book re Australian branches 1911–30, out-letter book of G H B Gibbs 1911–34, general private out-letter books re N American business (2) 1912–31, chartering ledgers (2) 1913–30, general private out-letter book re Mexican loans 1914–28, letters from Australian partners 1918–20, papers re Chilean nitrate of soda sales 1918–28, commission ledger (S America) 1919–23, partners' & special west coast letters to/from London (23 files) 1921–54, consignment ledger 1927–36, 'small trading account ledger' 1928–30, registers of bills receivable & payable (2) 1936–41, minutes of directors' meetings 1946–63

Arequipa: accounts (7 files) 1819–72, private letters to London (1 bdl) 1873–79

Australian branches: letters from V Gibbs

to London 1873, private letter books (12)
1910–30, annual accounts (15 files) 1910–
24, annual accounts 1881–1909, general
private out-letter book 1911–30
Bristol: sales day book 1775–1875,
partnership agreements & papers 1839–72,
partnership accounts 1844–80, annual
accounts 1881–1909
Concepcion: accounts 1938–39
Guyaquil: accounts (1 file) 1819–39
Iquique: private letters to London re fire
insurance (1 file) 1873 1877, private letter
books to London (4) 1878–81, annual
accounts 1882–1909
Lima: annual accounts (6 files) 1819–72,
private ledgers & journals (2) 1843–75,
letter books to S American branches (3)
1848–62, private letters to Valparaiso (1
bdl) 1873–79, letter books (3) 1912–20
Liverpool: papers re Jamaican plantations
1828–54, rough cash book 1827–28, private
ledgers (3) 1833–1903, partnership
agreements & papers 1839–72, papers re
ships (3 files) 1839–63, current account
ledger (N American clients) 1839–41,
commodity information book 1853–90,
private journal 1871–82, clerks' book 1881–
1909, annual accounts 1881–1909, reports
on standing of merchants 1884–1908, papers
re closure of Liverpool house 1908–09
Melbourne: papers re sheep farming (1 file)
1883–87, letter book 1897–98, papers re
New Zealand Exploration Co (1 parcel)
1897–98
New York: journal 1913–20, ledger 1913–20,
annual accounts 1913–28
Santiago: private ledger & journal (2) 1911–
39, letters to London (10 files) 1941–69
South American branches: annual accounts
(15 files) 1910–24
Tacna: annual accounts (3 files) 1847–71
Tarapaca: private letters to Lima (1 bdl)
1873–79
Valparaiso: annual accounts (6 files) 1819–
72 1882–1909 1938–39, private ledger &
journal 1847–66, private letter books
London to Valparaiso (83) 1852–66 1875–
1913, private letters to Lima (1 bdl) 1873–
79, private letters to Tarapaca (1 bdl)
1873–79, private letter books to London
(31) 1876–1933 inc, private letters to/from
London (48 files) 1919–52
Records' Location: Guildhall Library,
Aldermanbury, London EC2P 2EJ

235   GIBSON, TUKE & GIBSON
Location: Saffron Walden, Essex
History: est 1824 as Gibson & Co; known as
above 1863; incorporated with Barclay &
Co Ltd 1896; otherwise known as Saffron
Walden & North Essex Bank
Records: amlg papers 1896
Records' Location: Barclays Bank Ltd

236   GIBSON, WILSON & GREGSON
Location: Kirby Lonsdale, Cumbria
History: est 1810; amlg with Lancaster
Banking Co 1844
Records: declaration of confidence 1825,
amlg notice 1843
Records' Location: National Westminster
Bank Ltd

237   GILL, MORSHEAD & CO
Location: Tavistock, Devon
History: est 1791; absorbed by Fox Brothers
& Co 1889
Records: customer ledger 1822–24
Records' Location: Lloyds Bank Ltd

**238   GILLETT BROTHERS
DISCOUNT CO LTD**
Location: London
History: discount house; est 1867 as Gillett
Brothers & Co; known as above 1919; amlg
with Jessel Toynbee & Co Ltd 1982
Records: partnership agreements 1867–94,
papers re Bankers' Discount Association
Ltd 1873, general accounts weekly balance
books (3) 1875–1928, private ledgers (9)
1887–1918, statistics of bank returns &
tenders 1889–99, monthly balances (?) of
customer accounts, weekly statistics, bill
transactions, etc 1892–1916, papers re legal
case concerning partnership matters 1893–
94, printed balance sheets 1893–1947,
papers re increase in capital 1903–19,
statistics re bill transactions 1904–21 1926–
28 1951–54, 'weekly sheets' with bill
statistics & notes on profits 1915–27, papers
re proposed amlgs & liquidations 1920–40,
papers re bills rediscounted with & without
guarantees 1922–35, papers re purchase of
Hohler & Co 1942, reminiscences of senior
partner (1 file) c1930

Records' Location: Guildhall Library,
Aldermanbury, London EC2P 2EJ

239 GILLETT & CO

Location: Banbury, Oxon

History: est 1784 and operated under several
titles; known as above 1894; absorbed by
Barclay & Co 1919

Records 1: accounts of remittances to London
agents 1820–23, securities for loans 1821
1829, J A Gillett's account of Financial
Crisis 1825, papers re transactions with
Birmingham banks 1825–28, list of
customers 1840, extracts from A R
Tawney's diaries 1847, balance sheets 1853
1910–18, partnership agreements (7) 1845–
1904, partners' wills (2) 1856 1884, discount
ledger 1865–68, note registers (2) 1884–
1915, security book 1890–1919, amlg papers
1912–43, letter books (2) 1914–19, papers re
wartime banking policy 1914–20

Records' 1 Location: Barclays Bank Ltd

Records 2: Gillett family estate papers 1795–
1945, papers re debts 1819–96, papers re
treasurership of local authority 1838–1921,
securities for loans 1847–88, Gillett family
papers 1846–93

Records' 2 Location: Oxfordshire County
Record Office, County Hall, New Rd,
Oxford OX1 1NL Ref: Gil

240 GLAMORGANSHIRE BANKING CO

Location: Neath, W Glamorgan

History: est 1836; amlg with Capital &
Counties Bank Ltd 1898

Records: deed of settlements with
supplements 1836–77, board minute books
(7) 1836–84, private letter book 1871–75,
branch correspondence with managing
director 1876–83, staff applications 1877–
79, private memoranda book 1877–90,
monthly balance books (3) 1877–85, rough
minute books (2) 1878–84, managing
directors' diaries (3) 1880–83, list of
overdrawn accounts etc 1884–85, papers re
reconstruction 1884, monthly balance sheets
1886, amlg papers 1898

Records' Location: Lloyds Bank Ltd

241 GLASGOW JOINT STOCK BANK

Location: Glasgow, Strathclyde

History: est 1840; absorbed by Edinburgh &
Glasgow Bank 1844

Records: board minutes 1840–48

Records' Location: Clydesdale Bank Ltd,
Head Office, 30 St Vincent Place, Glasgow
G1 2HL

242 GLASGOW & SHIP BANK

Location: Glasgow, Strathclyde

History: est 1809 as Glasgow Bank Co; amlg
with Ship Bank to form above 1837;
absorbed by Glasgow Union Banking Co
1838

Records 1: private ledger 1836–50, deposit
receipt registers (3) and indexes (2) c1838–
43, customer ledgers (8) and indexes (2)
1837–44

Records' 1 Enquiries: National Register of
Archives (Scotland), HM General Register
House, Edinburgh EH1 3YY Ref: list 1110

Records 2: bills of exchange (books?) 1809–
45, miscellaneous papers re routine
transactions 1834–44

Records' 2 Location: Scottish Banking
Collection, University of Glasgow Archives,
The University, Glasgow G12 8QQ

243 GLENCROSS, HODGE & NORMAN

Location: Plymouth, Devon

History: est 1804; failed & resumed as Hodge
& Co 1824; otherwise known as Plymouth
Dock, Naval & Commercial Bank

Records: customer & general ledger 1809–20,
balance sheet 1889

Records' Location: Barclays Bank Ltd

244 GLOUCESTER COUNTY & CITY BANK

Location: Gloucester, Gloucs

History: est 1834; absorbed by County of
Gloucester Bank 1836

Records 1: deed of settlement & re papers
1835

Records' 1 Location: Gloucestershire
Collection, Public Library, Brunswick Rd,
Gloucester GL1 1HT
Ref: 2152 JF 13.51

Records 2: deed of settlement 1834
Records' 2 Location: Lloyds Bank Ltd

245 GLOUCESTERSHIRE BANKING CO

Location: Gloucester, Gloucs

History: est 1831; amlg with Capital & Counties Bank Ltd 1886

Records 1: deed of settlement & supplements 1831–63, rules for branch managers 1831–86, board minute books (6) 1836–86, weekly committee minute books (3) 1843–86 inc, annual reports 1868–85, private ledger 1870–85, amlg papers 1883–86, salary records f1884
Cheltenham: profit & loss accounts 1840–c60
Cirencester: profit & loss accounts 1842–63
Evesham: private ledgers (3) 1834–85, profit & loss accounts 1840–60s
Gloucester: profit & loss accounts 1840–55
Hereford: signature book 1862–87, letter book 1884
Newnham: profit & loss accounts 1837–58
Ross on Wye: private ledger 1859–85, security register 1859–76, profit & loss accounts 1854–61
Stroud: profit & loss accounts 1837–67
Stow on the Wold: profit & loss accounts 1854–61, security ledger 1854–76
Tewkesbury: profit & loss accounts 1840–64

Records' 1 Location: Lloyds Bank Ltd

Records 2: deed of settlement 1831, annual reports 1836, 1851, 1884

Records' 2 Location: Gloucestershire Collection, Public Library, Brunswick Rd, Gloucester GL1 1HT Ref: 2150–51

Records 3: receipts, accounts & vouchers c1850s

Records' 3 Hereford & Worcester Record Office, Shire Hall, Worcester WR1 1TR *Ref:* 750:66 BA4221/32

246 GLYN, MILLS & CO

Location: London; Lombard St

History: est 1753 as Vere, Glyn & Hallifax; known as Hallifax, Glyn, Mills & Mitton 1766; as Glyn, Mills, Hallifax & Co 1796; as Glyn, Mills & Co 1851; as Glyn, Mills, Currie & Co 1864; as Glyn, Mills, Currie, Holt & Co 1923; as Glyn, Mills & Co 1924; merged with National Bank Ltd & Williams Deacon's Bank Ltd to form Williams & Glyn's Bank Ltd 1970

Records 1: scrapbooks & press cutting books 1753–1950, staff Christmas box books (41) 1754–1925, partnership agreements 1760, bad debt book 1795–1807, papers re Glyn, Hallifax & Mills families 18–19 cent, customer ledgers (2) 1800–01, profit & loss books (6) 1809–31, salary books (10) 1810–48, staff lists 1815–1931, balance sheets 1819–85, register of exchequer bills purchased 1819–60, staff address books 1833–51, quarterly balances 1841–45, discount office weekly returns 1844–1910, guarantee books (2) 1846–1940, private letter books (19) 1848–1919, status enquiry/information books 1853–1934, loans book 1854–56, weekly balance books (2) 1864–1890, private letter books of B W Currie (2) 1864–81, daily summary of loans & discounts 1874–85, register of unpaid bills 1876–1930, papers re staff guarantee & provident fund f1880, trustee accounts 1880–1908, papers re loans to local authorities & companies (3 boxes) 1880–90, in-letter books (11) 1883–1900, balance books (8) 1888–1925, advances & management books (7) 1890–1927, hypothecation letters 1895–1921, money at call with brokers' accounts 1896–1934, probate register 1897–1914, safe custody registers (2) 19 cent, discount office collateral security registers 19 cent, solicitors' letter books (7) 19 cent, papers re country banks (7 boxes) 19 cent, papers re Canadian agency 19 cent, papers deeds accounts re Lombard St premises 19–20 cent, brokers outstanding bills record 1909–34, minutes & papers of staff clubs 1911–54, letters of introduction granted register 1914–35, security registers (14) 1915–20

Records' 1 Location: Williams & Glyn's Bank Ltd

Records 2: papers re financial difficulties (c15 letters) 1772

Records' 2 Location: Northumberland Record Office, Melton Park, North Gosforth, Newcastle upon Tyne NE3 5QX *Ref:* 2DE36/2/1–88

247 GODFREY & RIDDELL

Location: Newark, Lincs
History: est 1801; amlg with Samuel Smith & Co, Derby, 1880; otherwise known as Newark New Bank
Records: papers re partnership dispute 1802–08
Records' Location: Nottinghamshire Record Office, County House, High Pavement, Nottingham NG1 1HR
Ref: CP5/6133–222

248 GODWIN, MINCHIN & CO

Location: Portsmouth, Hants
History: est c1797; failed 1819; known otherwise as Portsmouth, Portsea & Hampshire Bank
Records: counsel's opinion on liability of estate of deceased partner 1819
Records' Location: Portsmouth City Record Office, 3 Museum Rd, Portsmouth PO1 2LE
Ref: 16A/19

249 GOODCHILD, JACKSON & CO

Location: Sunderland, Tyne & Wear
History: est 1800; failed 1815; otherwise known as Wear Bank
Records: papers re failure c1815–19
Records' Location: Dept of Palaeography, Prior's Kitchen, The College, Durham DH1 3EQ
Ref: Fenwick Collection 32

250 GOSCHENS & CUNLIFFE

Location: London
History: est 1814 as Fruhling & Goschen; amlg with Cunliffe Brothers 1920 to form above; ceased trading 1940
Records: copy out-letter books Hamburg agents (2) 1903–08, copy out-letter books Government Depts (7) 1915–29, copy book confidential out-letters 1926–36, registers of open policies 1928–40, copy books of out-telegrams (2) 1938–41
Records' Location: Guildhall Library, Aldermanbury, London EC2P 2E3

251 GOSLING & SHARPE

Location: London; Fleet St
History: est 1671 as Gosling & Bennet; known as Gosling, Bennet & Co 1754; Gosling, Gosling & Clive 1763; Gosling & Clive 1768; Gosling, Clive & Gosling 1772; Robert & Francis Gosling 1778; Robert, Francis & William Gosling 1786; as above 1794; incorporated with Barclay & Co Ltd 1896
Records: customer ledgers (c658) fl717, profit & loss ledgers (13) 1727–1845, letters re loans, securities, powers of attorney, wills, etc fl720s, waste books with country bankers' accounts (24) 1787–1834, sundry ledgers (3) 1803–27, security registers (3) 1831–77, stamp accounts 1866–96, amlg papers 1896
Records' Location: Barclays Bank Ltd

252 JOHN C GOTCH & SONS

Location: Kettering, Northants
History: est 1792; failed 1857
Records: papers re Gotch family 1795–1865, bankers' licences 1808–24, miscellaneous customer papers 1810–24, papers re proposed bank act 1815–18, partnership agreement 1822, papers re bank's indebtedness 1825–57, 'account of Gotch' being manuscript history
Records' Location: Northamptonshire Record Office, Delapre Abbey, Northampton NN4 9AW
Ref: GK691–928, 2001–2366

253 GRANT & MADDISON'S UNION BANKING CO LTD

Location: Portsmouth, Hants
History: est 1787 as Grant, Gillman & Long; amlg with Maddison, Hankinson, Darwin & Hankinson to form above 1888; amlg with Lloyds Bank Ltd 1903
Records 1: instruction book 1882–88, asset valuation book 1888, shareholders' register 1889–95, profit & loss accounts 1897–1903, amlg papers 1902–03
Records' 1 Location: Lloyds Bank Ltd
Records 2: ledger 1841–44
Records' 2 Location: Portsmouth City Record Office, 3 Museum St, Portsmouth PO1 2LE

254 GREENWAY, SMITH & GREENWAY

Location: Warwick & Leamington, Warws
History: est 1791; liquidated & business acquired by Staffordshire Joint Stock Bank 1887

Records 1: agreement for acquisition 1887
Records' 1 Location: Midland Bank Ltd
Records 2: papers re liquidation 1887
Records' 2 Location: Warwick County Record Office, Priory Park, Cape Rd, Warwick CV34 4JS

255   W GREGSON, SONS, PARK & MORLAND
Location: Liverpool, Merseyside
History: est c1793; wound up 1807
Records: papers re winding up 1807–38
Records' Location: Lancashire Record Office, Bow Lane, Preston PR1 8ND Ref: DDCm/7/23–40 inter alia

256   GRINDLAY BRANDTS LTD
Location: London
History: merchant bank; est 1805 as Wm Brandt's Sons & Co; known as Brandts Ltd 1974; known as above 1976
Records 1: letters, shipping lists, bills, contracts (several bdls) 1810–18, trade circular books (40) 1829–1934, American consular reports Archangel 1832–61, miscellaneous correspondence 1833–80, Russian letter books (4) 1914–22 inc, Petrograd letter books (5) 1914–23 inc, inland letter books (18) 1916–19 inc
Records' 1 Location: Dept of Economic History, University of Nottingham, University Park, Nottingham NG7 2RD
Records 2: general (?) ledgers (14) 1871–1903 inc, Russian current account ledgers (48) 1876–1947, Eastern & inland current account ledgers (61) 1878–1947, continental inland current account ledgers (2) 1883–87, day books (2) 1901–16, private & trust account ledgers (22) 1905–26, H H Brandt & A P Brandt accounts (10) 1906–26, N American current account ledgers (26) 1912–47, S American current account ledgers (18) 1913–47, general continental current account ledgers (17) 1914–47, German current account ledgers (39) 1914–26, register of bills accepted before due date 1914, Dutch current account ledgers (14) 1915–27, cash books (20) 1916–17, bills payable journals (2) 1919–24, nostro ledgers (19) 1921–47, foreign exchange sterling account ledgers (8) 1922–47, foreign

exchange inland customer account ledgers (5) 1922–26, timber account ledgers (2) 1923–26, Scandinavian current account ledgers (2) 1925–26, bills payable & receivable registers (47) 20 cent, foreign exchange journals (6) 20 cent, bills receivable & payable journals (7) 20 cent, insurance journals (6) 20 cent, investment journals (2) 20 cent, dividend journals (5) 20 cent, cash receivable & payable journals (29) 20 cent, American German Eastern & Inland journals (27) 20 cent
Records' 2 Location: British Library of Political & Economic Science, London School of Economics, 10 Portugal St, London WC2A 2MD
This list is approximately accurate as the records are awaiting cataloguing

257   GUERNSEY BANKING CO
Location: Guernsey, Channel Islands
History: est 1827 as Priaulx le Marchant & Co; reconstructed as a joint stock bank under above title 1847; absorbed by National Provincial Bank Ltd 1924
Records 1: minute books (3) 1827–1920, customer ledgers (5) 1827–1924 inc, waste books (2) 1827–28, journals with balance sheets 1827–34, letter books (2) 1827–38 inc, list of sundry creditors 1836–42, articles of partnership 1846, note registers (2) 1847–1906 inc, bills discounted register 1871–1948, advances ledger 1892–1924, articles of association 1898, committee minute book 1898–1927, share register 1898–1924, list of shareholders 1911–24, amlg papers 1924
Records' 1 Location: National Westminster Bank Ltd
Records 2: papers re proposed amlg 1923–24
Records' 2 Location: Lloyds Bank Ltd

258   GUERNSEY COMMERCIAL BANKING CO LTD
Location: Guernsey, Channel Islands
History: est 1835; absorbed by Westminster Bank Ltd 1924
Records: deed of incorporation 1835, board minute books (5) 1835–1924, rough minute books (2) 1835–1924 inc, letter books (2) 1835–46 inc, amlg papers 1924
Records' Location: National Westminster Bank Ltd

259 GUINNESS, MAHON & CO

Location: Dublin & London

History: merchant bank; est 1836

Records: papers re Guinness family (20 bdls) 1753–1887, partnership agreements (42) 1831–1947, balance sheets, profit & loss accounts, etc, 1840–46 1883–1956, papers re partnership matters (c30 files) 1848–1950s, papers re general business (c120 files) 1853–1954

Records' Location: Guinness, Mahon & Co Ltd, 32 St Mary At Hill, London EC2R 8DH

260 GUNDRY & CO

Location: Bridport, Dorset

History: est 1790; failed 1847

Records: partnership agreement 1797, papers re partnership matters 1797

Records' Location: Dorset Record Office, County Hall, Dorchester DT1 1XJ

Ref: D203/A55

261 GUNNER & CO

Location: Bishops Waltham, Hants

History: est 1809; acquired by Barclays Bank Ltd 1953; known also as Bishops Waltham & Hampshire Bank

Records 1: partnership agreements (11) 1809–50, current & deposit account ledgers f1809 inc, profit & loss ledger c1809, money register c1809, letter book 1873–78

Records' 1 Location: Barclays Bank Ltd

Records 2: waste book 1809–10, balance book 1813–33, bill register 1815–1939, profit & loss accounts 1854–82, security registers 20 cent

Records' 2 Location: Hampshire Record Office, 20 Southgate St, Winchester SO23 9EF

Ref: 44M73

262 GURNEYS, BIRKBECK, BARCLAY & BUXTON

Location: Fakenham, Norfolk

History: est 1790; incorporated with Barclay & Co Ltd 1896

Records: customer ledgers (2) 1792 1798–1801, private ledgers (2) 1816–39, details of managers' terms & service 1854, report on overdrawn accounts 1896, investment & estates ledger 1895

Holt: customer ledgers (2) 1801 1818–23

Records' Location: Barclays Bank Ltd

263 GURNEYS, BIRKBECK, BARCLAY & BUXTON

Location: Wisbech, Cambs

History: est 1774; known otherwise as Wisbech & Lincolnshire Bank; incorporated with Barclay & Co Ltd 1896

Records: partnership agreement 1792; abstract of advances 1837; amlg papers 1896

Records' Location: Barclays Bank Ltd

264 GURNEYS, BIRKBECK, BARCLAY, BUXTON & CRESSWELL

Location: King's Lynn, Norfolk

History: est 1782; incorporated with Barclay & Co Ltd 1896

Records: 'Vancouver ledger' 1783, book with details of partnership rearrangement 1806, memoranda book f1860, deposit account ledgers (2) 1873 1888, salary book f1877, letter books (3) 1880–90s, amlg papers 1896, private journal 1894

Records' Location: Barclays Bank Ltd

265 GURNEYS, BIRKBECK, BARCLAY, BUXTON & ORDE

Location: Gt Yarmouth, Norfolk

History: est 1781; incorporated with Barclay & Co Ltd 1896

Records: customer ledger 1781–85, partnership agreement 1793, private ledger 1840–96, profit & loss ledger 1856, amlg papers 1896

Records' Location: Barclays Bank Ltd

266 GURNEYS, BIRKBECK, BARCLAY, BUXTONS & ORDE

Location: Halesworth, Norfolk

History: est 1782 as Gurneys & Turner; known as Turner, Brightwen & Lloyd 1820; later known as above; incorporated with Barclay & Co Ltd 1896

Records: papers re fraudulent issue of notes 1830–39, balances of branch accounts 1855–56, legal opinion re status of bank agent 1859, amlg papers 1896

Records' Location: Barclays Bank Ltd

267   GURNEYS, ROUND, GREEN & CO

Location: Colchester, Essex

History: est 1787 as Crickitt & Co; known as Crickitt & Round 1793; as Round, Green & Co on failure of Crickitt 1825; as Round, Green & Hoare & Co 1883; business taken over by Gurneys & Co of Norwich under title Gurneys, Round, Green & Co 1891; incorporated with Barclay & Co 1896

Records 1: customer ledgers (2) 1787–89 1806–07, partnership agreements (5) 1842–82, amlg papers 1896, plans & notes re premises

Records' 1 Location: Barclays Bank Ltd

Records 2: papers re failure 1826

Records' 2 Location: Essex Record Office, County Hall, Chelmsford CM1 1LX

Ref: D/DOP B1–2, 1065–9

268   JAMES GUTHRIE

Location: Newark, Notts

Records: grant of commission of bankruptcy 1793

Records' Location: Nottinghamshire Record Office, County House, High Pavement, Nottingham NG1 1HR

Ref: DDT 126/5

269   HALIFAX COMMERCIAL BANKING CO LTD

Location: Halifax, W Yorks

History: est 1836; amlg with Bank of Liverpool & Martin's Bank Ltd 1920

Records: board minutes 1836–1921 inc, securities for loans 1836, income tax returns 1843–57, papers re securities for loans 1847, correspondence with customers 1848–51, correspondence with London agent 1848–50, correspondence re financial difficulties of a manager 1847–52, list of closed accounts 1855, minutes re establishment of Country Bankers' Clearing House 1858, memoranda re financial position 1861, half yearly balance sheets 1865–78 inc, annual reports 1893–1918 inc, press cutting books (2) 1894–1942, letter book re amlg 1919–20

Records' Location: Barclays Bank Ltd

270   HALIFAX & HUDDERSFIELD UNION BANKING CO

Location: Halifax, W Yorks

History: est 1836; business taken over by the Halifax Joint Stock Banking Co Ltd 1910

Records 1: deed of settlement 1836, proceedings of proprietors 1837–1910

Records' 1 Location: Lloyds Bank Ltd

Records 2: deeds, accounts, correspondence & bankruptcy papers c1836–1910

Records' 2 Location: Calderdale Metropolitan Borough Archives Dept, Central Library, Lister Lane, Halifax HX1 5LA

Ref: FW.108

271   HALL, BEVAN, WEST & BEVANS

Location: Brighton, Sussex

History: est 1805; amlg with Barclay, Bevan, Tritton, Ransom & Bouverie & Co 1896; otherwise known as Brighton Bank

Records: waste book 1805–06, London agent ledger 1805–08, letter book 1805–12, amlg papers 1896

Brighton, North St: instruction book f1894

Hove: authority book f1895

Records' Location: Barclays Bank Ltd

272   HALL & MORGAN

Location: Daventry, Northants

History: est 1809 as Hall, Oakden & Co

Records: cash book 1832–34

Records' Location: Natonal Westminster Bank Ltd

273   HAMBROS BANK LTD

Location: London; Bishopsgate

History: merchant bank; est 1839 as C J Hambro & Son; amlg with British Bank of Northern Commerce to form Hambros Bank of Northern Commerce Ltd 1920; known as above 1921

Records: 'correspondence' re miscellaneous business including Danish loan (1836–37), Sardinian loan (1851–52), business & family matters (1851–59), payments by Emperor of Russia to King of Denmark (1857), finance of Danish railways (1860–61), Norwegian bonds (1860–61), tour of Scandinavian banks (1912), 'general business papers' including papers re non payment of bills (1847), claims on companies in liquidation (1858–60), security for a debt due (1860–68), USA business (1889–1923), papers re settlement of enemy debts owed Hambros (1914–25), press cuttings (1889–1927), finance of Norwegian fish & oil purchases (1915–16) etc 1847–1925, list of debtors & creditors & profits & losses c1850, staff salary & bonus lists 1856–1924, correspondence of C J Hambro & E Hambro & partners re business, family & personal matters (32 bdls) 1861–92, annual balance book 1863–66, annual balance books with capital accounts of partners (29) 1864–1906, 'synopsis of journals' giving annual & monthly income & expenditure totals 1867–1916, loan papers including correspondence, agreements etc re issues & proposed issues for overseas governments, municipalities etc (c117 bdls) 1880–1918, Hambro family trust account ledger c1881–1918, annual states of balances of securities (33 bdls) 1887–1920, half yearly lists of stocks & shares (11 files) 1905–10, general ledger 1912, special advance accounts ledger 1914–22, journal 1921–38, annual reports f1921, capital accounts re clients' etc securities 1921–33, general ledgers (18) 1922–60

Records' Location: Guildhall Library, Aldermanbury, London EC2P 2EJ

274   HAMMERSLEY, GREENWOOD & BROOKSBANK

Location: London; Pall Mall

History: est 1795 as Hammersley, Montolieu, Brooksbank, Greenwood & Drewe; known as Hammersley, Greenwood, Drewe & Brooksbank 1805; as above 1821; failed & absorbed by Coutts & Co 1840

Records 1: signature book

Records' 1 Location: Coutts & Co, 440 Strand, London WC2R 0QS
All applications must be made in writing to the Archivist

Records 2: list of drafts on bank 1792–95

Records' 2 Location: Greater London Record Office, 40 Northampton Rd, London EC1 0HB

Ref: Acc 931/1

275   HAMMOND & CO

Location: Newmarket, Suffolk

History: est 1770; amlg with Barclay & Co Ltd 1905; known otherwise as Eaton, Hammond & Co

Records: customer ledgers (4) 1790–1912 inc, London agent ledgers (5) 1790–1841 inc

Records' Location: Barclays Bank Ltd

276   HAMMOND, PLUMPTRE, HILTON, McMASTER & FURLEY

Location: Canterbury, Kent

History: est 1788 as Gipps, Simmons & Gipps; became Payler, Hammond, Simmons & Gipps 1800; known as Hammond, Plumptre, Furley, Hilton & McMaster c1816; known as above 1898; amlg with Capital & Counties Bank Ltd 1903

Records: day book 1782–1803, notice of establishment 1788, summary of general accounts 1789–1901, customer & general account balance books (2) 1788–1802, salary & agreements book f1815, general ledger 1885–1905, partnership agreement 1898, amlg papers 1897–1904
Ramsgate: balance book 1874

Records' Location: Lloyds Bank Ltd

277   HAMPSHIRE BANKING CO

Location: Southampton, Hants

History: est 1834; amlg with North Wilts Banking Co to form Hampshire & North Wilts Banking Co 1877; known as Capital & Counties Bank Ltd 1878

Records: deed of settlement with supplements 1834–63, general memoranda book 1834–76, branch inspection report book 1834–77, register of shareholders 1835–84, annual reports 1836–76, private minute book 1876–93, amlg papers 1876
Andover: security register 1861–76
Jersey: letter books (2) 1873–78
Ryde: security registers (2) 1864–75
Southampton: signature books f1860, security register 1865–74

Records' Location: Lloyds Bank Ltd

278 HANBURY, LLOYDS & CO

Location: London

History: est 1784 as Taylor, Lloyd &
Bowman; known as Taylor, Lloyd,
Hanbury & Bowman 1790; as Hanbury,
Taylor & Lloyd 1815; as above 1857; amlg
with Barnett, Hoare & Co to form Barnetts,
Hoare, Hanbury & Lloyd 1864

Records: staff fidelity & indemnity bonds
1770–1815, partnership agreement 1790,
memoranda re partnership matters & profit
distribution 1787–1867, papers re Hanbury
& Taylor families fc1800, letter book of J
Taylor 1844–47, papers re premises
rebuilding 1852

Records' Location: Lloyds Bank Ltd

279 HANKEYS & CO

Location: London; Fenchurch St

History: est 1685 as Joseph Hankey Esq &
Co; known as Sir Joseph Hankey & Co
1739; Hankey, Hall, Hankey & Alers 1804;
known as above 1810; absorbed by
Consolidated Bank Ltd 1863

Records: waste book 1697–1705, signature
book c1790s, mandate book 1825–78, cash
book 1731

Records' Location: National Westminster
Bank Ltd

280 HARDCASTLE, CROSS & CO

Location: Bolton, Gt Manchester

History: est 1818; amlg with Manchester &
Salford Bank 1878; known otherwise as
Bolton Commercial Bank

Records: expenses ledger 1818–40, 'ledgers'
(12) c1818–80, private ledgers (2) 1819–20
1860–78, letter book re advances 1849–69,
private letter book 1856–80, balance books
(2) 1859–77, balance sheet 1875, 'household
accounts' (6) c1870s

Records' Location: Williams & Glyn's Bank
Ltd

281 HARDING & CO

Location: Bridlington & Driffield,
Humberside

History: est 1802; acquired by York City &
County Bank 1878; otherwise known as
Burlington & Driffield Bank

Records: petty cash book 1835–50, pass book
1836–37
Driffield: journals (2) 1825–29 1845–48

Records' Location: Midland Bank Ltd

282 HARDY & CO

Location: Grantham, Lincs

History: est 1819; acquired by Leicestershire
Banking Co Ltd 1895

Records: partnership agreements 1819 1859,
current account ledger 1819–21, receipt
registers (3) 1819–40, profit & loss books (5)
1837–1900, analysis of income tax payments
1839–43, general balance book 1845–57,
payments re new premises 1848–50, half
yearly comparative statements 1859–71,
security register 1857–84, balance books (3)
1860–94, analysis of accounts 1872–75, safe
custody book 1881–97, loan register 1883–
99, amlg papers 1895

Records' Location: Midland Bank Ltd

283 HARRIS, BULTEEL & CO

Location: Plymouth, Devon

History: est 1774; failed & absorbed by
Lloyds Bank Ltd 1914; known also as The
Naval Bank

Records 1: signature book 1892–1900, amlg
papers 1914, papers re failure 1914–16

Records' 1 Location: Lloyds Bank Ltd

Records 2: papers & correspondence 1808–55

Records' 2 Location: West Devon Record
Office, Unit 3, Clare Place, Coxside,
Plymouth Pl4 0JW
Ref: Acc 81/A29–31

284 HARRIS & CO

Location: Bradford, W Yorks

History: est 1804 as Peckover, Harris & Co;
known as Charles, Henry & Alfred Harris &
Co 1823; as H A & W M Harris 1840;
Harris & Co 1850; became a joint stock
bank as Bradford Old Bank Ltd 1864

Records: partnership agreements (2) 1804
1810, papers re Harris family

Records' Location: Barclays Bank Ltd

285 HART, FELLOWS & CO

Location: Nottingham, Notts

History: est 1824; taken over by Lloyds Bank
Ltd 1891

Records: amlg papers 1891
Records' Location: Lloyds Bank Ltd

286   HARTSINCK, HUTCHINSON & PLAYFAIR

Location: London; Cornhill
History: est c1790s
Records: papers re formation & failure 1797–99
Records' Location: Guildhall Library, Aldermanbury, London EC2P 2EJ

287   HARVEYS & HUDSONS

Location: Norwich, Norfolk
History: est 1783; failed 1871 when some branches taken over by Lacon, Youell & Co; known otherwise as The Crown Bank
Records: bankers' licence 1849
Bury St Edmunds: private ledger 1874–80
Framlingham: customer ledgers (7) 1860–70
Records' Location: Barclays Bank Ltd

288   HARWOOD & CO

Location: Thornbury, Gloucs
History: est 1808 as Ralph Yates & Parslaw; amlg with Prescott & Co to form Prescott, Dimsdale, Cave, Tugwell & Co 1891
Records: cash balance book 1858, signature book late 19 cent, amlg papers 1891
Records' Location: National Westminster Bank Ltd

289   J M HEAD & CO

Location: Carlisle, Cumbria
History: est 1804; acquired by Cumberland Union Banking Co 1865; known also as Carlisle Old Bank
Records: deposit account balance book 1854–64, security book 1854–65, current account balance books (3) 1859–64, discount ledger 1857–64
Records' Location: Midland Bank Ltd

290   HECTOR, LACY & CO

Location: Petersfield, Hants
History: est 1807; failed & amlg with London & County Bank 1841
Records: partnership agreement 1826
Records' Location: National Westminster Bank Ltd

291   HEDGES, WELLS & CO

Location: Wallingford, Berks
History: est 1797 as Wells, Allnatt & Co; known as above 1858; taken over by Lloyds Bank Ltd 1905
Records 1: declarations of confidence (2) 1825 1847, general correspondence (12 bdls) 1850–70, agreement for division of profits 1860, status opinions 1870–1900, amlg agreement 1905
Records' 1 Location: Lloyds Bank Ltd
Records 2: partnership agreements 1828–51, statement of confidence 1847, papers re premises alterations 1877, amlg papers 1891–92
Records' 2 Location: Berkshire Record Office, Shire Hall, Reading RG1 3EE
Ref: D/EH B29–33; W/Z 10/15

292   HELSTON BANKING CO

Location: Helston, Cornwall
History: est 1836; liquidated 1878
Records: liquidation agreement 1877
Records' Location: Cornwall County Record Office, County Hall, Truro TR1 3AY
Ref: DDX 393/135

293   HEMMING, NEEDHAM & CO

Location: Hinckley, Leics
History: est 1835; wound up 1840; known otherwise as Leicestershire & Warwickshire Banking Co
Records: agreement for liquidation 1842
Records' Location: Public Record Office, Ruskin Av, Kew, Richmond, Surrey TW9 4DU
Ref: J90/711

294   HENLEY, CLARKE, WHEADON & HALLETT

Location: Chard, Somerset
History: est c1790; closed c1800
Records: bill, waste, balance & money books 1791–95 (this bank?), misc Wheadon family papers re banking 1791–1866
Records' Location: Somerset Record Office, Obridge Rd, Taunton, Somerset TA2 7PU
Ref: DD/CN bxs 48–49; DD/SASC/909/27

295 HENTY & CO

Location: Worthing, Sussex

History: est c1790; amlg with Capital & Counties Bank Ltd 1896

Records: general & customer account balance book 1827–36

Records' Location: Lloyds Bank Ltd

296 HEREFORDSHIRE BANKING CO

Location: Hereford, Hereford & Worcester

History: est 1836; failed & purchased by Midland Banking Co Ltd 1863

Records 1: deed of settlement 1836, papers re liquidation etc 1863

Records' 1 Location: Barclays Bank Ltd

Records 2: list of shareholders 1843

Records' 2 Location: Lloyds Bank Ltd

297 HERRIES, FARQUHAR & CO

Location: London, St James's

History: est 1770 as Robert Herries & Co; known as Sir Robert Herries & Co 1775; Herries, Farquhar & Co 1797; amlg with Lloyds Bank Ltd 1893

Records: general ledgers (2) 1773–1813 inc, signature books 1774–1896, bad debt book 1789–1816, customer ledger 1794–1836, closed accounts' register 1795–1840, clerks' salary book 1796–1807, partnership agreements 1797–1807, correspondence re overdrafts 1808–15, note registers (3) 1814–64, security ledger 1835–60, standing order book 1840s, Royal London Militia ledger f1855, salary book 1862–95, amlg papers 1887–91, private ledger of A Farquhar 1890–1919

Records' Location: Lloyds Bank Ltd

298 HEYWOOD BROTHERS & CO

Location: Manchester, Gt Manchester

History: est 1788; amlg with Manchester & Salford Bank 1874

Records: customer ledgers (2) 1788–1800, statistics of business 1820–60, general statement books with papers re profits (2) 1820–61, balances with banks, investments record, details of lost notes etc (2) 1830–74, directory of old accounts 1830–46, statistics book re deposits, loans, cash, bills 1849–70,

building accounts 1849, decennial analyis of profits 1851–73, staff lists etc 1854–1913, charges & expenses ledger 1856–63, papers re unpaid bills 1857–72, press cuttings & notice re amlg 1874

Records' Location: Williams & Glyn's Bank Ltd

299 ARTHUR HEYWOOD, SONS & CO

Location: Liverpool, Merseyside

History: est 1773; amlg with Bank of Liverpool Ltd 1883

Records: private ledger of A Heywood 1753–60, customer (?) balance book 1787, customer (?) ledgers (2) 1791–94, balance sheet 1796, apprenticeship indenture 1817, signature books (4) 1836–59, circular re amlg 1882, press cuttings book 1883, manager's diaries 1883–84, extracts from Oliver Heywood's diary 19 cent

Records' Location: Lloyds Bank Ltd

300 HEYWOODS, KENNARD & CO

Location: London; Lombard St

History: est as Joseph Denison & Co 1800; known as Denison, Heywood, Kennard & Co 1836; known as above 1850; amlg with Bank of Manchester to form Consolidated Bank 1863

Records 1: signature book 1844–85, private ledger 1850–59

Records' 1 Location: National Westminster Bank Ltd

Records 2: correspondence with Sykes family re banking & financial matters 19th cent

Records' 2 Location: Brynmor Jones Library, University of Hull, Cottingham Rd, Hull HU5 7RX

Ref: DDSY/101/50,55

301 PHILIP HILL, HIGGINSON, ERLANGERS LTD

Location: London

History: merchant bank; est 1907 as Higginson & Co; name changed to Philip Hill, Higginson & Co Ltd 1951; name changed to above after acquisition of Erlangers Ltd 1959; merged with M Samuel & Co to form Hill, Samuel & Co Ltd 1965

Records: general accounts 1951–63, board & agm minutes f1950, amlg papers 1951

Records' Location: Hill, Samuel & Co Ltd, 100 Wood St, London EC2P 2AJ

302   HILL, SAMUEL & CO LTD

Location: London

History: est 1831 as M Samuel & Co; merged with Philip Hill, Higginson, Erlangers Ltd to form Hill, Samuel & Co Ltd 1965

Records: general ledgers 1853–67, partnership agreements 1881–1920, letter books 1904–28, papers re oil business 1905–08, agency agreements 1919 1953, board minutes f1920, private ledgers (2) 1920–63, analysis of accounts 1920–64, acceptance statistics 1925–28 1946–55, directors' private office notes 1928–32, papers re issues 1928–35, pension fund papers 1933–65, German standstill debtors 1939, cash book 1939, routine ledgers 1939–64, client dividend accounts 1956–63

Records' Location: Hill, Samuel & Co Ltd, 100 Wood St, London EC2P 2AJ

303   HILL & SONS

Location: London; West Smithfields

History: est 1825; taken over by Lloyds Bank Ltd 1911

Records: amlg papers 1911

Records' Location: Lloyds Bank Ltd

304   HILTON, RIGDEN & CO

Location: Faversham, Kent

History: est 1796 as Bax, Jones & Co; known as Jones, Wright & Co 1806; as Wright & Hilton 1812; as Hilton, Rigden & Co 1840; business acquired by Prescott, Dimsdale, Cave, Tugwell & Co Ltd 1892

Records: papers re partners 1863–68

Records' Location: National Westminster Bank Ltd

305   C HOARE & CO

Location: London, Cheapside (1672–90), Fleet St (f1690)

History: est 1672 as Richard Hoare; known as Richard Hoare & Partner(s) 1698; Henry & Benjamin Hoare 1718; Benjamin Hoare & Partners 1725; Henry & Richard Hoare & Partners 1750; Sir Richard Hoare & Partners 1785; Henry Hoare & Co 1787;

Henry Hugh Hoare & Co 1828; Charles Hoare & Co 1841; as above f1928

Records: customer current account ledgers f1673, notes on staff 1674–1906, loan ledgers & accounts 1677–85 f1696, analysis of bank's early business 1678–1740, daily cash books (2) 1677–85, goldsmith's debt book 1684–1702, goldsmith's work book 1684–87, bill book 1688–94, Sir W Benson's private ledgers 1690–1713, daily cash book 1692–95, goldsmith's engraver book 1693–98, Hoare family correspondence f1695, customers' addresses 1685–87 1800–83, goldsmith's plate ledger 1697–1736, goldsmith's day books (2) 1700–44, copy letters to customers 1701–06, daily cash book 1701–02, annual signed balance sheets f1702, annual signed division of profit accounts f1702, partnership agreements 1702–1928, daily balance books (39) 1707–1848, miscellaneous letters to customers 1708–1869, Queen Anne's Privy Purse accounts 1710–14, accounts & papers re South Sea Co 1712–25, Hoare family wills 1718–1884, annual shop expenses 1718–1891, private ledgers 1719–1891, mortgage deeds & receipt book 1734–77, private accounts of Henry Hoare 1749–84, miscellaneous letter books (5) 1758–59, private accounts of clerk to House of Commons 1760–1820, daily cash book 1762–63, general orders 1766–1807, Michaelmas Papers (working papers) f1770, letters from overseas agents 1767–78, private account of chief clerk 1788–1826, partners' memoranda books f1793, applications for employment 1795–1863, signature books 1796–1893, brokerage books (6) 1805–45, Lord Chamberlain's Dept accounts 1807–11, business diaries of H Hoare 1828–31, papers re rebuilding of premises 1829–31, household accounts 1912–21

Records' Location: C Hoare & Co, 37 Fleet St, London EC4

306   HODGKIN, BARNETT, PEASE, SPENCE & CO

Location: Newcastle upon Tyne, Tyne & Wear

History: est 1859; amlg with Lloyds Bank Ltd 1903

Records: customer ledger 1860s, safe custody registers f1863, security registers f1865, investment & liquidation book 1885–1902, private memoranda books 1890s, amlg papers 1903

Records' Location: Lloyds Bank Ltd

307   HOLLINGS, DALLAWAY & CO

Location: Stroud, Gloucs

Records: partnership agreement 1779

Records' Location: Gloucestershire Record Office, Worcester St, Gloucester GL1 3DW

Ref: NRA 10491

308   HOLSWORTHY BANK

Location: Holsworthy, Devon

Records: personal & business letters of bank's agent 1793–1812

Records' Location: Devon Record Office, Castle St, Exeter EX4 3PQ

Ref: 1038M/F2/7–46

309   HOLT & CO

Location: London; Whitehall Place

History: est 1809 as Holt, Lawrie & Co; known as above 1892; absorbed by Glyn, Mills, Currie & Co 1923

Records: letter books 1887–1908, signature books 1900–20, sports club minute books (2) 1907–23, Holt family papers 1914–33

Records' Location: Williams & Glyn's Bank Ltd

310   HONGKONG & SHANGHAI BANKING CORP

History: overseas bank; est 1864

Records 1: private papers of Sir C Addis inc, diaries 1881–83 1886–1945, letterbooks 1886–1904, personal papers 1878–1945, business papers 1904–45, letters from M Norman 1912–43

Records' 1 Location: School of Oriental & African Studies, Malet St, London WC1

Records 2: papers re extension of powers & amendment of ordinance 1920–29

Records' 2 Location: Public Record Office, Ruskin Av, Kew, Richmond, Surrey TW9 4DU

Ref: T160/2866

311   HOSKINS & CO

Location: Crewkerne, Somerset

History: est c1790; amlg with Perham, Phelps & Co 1819

Records: ledger of account with Stuckey & Co, Langport

Records' Location: National Westminster Bank Ltd

312   HUDDERSFIELD BANKING CO LTD

Location: Huddersfield, W Yorks

History: est 1827; acquired by Midland Bank Ltd 1897

Records: prospectus 1827, deeds of settlement (3) 1827–41, board minute books (8) 1827–98, share register 1827–97, share transfer jornal 1827–96, shareholders' minute books (2) 1828–97, security registers (4) 1830–97, bad debt ledger 1840–81, safe custody register 1855–97, pass books (3) 1862–87, annual reports 1870–96, salary book 1873–93, branch balance abstract books (2) 1871–97, summary of loan limits & securities 1877, half yearly balance sheets 1880–96, interview book 1882–83, letter books (2) 1883–89, general ledgers (5) 1885–97, board agenda 1890–97, amlg papers 1897
Cleckheaton: discount ledger 1879–89
Dewsbury: security registers (6) 1864–98, register of deeds 1880–89
Heckmondwike: security register 1885–97

Records' Location: Midland Bank Ltd

313   HUDDLESTON & CO

Location: Bury St Edmunds, Suffolk

History: est 1835 as Worlledge & Co; known as above 1866; taken over by Gurney & Co (Norwich) 1880

Records: papers re take over 1879–80

Records' Location: Barclays Bank Ltd

314   HULL BANKING CO LTD

Location: Hull, Humberside

History: est 1833; acquired by York City & County Bank 1894

Records: prospectus 1833, board minute books (18) 1833–94, shareholders' minute books (2) 1833–94, deed of settlement 1834,

share ledgers (3) 1835–79, balance books (2) 1834–35
Barton: general ledger 1844–50, deposit ledger 1846–60
Grimsby: general ledgers (8) 1836–69
Lincoln: deposit ledger 1835–45
Records' Location: Midland Bank Ltd

315   FREDERICK HUTH & CO

Location: London
History: merchant bank; est 1809; absorbed by the British Overseas Bank Ltd 1936
Records 1: papers re foreign investments (7 boxes) c1820–1900, papers re lawsuits (5 boxes) 1932–56, remittance (London from S American offices) & stock account ledger 1849–1902, partnership agreements (S America) 1853–83
Lima: balance sheets 1872–77, accounts & letters (2 bdls) 1875–78
Valparaiso: private ledgers (2) 1854–1933, balance sheets 1872–85, correspondence (1 bdl) 1876
Records' 1 Location: Guildhall Library, Aldermanbury, London EC2P 2EJ
Records 2: cash books Glyn Mills account (13) 1814–49, in-letters (2 boxes) 1814–50, Spanish letter books (29) 1812–52 inc, insurance ledgers (6) 1819–51 inc, bills payable & receivable ledgers (40) 1820–51, general ledgers 1821–40, journals (12) 1822–50 inc, German letter books (84) 1822–55, Spanish customer ledgers (2) 1822–41, European customer ledgers (2) 1823–32, English letter books (69) 1827–51, sales & returns books (3) 1835–61, personal letter book 1839, German customer ledgers (2) 1839–43, English customer ledgers (2) 1841–46, memoranda books (2) 1867–1904
Liverpool: customer ledgers (2) 1839–55
Records' 2 Location: University College, Gower St, London WC1E 6BT

316   IDEAL BANK LTD

Location: Birmingham, W Midlands
History: taken over by Barclays Bank Ltd 1958
Records: annual reports 1945–58, board minutes 1958, papers re take over 1957–58
Records' Location: Barclays Bank Ltd

317   IMPERIAL BANK LTD

Location: London
History: est 1862; acquired by London Joint Stock Bank 1893
Records: counter order books (30) 1862–93, signature books (6) 1862–99, security book 1866–74, country office counter order books (4) 1869–98, safe custody books (4) 1874–93, annual reports 1881–90, board minutes 1882–89, directors' attendance book 1887–1919, amlg agreement 1893
Westminster: security book 1866–73, counter orders 1867–1917
Records' Location: Midland Bank Ltd

318   INNES & CLERK

Location: London
Records: in-letters 1748–57
Records' Location: Guildhall Library, Aldermanbury, London EC2P 2EJ

319   INTERNATIONAL BANK OF LONDON LTD

History: est 1880; liquidated 1905
Records: liquidation papers 20 cent
Records' Location: Williams & Glyn's Bank Ltd

320   IONIAN BANK LTD

Location: London
History: overseas bank; est 1840; ceased business 1977
Records: court minutes f1839, conventions re bank 1839–97, establishment books 1839–1900, correspondence re early business 1839–42, deed of settlement 1840, share registers f1840, general ledgers (16) 1840–1968 inc 1848–1945, agm minutes 1842–1906, papers re charter 1848–1903, cases for legal opinions 1850–88, papers re note issue 1868–1901, minutes of balances & investments committee 1886–99, articles of association & related papers 1886–1950, profit & loss accounts 1891–1944, salary committee minutes 1891–1926, salary committee agenda 1892–1921, registers of letters (2) 1891–1911, registers of directors (2) 1901–55, particulars re shareholdings 1902–30, balance sheets 1908–27, monthly balance sheets 1917–19 1927–29, monthly statements of general accounts 1921–26,

general business correspondence 1920s-50s, share applications 1923–51, head office ledgers (9) 1927–56, head office journal 1937–42, head office profit & loss account 1945–54, lists of shareholders 1936–42
Cyprus branches: general business papers f1920s
Egypt: general business papers f1920s
Greece: general business papers f1920s
Records' Location: British Library of Political & Economic Science, London School of Economics, 10 Portugal St, London WC2A 2HD
The above list is not wholly accurate as the records are awaiting cataloguing

321   ISLE OF MAN JOINT STOCK BANK

Location: Isle of Man
History: est 1836; closed 1843
Records: papers re winding up 1839–50s
Records' Location: Cumbria Record Office, County Offices, Kendal, Cumbria LA9 4RQ

322   ISLE OF WIGHT JOINT STOCK BANKING CO

Location: Newport, Isle of Wight
History: est 1836; amlg with National Provincial Bank 1844
Records: amlg papers 1844
Records' Location: National Westminster Bank Ltd

323   JENNER & CO

Location: Sandgate, Kent
History: est 1872; taken over by Lloyds Bank Ltd 1898
Records: amlg papers 1898
Records' Location: Lloyds Bank Ltd

324   F W JENNINGS

Location: Leek, Derbys
History: est 1855; amlg with Parr's Banking Co Ltd 1877
Records: amlg agreement & circulars 1877
Records' Location: National Westminster Bank Ltd

325   JERSEY BANKING CO LTD

Location: Jersey, Channel Islands
History: est 1828; failed 1886
Records: report on failure 1886
Records' Location: Lloyds Bank Ltd

326   JESSEL, TOYNBEE & CO LTD

Location: London
History: discount house; est 1922; amlg with Gillett Brothers Discount Co Ltd 1982
Records: annual reports & partners' accounts f1922, general ledgers f1922, money books f1922, private ledgers f1922 inc, correspondence with German banks (20 files) f1930s, papers re formation of public company f1943, board minutes f1946
Records' Location: Jessel, Toynbee & Co Ltd, 30 Cornhill, London EC3V 3LH

327   JONES & BLEWITT

Location: Chepstow, Newport & Pontypool, Gwent
History: amlg with Monmouthshire & Glamorganshire Banking Co before 1845
Records: partnership agreement 1833
Records' Location: Public Record Office, Ruskin Av, Kew, Richmond, Surrey TW9 4DU
Ref: J90.1826(65)

328   DAVID JONES & CO

Location: Llandovery, Dyfed
History: est 1799; taken over by Lloyds Bank Ltd 1899
Records: customer ledger 1803–26, private memoranda book 1874–75, registers of current & deposit accounts (4) 1909, amlg papers (26 files) 1909
Records' Location: Lloyds Bank Ltd

329   JONES & DAVIS

Location: Monmouth, Gwent
History: est 1813; formed into Monmouthshire & Glamorganshire Banking Co 1836
Records: notices of dissolution (2) 1837 1814, partnership agreements (2) 1812 1829
Records' Location: Gwent County Record Office, County Hall, Cwmbran NP4 2XH
Ref: D1110.256–8, 260

330 WILLIAM JONES & SON

Location: Bilston, W Midlands

History: est 1824 as Jones & Forster; also Bilston & Staffordshire Bank; reconstructed 1845; acquired by Staffordshire Joint Stock Bank 1863

Records: partnership agreement 1845, agreement for acquisition 1863

Records' Location: Midland Bank Ltd

331 KELLOW & CO

Location: Southampton, Hants

History: est 1801 as Hunt, Trim & Co; known as Trim & Toomer 1809; as above 1823; failed 1825

Records: partnership agreement 1800

Records' Location: Southampton City Record Office, Civic Centre, Southampton S09 4XL *Ref:* D/2 51

332 KENSINGTONS & CO

Location: London

History: est 1774; failed 1812

Records: papers re failure c1803–12

Records' Location: Nottinghamshire Record Office, County House, High Pavement, Nottingham NG1 1HR *Ref:* CP 5/8/85–135

333 A KEYSER & CO LTD

Location: London

History: merchant bank; est 1868; merged with Ullmann & Co to form Keyser Ullmann Ltd 1966

Records: private ledgers (4) 1865–1922, partnership agreements (52) 1868–1937, miscellaneous correspondence (c250 items) 1870–1920, agreements with clerks (c20) 1873–1915, salary list 1888–1929, private balance books (2) 1890–1929, correspondence with Ministry of Blockade 1914–18, property ledger 1917–22, papers re will of A Keyser 1920–22, papers re proposed amlg 1929

Records' Location: Charterhouse Japhet Ltd, Paternoster Row, St Paul's, London EC4M 7DH

334 HENRY S KING & CO

Location: London

History: est 1868; absorbed by Lloyds Bank Ltd 1923

Records: reports on Delhi & Simla branches 1923; amlg papers 1923

Records' Location: Lloyds Bank Ltd

335 KINNERSLEY & SONS

Location: Newcastle under Lyme, Staffs

History: est c1780; amlg with National Provincial Bank of England 1854

Records 1: accounts with London Agent 1799–1805

Records' 1 Location: National Westminster Bank Ltd

Records 2: papers re amlg 1855

Records' 2 Location: Staffordshire Record Office, Eastgate St, Stafford ST16 2LZ *Ref:* D593/T/1/14

336 KLEINWORT, BENSON LTD

Location: London

History: merchant bank; est 1792 as Kleinwort Sons & Co; known as above 1961 on reorganisation to combine with Robert Benson, Lonsdale & Co Ltd

Records: Liverpool clients accounts ledgers (14) 1863–1924, West Indies clients accounts ledgers (23) 1863–1926, monthly balance books (41) 1865–1961, China Japan Australia clients accounts ledgers (2) 1865–75, US clients accounts ledgers (39) 1865–1929, partners' private accounts ledgers (37) 1866–1963, France clients accounts ledgers (23) 1866–1926, Russia Poland Switzerland Austria Italy Spain Turkey Egypt clients accounts ledgers 1866–1972, Brazil Argentina clients accounts ledgers (14) 1866–1923, Central America Mexico W coast of S America clients accounts ledgers (12) 1866–1924, UK clients accounts ledgers (42) 1868–1929, Germany clients accounts ledgers (103) 1870–1929, Belgium & Holland clients accounts ledgers (6) 1871–93, Cape Colonies E India China Japan Australia clients accounts ledgers (12) 1871–1928, Switzerland Austria Turkey Egypt Italy clients accounts ledgers (13) 1871–1912, Spanish clients accounts ledgers (39) 1873–1924, Germany information books (6) 1875–1911, UK information books (3) 1875–1910, France Belgium Holland information books (6) 1875–1911, Switzerland Austria Turkey Egypt Italy information books (3) 1875–1910, US information books (7) 1875–1915, Denmark Sweden Norway Russia information books (10) 1875–1910, Cape Colonies E India China Japan Australia information books (2) 1875–1911, Brazil River Plate information books (2) 1875–1911, Spain information books (4) 1875–1912, Denmark Sweden Norway Russia clients accounts ledgers (17) 1876–1923, Austria clients accounts ledgers (12) 1881–1922, Prussia clients accounts ledgers (13) 1880–1922, Manchester accounts ledgers (3) 1883–96, sundry debtors & creditors accounts ledgers (15) 1884–1932, securities ledgers (4) 1885–1913, advance accounts ledgers (15) 1892–1931, Switzerland Italy clients accounts ledgers (4) 1892–1903, Russia clients accounts ledgers (8) 1892–1924, Belgium clients accounts ledgers (13) 1893–1923, Holland clients accounts ledgers (11) 1893–1924, commission balance books (2) 1899–1944, US joint exchange accounts (19) 1899–1930, statistics books (8) 1900–38, 'stock ledger accounts' 1903–42, US credit accounts ledgers (6) 1902–29, US banks' accounts ledgers (6) 1903–23, US special joint account ledgers (14) 1906–31, foreign exchange accounts (50) 1904–28, Russia Poland clients accounts ledgers (4) 1905–24, supertax returns books 1909–19, issuing dept syndicate & underwriting accounts ledgers (5) 1910–15, clients securities ledger American issues 1911–12, agents' commission accounts ledgers (6) 1912–65, Bank of England moratorium account ledger 1914–22, private journals (3) 1915–64, 'private' accounts (8) 1918–29, trust companies accounts ledgers (3) 1920–41, Austria Hungary Czechoslovakia clients accounts ledgers (6) 1922–23, partners' joint investment accounts ledger 1922, property accounts ledger 1923, US sundry accounts ledgers (5) 1924–31, summary of monthly turnover books (2) 1924–28, returns on industrial securities etc book 1925–31, foreign exchange operations profit & loss ledgers (2) 1926–38, staff accounts 1943–46, 'particulars of charges accounts' (3) 1950–61, charges account book 1953–63

Records' Location: The Guildhall Library, Aldermanbury, London EC2P 2EJ

337   HENRY KNAPP & JOHN TOMKINS

Location: Abingdon & Wantage, Berks

History: est 1801; failed 1847

Records: partnership dissolution agreement 1846, balance sheet 1847

Records' Location: Berkshire Record Office, Shire Hall, Reading RG1 3EE

Ref: D/EM B16; D/EBr B3

338   KNARESBOROUGH & CLARO BANKING CO LTD

Location: Knaresborough, W Yorks

History: est 1831; amlg with National Provincial Bank of England Ltd 1903

Records: deed of settlement 1831, registers of notes issued & burnt (4) 1831–1918, amlg papers 1903

Records' Location: National Westminster Bank Ltd

339   KNEWNEY & KING

Location: Grantham, Lincs

History: est 1812 as Holt, King & Co; known as above 1835; failed 1848

Records: partnership agreement 1824, balance sheets & accounts 1824–25

Records' Location: Nottinghamshire Record Office, County House, High Pavement, Nottingham NG1 1HR

Ref: DDFM 49/3–4

340   KNIGHT, JENNER & CO

Location: Farnham, Surrey

History: est 1828; amlg with the Capital & Counties Bank Ltd 1886

Records: securities & re papers 19 cent, amlg papers 1886

Records' Location: Lloyds Bank Ltd

341   LACONS, YOUELL & KEMP

Location: Gt Yarmouth, Norfolk

History: est 1791 as Lacons, Youell & Co; amlg with Capital & Counties Bank Ltd 1901

Records: amlg papers 1901

Records' Location: Lloyds Bank Ltd

342 LACY, HARTLAND, WOODBRIDGE & CO

Location: London, W Smithfield

History: est as Pocklington & Lacy 1809; renamed Lacy & Son 1851; as above 1880; acquired by Midland Bank 1891

Records: balance sheet 1873, amlg papers 1891

Records' Location: Midland Bank Ltd

343 LAMBTON & CO

Location: Newcastle on Tyne, Tyne & Wear

History: est 1790; amlg with Lloyds Bank Ltd 1908

Records: Lambton family correspondence 1780–1840, bills discounted registers (2) 1788–1861 inc, partnership agreements (8) 1797–1891, securities for loans registers f1797, salary book 1818–1908, list of clerks 1818–1908, profit & loss accounts 1822–40 inc, balance books 1839–57, note register 1841–55, safe custody receipt book 1850–1908, interest rate book 1854–1967, waste book 1855, letter books (3) 1855–60 1900–08, general ledgers (4) 1856–1920, inventory of securities & deeds 1858–90, status enquiry reply book 1860–67, standing order books (25) 1868–1908, discount ledger 1870–1908, deposit account ledger 1870s, signature books 1870s, probate register 1877–1908, security ledger 1886–1908, managers' diaries (14) 1888–1904, safe custody register 1889–1903, partners' ledger monthly balance book 1892–1901, papers re proposed amlg 1902, amlg papers 1907–08
Alnwick: statistics book 1867–1907
Newcastle, Byker: arrangement book 1898–1907, signature book 1898–1908
Newcastle, Quayside: signature books (2) 1866–70s, probate register 1866–70s, security register f1904, private memoranda book f1904
North Shields: status enquiry reply book 1859–74, security book 1858–1900
Ponteland: signature book 1906–08
Sunderland: letter book 1900–08

Records' Location: Lloyds Bank Ltd

344 LANCASHIRE & YORKSHIRE BANK LTD

Location: Manchester, Gt Manchester

History: est 1872; amlg with Bank of Liverpool & Martins Bank Ltd 1928

Records: board minute books (11) 1872–1924, private minute book 1886–1927, managers' diary 1889, agm minutes 1904–28, widows & orphans fund minutes 1922–29, press cuttings re amlg 1927
Accrington: drafts issued register f1899
Preston: authorities book 1894–1912

Records' Location: Barclays Bank Ltd

345 LANCASTER BANKING CO

Location: Lancaster, Lancs

History: est 1826; amlg with Manchester & Liverpool District Banking Co Ltd 1907

Records 1: deed of partnership 1826, directors' resolution & order books (9) 1826–1909, customer ledger 1826–29, investment ledger 1827–57, agm report books (2) 1828–1907, note circulation statistics 1833–39, investment & profit & loss ledger 1836–94, investment journal 1835–76, lists of directors & proprietors 1838–94 inc, papers re share capital 1841, deeds of settlement 1852 1882, dividend & salaries register 1863–1918, management committee minutes 1862–66, note register 1839–41, profit & loss & expenses ledger 1842–58, half yearly balance sheets 1873–94, half yearly balance book 1886–1900, annual reports 1889–1906 inc, branch overdraft registers (9) 1885–96, branch profit statistics 1899–1902, managers' diary & other papers 1899–1903, applications for advances 1906–11, amlg papers 1906–07
Barrow in Furness: managers' letter books (4) 1880–1911, applications for overdrafts 1898–1919
Chorley: profit & loss ledgers (2) 1867–1907, general ledger 1879–80
Fleetwood: general ledger 1875–92
Lancaster: managers' memoranda books (4) 1831–1908 inc, managers' letter books (6) 1832–1908 inc, managers' diaries (11) 1877–1908
Preston: deposit register f1869, information book 1885–94
Ulverston: managers' letter books (5) 1883–1907, half yearly balance sheets 1897–1907
Windermere: general letters 1883–1913

Records' 1 Location: National Westminster Bank Ltd

Records 2: deed of settlement 1826–96, list of directors, branches, agents 1832–85 (11 items), extracts from annual reports 1869–1907, directors' reports 1892–1900

Records' 2 Location: Lancaster District Library, Market Sq, Lancaster LA1 1HY

346　J & J LARGE

Location: Wootton Bassett, Wilts

History: est 1807; failed 1822

Records: assignment & sale of estates of Joseph Large banker (1808–16) 1822

Records' Location: Gloucestershire Record Office, Worcester St, Gloucester GL1 3DW

Ref: D182/V/21

347　LEACH, POLLARD & HARDCASTLE

Location: Bradford, W Yorks

History: est c1760; failed 1780

Records: partnership agreement 1777, bankruptcy petition 1781

Records' Location: Barclays Bank Ltd

348　LEAMINGTON BANK

Location: Leamington, Warws

History: est 1835; failed 1837

Records: deed of settlement 1835

Records' Location: Central Library, Leamington Spa, Warwickshire

349　LEAMINGTON PRIORS & WARWICKSHIRE BANK LTD

Location: Leamington, Warws

History: est 1835; acquired by Midland Bank 1889

Records: deed of settlement 1835, board minute books (4) 1835–89, reports of shareholders' meetings 1837–64, shareholders' minute book 1845–71, weekly balance sheets (14) 1845–89, general ledgers (6) 1854–89, security register 1864–83, annual reports 1886–88, amlg papers 1889–90

Records' Location: Midland Bank Ltd

350　LEATHAM, TEW & CO (EAST RIDING BANK)

Location: Doncaster, S Yorks

History: est 1800; purchased by Sir W Cooke Bart & Co 1848

Records: papers re purchase of bank 1843–47

Records' Location: National Westminster Bank Ltd

351　LEATHAM, TEW & CO (WEST RIDING BANK)

Location: Wakefield & Pontefract, W Yorks

History: est 1800; amlg with Barclay & Co Ltd 1906

Records: memoranda book 1800, customer ledgers (3) 1800–35 inc, partnership agreements (21) 1801–1905, private letter books (12) & loose letters 1805–1906, minute book 1806–32, small expenses book 1808–39, private ledgers (12) 1809–75, cash book 1809–11, bankers' licences (3) 1821–43, note registers (4) f1822, declaration of confidence 1825, apprenticeship agreements 1831–34, diaries re advances (7) f1844, monthly abstract books (2) 1844–1906, papers re Sir W B Cooke & Sons 1848, investment ledger 1880–90, general ledger 1886–94, balance sheets 1894–1906, amlg papers 1906

Records' Location: Barclays Bank Ltd

352　LECHMERE, ISAAC, MARTIN & CO

Location: Tewkesbury, Hereford & Worcester

History: est 1790; amlg with Capital & Counties Bank Ltd 1906

Records: partnership agreements (7) 1797–1805

Records' Location: Hereford & Worcester Record Office, Shire Hall, Worcester WR1 1TR

Ref: 705:134 BA1531/93(ii)

353　LECHMERE, WALL & ISAAC

Location: Worcester, Hereford & Worcester

History: est as Joseph Berwick, Wall & Isaac 1785; known as Lechmere, Wall & Isaac c1811; as Berwick, Lechmere & Co 1869; amlg with Capital & Counties Bank Ltd 1906

Records: partnership agreements (5) 1766–1888, customer ledgers (9) 1781–1841, discount ledgers (26) 1803–38, general ledgers (11) 1804–96, miscellaneous correspondence f1825, memoranda books (4) 1826–1906 inc, deposit ledgers (5) 1835–1905 inc, signature books (9) 1852–1906, dormant balance book 1858–78, security registers (2) 1860–1900 inc, amlg papers 1905–07
Malvern: private memoranda book 1904–08
Tewkesbury: private memoranda books (2) 1859–68 1904–08

Records' Location: Lloyds Bank Ltd

354 LEDGARD & SONS

Location: Poole, Dorset
History: est 1821; failed & absorbed by Wilts & Dorset Banking Co 1861; alias Town & County of Poole Bank, & Ringwood & Poole Bank
Records: customer ledger 1808, partnership agreement 1821
Records' Location: Lloyds Bank Ltd

355 LEEDS & COUNTY BANK LTD

Location: Leeds, W Yorks
History: est 1862; acquired by Midland Bank 1890
Records: notices to shareholders 1862–90, board minute books (7) 1863–90, shareholders' minutes 1863–92, annual lists & summaries of shareholdings books (3) 1863–85, seal books (4) 1863–91, declarations of secrecy 1863–90, index of securities 1864–90, amlg papers 1890
Records' Location: Midland Bank Ltd

356 LEEDS & WEST RIDING JOINT STOCK BANKING CO

Location: Leeds, W Yorks
History: est 1835; dissolved 1846
Records: letters, bills, etc 1839–45, list of shareholders 1842
Records' Location: Leeds Archives Dept, Chapeltown Rd, Sheepscar, Leeds LS7 3AP
Ref: Acc 2205

357 LEICESTERSHIRE BANKING CO LTD

Location: Leicester, Leics
History est 1829; acquired by Midland Bank Ltd 1900
Records 1: deed of settlement 1829, board minute books (21) 1829–1900, profit & loss ledgers (6) 1829–1900, declarations of secrecy 1829–96, deeds of covenant (5) 1836–73, general ledgers (13) 1842–1901, shareholders' minute book 1845–72, staff list 1871–99, security books (22) 1873–90, general managers' memoranda 1874–79, general managers' letter book 1876–1900, bills of exchange diaries (6) 1877–99, customers' bills discounted books (11) 1878–1900, note circulation ledger 1878–1900, returned bills book 1879–85, loan register 1883–99, bill balance book 1885–96, country bills for collection books (8) 1888–1900, weekly balance sheets 1890–94, abstract of balance sheets 1894–99, discount ledger 1895–1901, bill register 1895–1901, shareholders' minute book 1897–98, foreign bills for collection 1897–1908, branch receipts & expenditure 1896–1905, amlg papers 1900
Ashby: board minutes 1837–57
Grantham: general ledger 1883–96
Hinckley: private ledger 1848–53
Records' 1 Location: Midland Bank Ltd
Records 2: prospectus 1829, shareholders' resolutions with deeds of settlement & names of shareholders (1873) 1829–80, shareholders' minutes re amlg 1900
Records' 2 Location: Leicestershire Record Office, 57 New Walk, Leicester LE1 7JB
Ref: 3D42/3

358 LEITH BANKING CO

Location: Leith, Lothian
History: est 1792; failed 1842
Records: general ledgers 1797–1813, discount ledgers 1799–1842, weekly transactions record 1812–16
Records' Enquiries: National Register of Archives (Scotland), PO Box 36, HM General Register House, Edinburgh EH1 3YY
Ref: list 945

359 WILLIAM LEWIS & THOMAS SALT

Location: Birmingham, W Midlands

Records: partnership agreement 1760

Records' Location: William Salt Library, Eastgate St, Stafford ST16 2LZ
Ref: D1716 bdl 7/22

360 LEWIS'S BANK LTD

Location: Liverpool, Merseyside

History: est 1909 as Lewis's Ltd; purchased by Martins Bank Ltd 1958

Records: board minutes 1934–41

Records' Location: Barclays Bank Ltd

361 LEY & CO

Location: Bideford, Devon

History: est c1790; amlg with National Provincial Bank of England 1843

Records: notice of amlg 1844

Records' Location: National Westminster Bank Ltd

362 LEYLAND & BULLINS

Location: Liverpool, Merseyside

History: est 1807; acquired by North & South Wales Bank 1901

Records 1: customer balance books (2) 1807–32, pass books (13) 1807–36, profit & loss ledgers (3) 1807–60, bills sent for acceptance books (7) 1807–24, cash books (3) 1811–31, cash balance book 1815–19, commission ledger 1818–22, profit & loss settlements (2) 1819–78, private ledger 1826–90, cash book Masterman & Co 1833–39, pass books Bank of England (2) 1836–39, investment ledger 1850–62, profit & loss ledger 1865–78, loan ledger 1878–88, general ledgers (7) 1879–1901, advances ledgers (2) 1885–94, cash books (12) 1887–94, rough office diaries (5) 1889–93, private ledgers ('day book blotters') (5) 1889–93, private ledgers containing accounts with other banks (2) 1890–93, suspense account ledgers (2) 1890–96, weekly balances private deposit accounts 1899–1901, amlg agreement 1901

Records' 1 Location: Midland Bank Ltd

Records 2: diaries of J Leyland (2) 1829–82, letters to J Leyland (8 vols) 1830–69, cash book 1870–75, ledger 1849–71

Records' 2 Location: Hindley Public Library, Market St, Wigan, Greater Manchester WN2 3AN

363 LICHFIELD, RUGELEY & TAMWORTH BANKING CO

Location: Lichfield, Staffs

History: est 1835; absorbed by National Provincial Bank 1837

Records: board minutes re absorption 1837

Records' Location: National Westminster Bank Ltd

364 LINCOLN & LINDSEY BANKING CO LTD

Location: Lincoln, Lincs

History: est 1833; acquired by Midland Bank Ltd 1913

Records: deed of settlement 1833, board minute books (15) 1833–1914, shareholders' minute books (2) 1833–1913, register of deeds (2) 1834–84, balance sheets 1834–1912, half yearly balances 1877–1907, articles of association 1902, amlg papers 1913
Barton: general ledger 1835–43
Gainsborough: agreement for purchase of business of Nottingham & Notts Joint Stock Bank 1878
Louth: board minute book 1833–78
Spilsby: profit & loss book 1869–1900

Records' Location: Midland Bank Ltd

365 LIVERPOOL BOROUGH BANK

Location: Liverpool, Merseyside

History: est 1836; failed 1857

Records: liquidator's report 1859

Records' Location: Barclays Bank Ltd

366 LIVERPOOL COMMERCIAL BANKING CO

Location: Liverpool, Merseyside

History: est 1832; amlg with Bank of Liverpool 1889

Records: provisional committees minutes 1832, deed of settlement 1833, board minute books 1832–35 1883–89, synopsis of board minutes 1832–86, declarations of secrecy register 1833–90, papers re limited liability 1860–61, agreement re provident fund 1894

Records' Location: Barclays Bank Ltd

367   LIVERPOOL UNION BANK LTD

Location: Liverpool, Merseyside

History: est 1835; amlg with Lloyds Bank Ltd 1900

Records: deed of settlement 1835, board minute books (3) 1835–1913, amlg papers 1900

Liverpool, London Rd: security register 1884–1908, signature book 1884–1900

Records' Location: Lloyds Bank Ltd

368   LIVERPOOL UNITED TRADES BANK

Location: Liverpool, Merseyside

History: est 1836; wound up c1838

Records: notice re application for shares c1836

Records' Location: Lancashire Record Office, Bow Lane, Preston PR1 8ND
Ref: DDTs Bx33

369   LLOYDS BANK LTD

Location: London & Birmingham

History: est 1765 as Taylor & Lloyd; known as Lloyds & Co 1853 & otherwise as Birmingham Old Bank; amlg with J L Moilliet & Sons to form Lloyds Banking Co Ltd 1865; known as Lloyds, Barnetts & Bosanquets Bank following amlg with Barnetts, Hoares, Hanbury & Lloyd & Bosanquet, Salt & Co, 1884; title changed to Lloyds Bank Ltd 1889

Records: private ledger 1765–1865, rough cash book 1765–71, daily balances of receipts & payments 1835–64, note registers (2) 1842–65, customer ledger 1863–65, articles of association f1865, register of share applications 1865–67, share allotment book 1865, board minutes f1865, agm minutes f1865, annual reports f1865, share registers f1866, private letter books (2) 1865–77, widows' fund ledgers (2) 1865–1915, chairman's agenda books (14) 1866–1902, 'reference' (later 'county') committee minutes & agenda books (27) 1867–1901, profit & loss account books (7) 1866–1903, shareholders' cash book 1866, balance sheets 1865–85, premises ledger 1865–71, letter books (2) & other correspondence of Howard Lloyd 1868–1902, secretary's private memoranda book 1868–71, special committee minutes 1871–1900, senior staff salary book 1876–1918, bill committee memoranda book 1878–84, seal register 1883–95, properties & investments ledger 1884–99, London (later weekly) committee minute books (5) 1884–1901, Birmingham committee minutes & agenda books (6) 1884–92, daily committee minute books (10) 1886–1901, building committee minutes 1886–87, rules for branch managers 1889, private minute book 1889–1923, premises committee minute books (31) 1890–1937, properties committee minutes 1891–1902, investment committee minute books (14) 1891–1947, county committee minutes 1892–93, widows' fund subscription book 1900–16, staff rules & instructions 19 cent, comparative statistics of banks subsequent to amlg 1902–14, letter book of South Wales inspector 1902–15, letters to branch managers re bonds 1906–14, law & sealing committee minute books (9) 1908–51, staff committee minute books (47) 1909–64, general manager's letter books re staff (7) 1919–22, W Yorkshire committee minute books (2) 1920–30, W Yorkshire chairman's committee minute books (5) 1921–30, secretary's dept procedure book 1924–61

Birmingham, Colmore Row: private memoranda books (2) 1890–1902, staff attendance book 1883–84

Birmingham, High St: private memoranda books (4) 1868–1905

Birmingham, New St: private memoranda books 1890–1907

Birmingham, Small Heath: letter book 1914–31

Blackburn: salary book 1900–16

Burton on Trent: private memoranda book 1876–98

Droitwich: private memoranda book 1889–1940

Gloucester: letter books (2) 1891–1918 inc, private memoranda books (2) 1889–1906

Ironbridge: private memoranda book 1874–1906

Kidderminster: private memoranda books (2) 1889–1902

Shrewsbury: private memoranda book 1877–78

Swadlincote: profit & loss book 1899–1927

Tenbury Wells: private memoranda book f1889

Records' Location: Lloyds Bank Ltd

370   LLOYDS BANK (FOREIGN) LTD

Location: London

History: overseas bank; est as Lloyds Bank
(France) Ltd 1911; name changed to Lloyds
Bank (France) & National Provincial Bank
(France) Ltd 1917; as Lloyds & National
Provincial Foreign Bank Ltd 1919; as
Lloyds Bank (Foreign) Ltd 1955

Records 1: profit & loss accounts 1911–15,
secretary's letter book 1911–14, agreement
for sale of Colis business 1916, agreement
with National Provincial Bank 1917, papers
re investigation of French business 1937

Records' 1 Location: Lloyds Bank Ltd

Records 2: board minute books (44) 1911–68,
shareholders' minute book 1911–59, register
of members 1911, committee minutes 1917,
annual reports 1917–72, balance sheets
f1917, standstill agreements files (3 boxes)
1930s

Records' 2 Location: Lloyds Bank
International Ltd, Head Office, 40 Queen
Victoria St, London EC4P 4EC

Records 3: balance sheets & statistics 1931–
54, chairman's correspondence (2 dossiers)
1932–55, papers re legal case 1935–38,
investigation report 1938, papers re cash &
currency position 1936–37
City Office: inspection papers 1937–39
Paris: special report 1935, inspection papers
1938

Records' 3 Location: National Westminster
Bank Ltd

371   LOCKE, TUGWELL & MEEK

Location: Devizes, Wilts

History: est 1803; amlg with Capital &
Counties Bank Ltd 1883

Records: amlg agreement 1883

Records' Location: Lloyds Bank Ltd

372   LONDON & BRAZILIAN BANK LTD

Location: London

History: overseas bank; est 1862; known as
New London & Brazilian Bank 1871–85;
absorbed by London & River Plate Bank
Ltd 1923 to form Bank of London & South
America Ltd

Records 1: secretary's reports 1866–1920,
letter books (39) Rio de Janeiro to London

& elsewhere 1868–1924, letter books (13) &
pkts (22) London to Rio 1873–79 1892–1912
1917–18 1920–24, letter books (11)
Pernambuco to London & elsewhere 1876–
80 1897–1924, letter books (3) to/from
various 1878–80 1920–24, cable books (5)
Rio 1879–1924, letter books (24) Sao Paulo
to various 1887–1927, letter books (16)
Buenos Aires to London & elsewhere 1890–
1925, letter books (10) Rosario to London &
elsewhere 1897–1927, letter books (6 file)
London to Para & elsewhere 1902–24, letter
books (5) & files (5) London to Buenos
Aires & elsewhere 1906–28

Records' 1 Location: DMS Watson Library,
University College, Gower St, London
WC1E 6BT

Records 2: general ledger 1860s, day book
1860, annual reports 1872–1923

Records' 2 Location: Lloyds Bank
International Ltd, Head Office, 40 Queen
Victoria St, London EC4P 4EL

373   LONDON, COMMERCIAL & CRIPPLEGATE BANK LTD

Location: London; Fore St

History: est 1819 as Cripplegate Bank; name
changed 1900; absorbed by Union Bank of
London Ltd 1900

Records: articles of association 1879, minute
books (2) 1896–1906

Records' Location: National Westminster
Bank Ltd

374   LONDON & COUNTY BANKING CO

Location: London

History: est 1836 as Kent, Surrey & Sussex
Bank; known as London & County Joint
Stock Banking Co 1838; as London &
County Banking Co 1866; amlg with
London & Westminster Bank Ltd to form
the London, County & Westminster Bank
Ltd 1909

Records: deed of settlement 1836, board
minute books (23) 1836–1909, list of
directors 1836–1905, annual reports 1837–
1908, committee minutes 1838–39, deposit
receipt book 1837, agm minute books (3)
1838–1905, bad debts register 1838–1931,
general accounts 1836–38, general purpose

committee minutes 1839–41, board agenda books 1839–43, instructions to managers 1839–1911 inc, branch committee minute books (7) 1839–48, notes on half yearly meetings (2) 1840–59, register of board instructions to general manager 1841–62, standing orders of the board books (2) 1841–93 inc, special committee minutes 1842–49, branch inspector's letter book 1841–46, daily committee minute books (60) 1848–1909, register of mortgaged property 1850s, rules for staff 1853 1908, general memoranda book 1856–62, general meeting report books (9) 1860–1908, authorised expenditure at branches books (2) 1862–1905, directors' attendance & fee register 1863–75, special committee rough minutes 1863, Lombard St committee minutes 1864–69, general managers' information books (3) 1865–85, general meeting agenda book 1867–94, signature books 1867–80s, general statistics book 1868–1911, staff records 1873–1942 inc, authorities to prove debts 1874–1909, list of shareholders 1887, staff letter book 1877–1919, general meetings agenda book 1895–1954, head office committee minutes 1896–1914, daily committee agenda book 1904–05, managers' information books (8) 1908–32, amlg papers 1909

Ashford: branch minute books (2) 1847–58
Aylesbury: information book 1878–1932, minute books (3) 1900–31
Bishop's Stortford: salary sheets 1867–1911
Braintree: quarterly returns f1858, annual returns f1872
Brentford: information books (2) 1885–1936
Brighton: minute books (18) 1852–1926
Buckingham: quarterly returns f1856
Cambridge: minute books (5) 1845–90
Chelmsford: letter book 1843–47
Croydon: minute book f1878
Godalming: quarterly returns 1877
Halstead: report on overdrafts 1872, quarterly returns 1874 1907
Hastings: quarterly returns 1848
Hertford: managers' letters 1879–1930
Hitchin: status reports 1883–98
Hoddesdon: minute book 1898–1903
Leighton Buzzard: deposit account ledger 1837
London, Barnet: letters 1889–1926
London, Greenwich: quarterly returns f1842, minute book 1845–75

London, Hammersmith: minute book 1901–08
London, Hanover Sq: correspondence with head office 1868–72
London, Holborn:minutes re advances between branch & country branches 1876–1914
London, Kensington: information books (2) 1878–1904
London, Marylebone: minute book 1904–14
London, St Mary Axe: minute book 1906–16
London, Upper Clapton: minute book f1901
Maldon: memoranda re bad debts 1866
Newbury: quarterly returns 1851
St Albans: branch correspondence registers f1848
Teddington: minute book 1905–30, impersonal ledger 1905–15
Windsor: correspondence re premises 1853–89, correspondence re staff 1858–1900, opinion letters (5 items) 1867–75, memoranda book 1889–1908

Records' Location: National Westminster Bank Ltd

375   LONDON JOINT STOCK BANK LTD

Location: London

History: est 1836; amlg with Midland Bank 1918

Records 1: deed of settlement 1836, board minute books (10) 1836–1917, profit & loss ledger 1836–41, daily balance books (8) 1836–55, signature books (10) 1836–71, shareholders' minute books (4) 1837–1918, annual reports 1837–1918, country office standing order books (14) 1840–98, supplemental deeds of settlement 1840–68, private ledgers (45) 1842–1924, counter order books (22) 1842–73, monthly balance books (2) 1848–65, weekly balance book 1855–79, deposit account signature index books (5) 1859–81, indexes to house committee minutes (3) 1871–1918, indexes to departments committee minutes (3) 1871–1918, cricket club minute book 1872–1900, register of leases & agreements 1872–97, regulations 1879–1900, extracts from diary of Lord Harlech, director 1892, departments committee minute books (2) 1899–1905, general ledgers (2) 1908–16, analysis of customer accounts 1909–19,

house committee minute books (2) 1909–18, weekly balance books (3) 1913–18, amlg & liquidation papers 1918–66
Knaresborough: manager's reports 1901–20
London, Lambeth: directors' attendance book 1911–19
London, Leadenhall St: salary register 1889–1920
London, Limehouse: counter order book 1898–1912
London, Lothbury: counter order books (50) 1893–1918
London, Pall Mall: general ledger 1840–50, mandate book 1841–48, letter books (2) 1859, abstract of balance sheets 1864–1911, salary book 1903–20
London, Princes St: counter order books (50) 1878–1918
London, St Mary Axe: letter book 1901–12
Records' 1 Location: Midland Bank Ltd
Records 2: circular disclaiming connection with a second bank 1841
Records' 2 Location: Durham County Record Office, County Hall, Durham DH1 5UL
Ref: D/Sa/E 997

376   LONDON MERCHANT BANK LTD

Location: London
History: overseas bank; est 1873 as London & Hanseatic Bank Ltd; known as above 1916; certain parts of banking business acquired by Guinness, Mahon & Co 1939 when company converted to investment trust
Records: board & general minute books f1873, nominal & cash ledgers f1873, annual reports f1948
Records' Location: London Merchant Securities Ltd, Carlton House, 33 Robert Adam St, London W1M 5AH

377   LONDON & NORTHERN BANK LTD

Location: London
History: est 1898; failed 1899
Records: prospectus 1898
Records' Location: National Westminster Bank Ltd

378   LONDON & NORTHERN JOINT STOCK BANK

Location: Newcastle upon Tyne, Tyne & Wear
History: est 1862; absorbed by Midland Banking Co Ltd 1864
Records: list of branches 1864, liquidation papers 1864
Records' Location: Barclays Bank Ltd

379   LONDON, PROVINCIAL & SOUTH WESTERN BANK LTD

Location: London
History: est 1864 as Provincial Banking Corporation Ltd; became London & Provincial Bank Ltd 1870; amlg with London & South Western Bank Ltd to form London, Provincial & South Western Bank Ltd 1917; amlg with Barclay & Co Ltd 1918
Records 1: board minute books (c26) 1864–1918, annual reports 1864–1918, committee minute books (c7) f1870, half yearly accounts 1870–1917, articles of association 1871–1904, head office circulars 1876–1918, regulations for guidance of officers 1914, rules for branch managers 1915, registers of members 1918, amlg papers 1918
Brecon: probate register 1894–1926
Builth Wells, Brecknock: bills register f1882
Fishguard: security register f1884
Haverfordwest: security register f1885
Llanelli: head office circular book 1876–98
London, Anerley: bond register f1900, interview book 1904–06
London, Beckenham: request to establish branch 1874, weekly balances 1884–85
London, Bexleyheath Broadway: security register f1898
London, Carshalton: draft books (2) 1911–19
London, Catford: general authorities register 1890–1927
London, Forest Gate: inspection minutes & staff reports f1898
London, Hackney Triangle: general order book 1892–1901, security register 1898–1901
London, Lee Green: minute book f1900
London, Ponders Green: minute book f1892
London, Stoke Newington: customer ledger 1874–75, security book 1878–90

London, Walthamstow: minute book 1880–81

London, Woolwich: character books 1906–35

Merthyr Tydfil: appearance book 1878–85, customer authorities f1889

Penarth: inspection minutes 1884–1925

St Clear: inspection minute book 1887–1940

Swansea: deposit ledger 1863–69, customer ledger 1868–71, letters to general manager 1888–94

Treherbert: head office circulars 1876–1907

Records' 1 Location: Barclays Bank Ltd

Records 2: papers re amlg 1918–39

Records' 2 Location: University College, Singleton Park, Swansea, W Glamorgan SA2 8PP

Ref: Llanelly Tinplate Works Archives

380   LONDON & SOUTH AFRICAN BANK

Location: London

History: overseas bank; est 1860; amlg with Standard Bank of British South Africa 1875

Records: deeds of settlement 1861–65, allotment book nd, registers of shareholders (2) 1863–77, register of transfers 1877, general ledgers (2) 1869–76

Records' Location: Standard Chartered Bank Ltd, Head Office, 10 Clements Lane, London EC4 7AB
At the time of preparing this guide researchers can be given very limited access to records

381   LONDON & SOUTH WESTERN BANK LTD

Location: London

History: est 1862; amlg with London & Provincial Bank Ltd to form London, Provincial & South Western Bank Ltd 1917

Records: articles of association (3) 1862–1912, board minute books 1862–1918, share registers (18) f1862 inc, seal registers (5) 1863–1903, dividend book 1864, registers of issues 1897–1912 inc, head office circular books (7) 1890–1918, branch inspectors' report book 1892–1912, annual reports 1897 1899, rules & regulations for staff 1898–1901, staff report book 1899–1933, instructions to clerks 1909, regulations for

the gradation of salaries 1911

London, Barnes: bill register 1890–1929

London, Bow: minute book 1872–1908

London, Brentford: authorities book 1888–1907

London, Camberwell: impersonal ledger f1873

London, Charlton: profit & loss statements 1911–17

London, Chelsea: minute books (2) 1887–95 1901–20, loan ledger 1894–1932

London, Crofton Park: head office instruction book 1909, property valuation book 1914–36

London, Dulwich: minute book 1891–1937

London, Ealing Broadway: general order books (2) 1879–93

London, East Finchley: minute book f1892

London, East Sheen: staff book f1899

London, Finchley, Church End: order book 1885–1900

London, Forest Hill: quarterly returns 1883

London, Highgate: staff report book f1899

London, Holland Park: bad debts written off f1884, staff record book f1899

London, Ilford, Cranbrooke Rd: general order book f1898

London, Lavender Hill: minute book f1895

London, Lewisham Way: staff report book 1898–1949

London, Merton: staff report book f1898

London, Mile End: inspection reports 1894–1910

London, New Southgate: confidential letters 1890

London, Poplar: authorities book 1883–1920

London, South Ealing: manager's private letter book 1912

London, Streatham Common: staff book f1899

London, Tooting Broadway: manager's minute book f1879

London, Tulse Hill: minute book f1892

London, Upper Norwood: minute books (4) 1865–1910s

London, Vauxhall: inventory of fittings 1896

London, Wandsworth: minute book f1865, security register f1884

London, West Norwood: general order books (2) 1882–97

London, West Streatham: minute book 1908–50

London, Willesden Green: general order
books (4) 1891–1902
Southend on Sea: correspondence 1909,
loan increases 1910–14
Records' Location: Barclays Bank Ltd

382   LONDON & WESTMINSTER BANK LTD

Location: London

History: est 1834; amlg with London &
County Banking Co Ltd to form London,
County & Westminster Bank Ltd 1909

Records: prospectus 1833, board minute
books 1833–1909, deed of settlement 1834,
account with Coutts & Co 1833–34, balance
sheets 1834–82, correspondence of
provisional committee with prospective
general manager 1833, letter book 1833–36,
sundry board letters 1834–39, head office
circulars 1834–60, staff record books (2)
1834–1920 inc, staff appointments book
1834–55, annual reports 1835–1909,
correspondence re proposed association
with Agricultural & Commercial Bank of
Ireland 1835–36, general meetings minute
book 1835–1909, agreements with country
banks 1835–39, officers' appointment
registers (2) 1835–81, papers re increase in
capital 1836–80, private minutes 1836–90,
undertakings books 1836–37, circulars to
branches 1836–1909, register of officers
1836–1909, staff list 1836, list of past due
bills 1837, book of weekly statements 1837–
40, signature book 1841–61, statements of
net profits 1840–48, list of properties 1838,
statements of bills discounted & number of
accounts as per branch 1845–48, stock book
1845–48, declarations of secrecy 1846–85,
daily committee minute books (7) 1846–
1907, State of Victoria loan letter books (2)
1859–79, register of country securities 1859,
register of country & overseas accounts
1860, solicitors' report books (6) 1860–86,
secretary's memoranda book 1861–1911,
instructions to branches from head office
1862–71, country manager's letter book
1864–69, statistics re current accounts
1871–1909, establishment committee
minute books (20) 1875–1909, articles of
association 1897, salary comparison 1909
London, Bloomsbury: officers' ledger f1836
London, Lothbury: customer ledger 1834,
general ledgers 1834–1909, loan ledger

1834–57, deposit ledger 1842–46
London, Marylebone: staff book f1834,
branch minutes f1836, general order book
f1840, letters to customers 1836–39
London, Southwark: general ledger 1836–
42, customer ledger 1836, officers' ledger
f1837, branch diary 1839, general balance
book 1844–48, guard book f1858
London, Temple Bar: officers' ledger f1837
London, West End Office: local board
minutes 1834
London, Westminster: day book 1834,
customer ledger f1837 (2) 1834–35, minute
book 1834–45

Records' Location: National Westminster
Bank Ltd

383   LONDON & YORKSHIRE BANK LTD

Location: London

History: est 1872; amlg with Union of
London & Smith's Bank Ltd 1903

Records: staff register 1872–1947, list of
shareholders 1897, amlg papers 1903

Records' Location: National Westminster
Bank Ltd

384   LOVEBAND & CO

Location: Torrington

History: est 1808 as Cooke & Co; known as
above 1821; amlg with National Provincial
Bank of England 1843

Records: letter re amlg 1833

Records' Location: National Westminster
Bank Ltd

385   LOYD, ENTWISLE & CO

Location: Manchester, Gt Manchester

History: est c1771 as Jones, Loyd & Co;
absorbed by Manchester & Liverpool
District Banking Co 1863

Records: papers re London agent 1793,
partnership agreements (4) 1809–51, papers
re securities, bankruptcies & unpaid bills
1816–53, papers re loans 1820–26, stock
registers (2) 1845–63, papers re capital
reconstruction 1848–49, papers re profits
1850–62, balance book & liquidation
accounts 1863, deposit ledger 1861–64, amlg
papers 1863–64, partner's diary 1864

Records' Location: National Westminster
Bank Ltd

386 SIR JOHN WILLIAM LUBBOCK, FORSTER & CO

Location: London

History: est 1772 as Sir John Lubbock, Lubbock, Forster & Co; known as above 1834; amlg with Robarts, Lubbock & Co 1860

Records 1: signature books 1841–60

Records' 1 Location: Coutts & Co
All applications for access must be made in writing to the Archivist

Records 2: Sir J Lubbock business account books (3) 1765–1805, partnership agreements 1763–1841, letter book 1771–73, partnership papers 1772–1841, misc correspondence 1773–1802, misc papers inc receipts, cheques, etc 1777–1842

Records' 2 Location: Kent Archives Office, County Hall, Maidstone ME14 1XH
Ref: U697 T37; U1979 B1–12

387 LUDLOW & TENBURY BANK

Location: Ludlow, Salop

History: est 1840; amlg with Worcester City & County Banking Co 1864

Records: annual reports 1840–59

Records' Location: Lloyds Bank Ltd

388 MACHELL, PEASES & HOARE

Location: Beverley, Humberside

History: est 1797 as Appleton, Machell & Co; known as above c1858; taken over by York Union Banking Co 1894

Records: customer ledgers (2) 1842–47, security & parcel register 1864–80, letters re staff 1878–99, private ledger 1882–92

Records' Location: Barclays Bank Ltd

389 MADDISON, ATHERLEY, HANKINSON & DARWIN

Location: Southampton, Hants

History: est 1869 by amlg of Atherley, Fall & Atherley, and Maddison & Pearce; amlg with Grant, Gilman & Long to form Grant & Maddison Union Banking Co 1888

Records: partnership agreement 1875, asset valuation book 1888

Records' Location: Lloyds Bank Ltd

390 MANCHESTER JOINT STOCK BANK LTD

Location: Manchester, Gt Manchester

History: est 1863 as Robertson, Fraser & Co; reconstructed under above title 1873; acquired by London & Midland Bank Ltd 1892

Records: board minute books (7) 1873–92, shareholders' minutes 1873–92, share transfer register 1873–92, share application ledgers (2) 1873–92, allotment of shares book 1873–91, general ledger 1873–92, half yearly balance sheets 1873–93, private letter book 1873–94, salaries ledger 1873–85, correspondence re accounts with Robarts, Lubbock & Co 1878, committee minute book 1882–92, list of shareholders 1890–92, proxy register 1892, amlg papers 1892

Records' Location: Midland Bank Ltd

391 MANCHESTER & SALFORD BANK

Location: Manchester, Gt Manchester

History: est 1836; amlg with Williams, Deacon, Thornton & Co to form Williams Deacon & Manchester & Salford Bank Ltd 1890

Records: deeds of settlement 1836–81, board minutes 1836–90, agm minutes 1836–90, balance sheets 1836–90, journal 1836–46, annual reports 1837–90, list of shareholders 1838, private notebook of general manager 1840s, salary papers 1845–90, reserves ledger c1850–80, charges accounts 1875–1917, profit & loss account books (3) 1881–90, property ledger 1887–90, private letter books 19 cent
Manchester, Heywoods Branch: profit & loss summaries 1871–90, summaries of business 1880–85
Manchester, Mosley St: information books 1870s
Rochdale: accounts opened books (2) 1880s, information books 1880–90

Records' Location: Williams & Glyn's Bank Ltd

392 MARGESSON, HENTY, HENTY & HOPKINS

Location: Worthing, W Sussex

History: est 1808; absorbed by Capital & Counties Bank Ltd 1896

Records: general & customer accounts balance book 1827–36, stock ledgers (4) 1842–96, security ledger with partnership accounts 1881–96, amlg papers 1896

Records' Location: Lloyds Bank Ltd

393   MARSH, SIBBALD, STRACEY & FAUNTLEROY

History: est 1792; known as Marsh, Stracey, Fauntleroy & Graham 1824; failed 1824

Records: papers, some re a former partner & embezzler 1811–25

Records' Location: University of London Library, Senate House, Malet St, London WC1E 7HU

Ref: ULL MS676

394   MARTEN, PART & CO

Location: St Albans, Herts

History: est 1773 as Pybus, Dorset & Cockell; known under several titles until 1813 when known as Marten, Hale & Call; known as Sir W P Call, Arnold & Marten 1826; as Call, Marten & Co 1829; as Smith Marten & Co 1865; as Marten, Part & Co 1898; amlg with Barclay & Co Ltd 1902

Records: balance sheets & profit & loss accounts 1892–1900 inc, private ledger 1898–1902, customer ledger 1901–02

Records' Location: Barclays Bank Ltd

395   MARTINS BANK LTD

Location: London & Liverpool

History: est 1712 as Martin & Co; known as Martin, Stone & Co 1769–1851; as Martin & Co 1851; as Martin's Bank Ltd 1891; amlg with Bank of Liverpool Ltd to form Bank of Liverpool & Martins Ltd 1918; known as Martins Bank Ltd 1928; merged with Barclays Bank Ltd 1968

Records 1: partnership agreements 1714–91, miscellaneous letter books (18) 1714–1916 inc, daily cash balance books (10) 1729–1852, discount book 1731–35, trial balances & balance sheet books (8) 1731–44 1761–1842, receipt books (3) 1744–75, general balance books with details of profit distribution & partners' investments (4) 1746–82 inc, profit & loss account books 1755–70, plan of banking premises 1748, private accounts of R Stone 1764–82, customer ledgers (111) 1772–1930 mostly inc, papers re E Blackwell (partner) 1782–

1909, general ledgers (5) 1796–1873 inc, papers re Lombard St premises 1798–1944, papers re Stone family (extensive) 18–19 cent, details of bills discounted 1802–15, signature books (40) 1811–1912 inc, information book 1812–44, safe custody register 1827–40, accounts open & closed &, information book c1840, bad & doubtful debt books (7) 1850–1926, customer weekly balance books 1847–71, staff guarantees & letters 1881–1918, clerk registers (2) 1882–1919, balance sheets 1891–1918, weekly balance sheets 1891–1939, 'securities, sundry loans' (3) 1891–1932, security registers (15) 1896–1932, papers re individual & corporate customers including papers re securities for loans, bankruptcies, prospectuses, legal cases etc (extensive) 19 cent, papers re George Stone (extensive) 19 cent, foreign exchange ledgers (8) 1913–20, amlg papers 1918, articles of association f1918, board minute books f1918, annual reports f1918, minutes & rules re widows & orphans funds 1922–58, superannuation fund minute books (2) 1940–58, head office rebuilding committee minutes 1926–33

Records' 1 Location: Barclays Bank Ltd

Records 2: papers re amlg with Lancashire & Yorkshire Bank & Equitable Bank 1928

Records' 2 Location: Public Record Office, Ruskin Av, Kew, Richmond, Surrey TW9 4DU

Ref: T160/10541

396   MAY, WYBORN, WHITE & MERCER

Location: Deal, Kent

History: est 1802; failed 1825

Records: letter books (3) 1771–77 1794–1801 1824–29, list of debts on failure 1825

Records' Location: Cambridge University Library, West Rd, Cambridge CB3 9DR

Ref: Joslin Papers

397   SIR CHARLES E McCRIGOR, BART & CO

Location: London

History: est 1840; suspended payments 1922

Records: government correspondence with creditors 1922

Records' Location: Public Record Office, Ruskin Av, Kew, Richmond, Surrey TW9 4DU

Ref: T172/1258

398   MEDITERRANEAN BANK

Records: papers re application for charter 1836

Records' Location: Public Record Office, Ruskin Av, Kew, Richmond, Surrey TW9 4DU

Ref: T1/3472

399   MEDLEY, SON & CO

Location: Aylesbury, Bucks

History: est 1833; failed 1837

Records: papers re failure 1837

Records' Location: Buckinghamshire Record Office, County Hall, Aylesbury HP20 1VA
Ref: D/X 1/42

400   MELLERSH & CO

Location: Godalming, Surrey

History: est 1814; amlg with Capital & Counties Bank Ltd 1893

Records: amlg papers 1893

Records' Location: Lloyds Bank Ltd

401   MERCANTILE BANK OF LANCASHIRE LTD

Location: Manchester, Gt Manchester

History: est 1890; amlg with Lancashire & Yorkshire Bank Ltd 1904

Records: articles of association 1890, board minutes 1890–1904, agm minutes 1890–1904, papers re share issue 1896, instructions to managers 1900, amlg papers 1903

Records' Location: Barclays Bank Ltd

402   METROPOLITAN BANK

Location: London

History: est 1839; amlg with Union Bank of London 1841

Records: notices of opening & amlg 1839–41

Records' Location: National Westminster Bank Ltd

403   METROPOLITAN BANK (OF ENGLAND & WALES) LTD

Location: Birmingham (1829), London (1889)

History: est 1829 as Birmingham Banking Co; amlg with Royal Exchange Bank to form Metropolitan & Birmingham Bank 1889; known as above 1893; acquired by Midland Bank 1914

Records 1: deed of settlement 1830, general ledgers 1829–49 1884–87, annual reports 1866–69 1885–1914, board minutes (9) 1866–68 1888–1914, statement of affairs 1870, conveyance of assets from Birmingham Banking Co to Birmingham Banking Co Ltd 1871, private minute book re staff 1876–1914, weekly balance sheets return books (8) 1878–1914, letter books (3) 1892–97, quarterly balance sheets 1897–1914, signature books (3) 1889–1914, security books (4) 1889–1914, shareholders' minutes 1900–14, press cutting books (2) 1894–1914, premises insurance register c1900–14, share ledgers (10) 1911–14, analysis of balance sheets books (3) 1913–14, amlg papers 1914
Neath: security book 1895–1905

Records' 1 Location: Midland Bank Ltd

Records 2: deeds of settlement 1830–37, prospectuses 1866–80, press cuttings 1866–69, investigation committee report 1868, directors' report 1873

Records' 2 Location: Birmingham Reference Library, Central Libraries, Birmingham B3 3HQ

404   METROPOLITAN BANK LTD

Location: London

History: est as Metropolitan & Provincial Bank Ltd 1861; known as above 1867; stopped payment & business carried on under Royal Exchange Bank Ltd 1879

Records: agreement for amlg of Macclesfield branch with Parr's Banking Co 1867

Records' Location: National Westminster Bank Ltd

405   MIDDLETON & CO

Location: Loughborough, Leics

History: est 1790; acquired by Leicestershire Banking Co 1878

Records: draft prospectus nd, annual reports 1850–77, list of creditors 1878, bankruptcy papers E W C Middleton 1878

Records' Location: Midland Bank Ltd

406   MIDLAND BANK LTD

Location: Birmingham (1836) London
(f1891)

History: est 1836 as Birmingham & Midland
Bank; amlg with Central Bank of London to
form London & Midland Bank 1891; amlg
with City Bank to form London City &
Midland Bank 1898; amlg with London
Joint Stock Bank to form London Joint City
& Midland Bank 1918; renamed Midland
Bank Ltd 1923

Records: prospectus 1836, deed of settlement
1836, board minute books (48) 1836–76
1879–1960, shareholders' minute books (4)
1836–1957, deposit account ledger 1836,
current account ledgers (2) 1836, cash book
1836, annual reports f1837, balance sheets
1847–72, secretary's notebooks (2) 1871–98,
press cuttings re annual meetings 1879–99,
finance committee rough minute book 1885–
88, overdraft committee minute book 1887–
91, branch office abstract of accounts books
(5) 1886–97, head office abstract of accounts
books (5) 1888–1900, branch balance sheet
ledgers (6) 1890–98, premises reference
book London branches 1890–1900, branch
managers' instruction book 1890,
Birmingham committee minute book 1891,
board agenda books (2) 1891–98, finance
committee minute books (2) 1891–1901,
summaries of doubtful debts books (6)
1891–1911, investment register 1892–96,
staff agreements 1894–1905, bill risks book
1895, projected amlgs working papers 1896–
1924, branch balance sheet books (32)
1898–1904, balance sheets 1898 1901–08,
arrangement books – overseas business (4)
1898–1914, investment register 1899,
discount ledger 1900, general ledgers (24)
1900–45, head office circulars (many vols)
1900–39, premises reference book 1900,
finance committee minute book 1905–19,
verbatim minute books shareholders'
meetings (4) 1906–53, overseas business
letter book 1906–09, analysis of interest
rates 1907–15, Liverpool committee papers
1908, staff refreshment club register 1911–
19, working papers staff guarantee fund
accounts 1911–19, branch balance sheet
ledgers (57) 1912–39, balance sheet working
papers (60 files) 1912–45, monies held
abroad books (10) 1915–19, reports &
correspondence re Petrograd office 1917,

overseas business letter books (6) c1920,
Birmingham committee papers 1923–54,
finance committee minute book 1929–46,
mutual provident fund reports & balance
sheets 1938–43, classification of advances
1933–39
Barnsley, Market Hill: reference books (3)
1920–32
Barnsley, Peel Sq: reference books (3) 1897–
1932
Bewdley: general ledgers (2) 1862
Coventry: letter book 1918–30
Dalton-in-Furness: private ledgers (13)
1918–44, cash books (4) 1922–44
Huddersfield: salary book 1900–37
Leeds, Park Row: letter books (8) & salary
book 1900–11
Liverpool, Walton: general ledger 1909–17
London, Angel Court: reference book 1912–
31
London, Chancery Lane: security registers
(3) 1890–1921
London, Chiswick: general charges analysis
1899–1951
London, Cornhill: salary books (2) 1891–
1932, security register 1892–1908, letter
book 1905–13
London, Covent Garden: reference book,
salary book & letter book 1899–1943
London, Lambeth: salary books (2) 1922–5
Lye: private ledgers (2) 1890
Morley: security register 1891–1902
Stourbridge: general ledger 1882
Wednesbury: security register 1877–84,
opened & closed accounts book 1877–1905

Records' Location: Midland Bank Ltd

407   MIDLAND BANKING CO LTD

Location: Birmingham, W Midlands

History: est 1863; amlg with Birmingham,
Dudley & District Banking Co 1881

Records: articles of association 1863, board
minute books (4) 1863–81, general purpose
committee minute books (7) 1863–81,
details of branch total credits 1863–81, agm
attendance book 1864–80, net profits record
1868–1904, summary of weekly returns
1874–81, premises ledger 1877–80, sealing
minute book 1880–81, amlg papers 1881–82
Derby: customer ledger 1875–76
Tunstall: impersonal ledger 1865

Records' Location: Barclays Bank Ltd

408 MILBANKE, WOODBRIDGE, GRUGGEN & GAUNTLETT

Location: Chichester, W Sussex

History: est 1809 as Hack, Dendy, Hack & Farenden; known under several titles 1817–1892 including Dendy, Comper & Gruggen, Dendy, Gruggen & Comper 1827; Comper, Gruggen & Comper 1849; Dendy Halstead & Gruggen 1867; Halstead, Woodbridge, Gruggen & Gauntlett 1885; known otherwise as Chichester Bank; amlg with Barclays & Co Ltd 1900

Records: letter book 1818–76, customer ledgers (c100) f1809, partnership agreements 1819–85, profit & loss ledgers (2) 1827–71, stock exchange day books (2) 1849–57 inc, investment book 1857–72, balance sheet book 1875–94, security register 1886, interview book 1892, London agent ledgers 19 cent, private ledgers 19 cent, amlg papers 1900

Records' Location: Barclays Bank Ltd

409 MILES, CAVE, BAILLIE & CO

Location: Bristol, Avon

History est 1750 as Baillie & Co; known as Cave, Baillie & Co 1866; as above 1877; amlg with Prescott & Co to form Prescott, Dimsdale, Cave, Tugwell & Co Ltd 1891

Records: general ledgers (4) 1772–1820, partnership agreements (3) 1820–24

Records' Location: National Westminster Bank Ltd

410 MILFORD, SNOW & CO

Location: Exeter, Devon

History: est 1776; amlg with Sanders & Co to form Sanders, Snow & Co 1901; known otherwise as The City Bank

Records: letters with London agent 1800–02, general ledgers (5) 1816–28 1846–83, partnership agreements 1820–89, papers re chief clerk 1827–43, private letter book 1843–87, premises valuation 1884, profit & loss accounts 1895–99, amlg papers 1901

Records' Location: National Westminster Bank Ltd

411 MILLION BANK

Location: London

History: est 1695; dissolved 1712

Records 1: lists of subscribers 1695–1700, general meetings orders 1695–96, cash ledgers (8) 1696–1720 1727–78, journal 1796–98, dividend books (11) 1701–96, ledgers 1709–16, general expenses books 1709–96, cash books (3) 1725–98, sub committee minute books (12) 1718–98, 'names of proprietors' 1732–34, 'annuities remaining' 1732, stock transferred account books (2) 1734–96, secretary's cash book 1748–96, receipt book 1748–96, rough journal 1786–98, miscellaneous papers inc, specimen dividend warrants, directors' affidavits, etc

Records' 1 Location: Public Record Office, Chancery Lane, London WC2
Ref: C114.9–23,153

Records 2: papers 1695–1712

Records' 2 Location: Barclays Bank Ltd (Martins Bank archives)

412 MILLS, ERRINGTON, BAWTREE & CO

Location: Colchester, Essex

History: est 1774; failed & business taken over by Sparrow, Tufnell & Co

Records: legal papers re J Mills 1821–22, deed of indemnity re note issue 1884, deed of security re partnership 1890

Records' Location: Essex Record Office, County Hall, Chelmsford CM1 1LX
Refs: D/DE1 B36, D/DE1 F47–8, D/DHt B10

413 MINET, FECTOR & CO

Location: Dover, Kent

History: est 1700; amlg with National Provincial Bank 1841; known otherwise as Dover Old Bank

Records 1: extracts from I Minet's letter book 1737–38, balances of notes issued 1777–79, balance sheet 1821, amlg papers 1842

Records' 1: Location: National Westminster Bank Ltd

Records 2: partner's will 1806, papers re partnership matters 1814–42, partner's private diary 1821–27

Records' 2 Location: Lincolnshire Archives
Office, The Castle, Lincoln LN1 3AB
Ref: Jarvis V/E passim; Jarvis V/B 7,9–10;
Jarvis V/A5, 11.1–10

414   MOGER & SON & JONES
Location: Bath, Avon
History: est 1819; amlg with Prescott & Co
to form Prescott, Dimsdale, Cave, Tugwell
& Co Ltd 1891; known otherwise as Bath
City Bank
Records: amlg agreement 1891
Records' Location: National Westminster
Bank Ltd

415   MOLINEUX, WHITFELD & CO
Location: Lewes, E Sussex
History: est c1789 as Molineux, Hurley,
Whitfeld & Dicker; thereafter operated
under many titles; known as Molineux,
Whitfeld & Co 1893; absorbed by Barclay &
Co Ltd 1896
Records: cash books (4) 1754–1826 inc,
journals 1780–95, partnership agreement
1789, cash account book 1804–12, private
ledger 1810–13, note registers (3) 1811–12
1854–84, security book 1860s, dividend
ledgers (2) 1879–92, stock order book 1894–
1900, disbursement ledgers 1891–97,
customer ledgers 1892–98, amlg papers
1896
East Grinstead: general ledgers (13) 1838–
1902 inc, ledgers of account with head office
(7) 1864–98, security journal 1868–96,
record of commission & interest charged
1897–1916
Tunbridge Wells: customer ledgers (13)
1848–70
Records' Location: Barclays Bank Ltd

416   MONMOUTHSHIRE & GLAMORGANSHIRE BANKING CO
Location: Newport, Gwent
History: est 1836; failed 1851
Records 1: agreement for payment of
creditors 1851, legal opinion re debts of
Coalbrookdale Iron Co 1856
Records' 1 Location: Gwent Couny Record
Office, County Hall, Cwmbran NP4 2XL
Ref: D43.545, 6396

Records 2: securities for loans, with relating
papers c1823–c26
Records' 2 Location: Public Record Office,
Ruskin Av, Kew, Richmond, Surrey TW9
4DU
Ref: J90/1823–1839

417   MONTROSE BANKING CO
Location: Montrose, Tayside
History: est 1814; absorbed by Dundee
Union Bank 1829
Records: 'minute book, ledger' 1814–28
Records' Enquiries: National Register of
Archives (Scotland), HM General Register
House, Edinburgh EH1 3YY
Ref: list 945

418   MOORE, HARRISON & CO
Location: Whitehaven, Cumbria
History: est 1793; failed 1825
Records: note register 1803–13
Records' Location: Cumbria County Record
Office, The Castle, Carlisle CA3 8UR
Ref: Allison MSS

419   MORGAN & ADAMS
Location: Hereford, Hereford & Worcester
History: est 1820; failed 1863; otherwise
known as Hereford, Ross & Archenfield
Bank
Records: press cuttings re failure 1863
Records' Location: National Westminster
Bank Ltd

420   MORGAN GRENFELL & CO LTD
Location: London
History: merchant bank; est 1838 as George
Peabody & Co; known as J S Morgan & Co
1864; as Morgan Grenfell & Co 1910
Records: The archives are extensive and date
from the second half of the nineteenth
century. In 1982 an Archivist was appointed
to sort and catalogue the collection
Records' Location: Morgan, Grenfell & Co
Ltd, 23 Great Winchester St, London EC2P
2AX

421   MORTLOCK & CO

Location: Cambridge, Cambs

History: est 1790; known as J Mortlock & Co Ltd 1889; incorporated with Barclay & Co Ltd 1896

Records 1: private ledgers (2) 1856–96, partners' ledger f1860, register of members 1889–96, amlg papers 1896

Records' 1 Location: Barclays Bank Ltd

Records 2: cash books 1776–1819, profit & loss ledgers 1791–1828, balance sheets 1793–97, misc papers & correspondence 1799–1885, Mortlock family & estate papers etc 18–20 cent, partnership records 1805–88, premises deeds 1805–77, Cambridge balance sheets 1807–15, bank notes 1807–15, Cambridge & Ely note register 1812–55, letter books 1816–20, in letters 1816–89, partners' ledgers 1820–56, balance books 1821 1842–58 1866–67, weekly account books 1826–28 1834–38, letters from Ely 1852–57, bankers' licences 1859–84, receipts for investments in Cambridge Savings Bank 1863–74
Bishop's Stortford: balance sheets 1813–26
Ely: balance sheets 1810–26
Royston: ledger 1825
Saffron Walden: balance sheets 1819–25

Records' 2 Location: Cambridgeshire Record Office, Shire Hall, Cambridge CB3 0AP

422   NATAL BANK LTD

Location: London

History: overseas bank; est 1854; amlg with National Bank of South Africa Ltd 1914

Records: out-letter book 1854–57, amlg agreement 1914

Records' Location: Barclays Bank International Ltd, 54 Lombard St, London EC3P 3AH

423   NATIONAL BANK LTD

Location: Dublin, London

History: est 1835 as National Bank of Ireland; known as National Bank 1856; merged with Glyn, Mills & Co & Williams Deacon's Bank to form Williams & Glyn's Bank Ltd 1970

Records: correspondence re formation 1834–46, prospectus 1835, court minute books 1835, deeds of settlement & supplements 1835, chairman's statements to agms 1836–60, annual reports 1843–96, general instructions & instructions to officers books (4) 1840–76, staff lists 1854 1875, register of branches 1856, balance sheets f1864, chairman's letter book 1874–87, list of shareholders 1907 1920, secretary's memoranda book 1912–25, inspectors' instruction books (2) 1914 1919, head office ledger 1921
London, Baker St: signature books (5) f1898, safe custody registers (2) f1898, security registers (2) 1920s-30s, loans ledger 1899–1919
London, Bayswater Rd: loans ledger f1862, signature books (15) f1862, information book 1876–1950
London, Camden Town: safe custody register 1872–1962
London, Cavendish Sq: safe custody registers (5) 1881–1956, security registers (2) 1897–1932
London, Charing Cross: signature books (2) 1904–19, press cuttings 1947–53
London, Grosvenor Gardens: signature books f1864, security registers (7) 1890–1939, safe custody registers (4) 1893–1938, bills registers (2) 1901–58, information book 1906–66, deposit account ledgers (2) f1922
London, Harrow Rd: signature books (12) f1882, safe custody registers (2) 1882–1960, information book 1882–1967, security register 1914–48, closed accounts register 1950–63
London, Holborn: signature books (4) 1920–62, safe custody registers (2) 1920–71, letters of instruction books (3) f1920, security ledgers (4) 1920–54
London, Islington: security registers (3) 1881–1930, signature books (8) 1881–1960, half yearly report book 1890–1901, safe custody registers (2) 1894–1930, past due bills registers (3) 1898–1940, bills discounted ledger 1912–49
London, King's Cross: signature books (6) 1868–1961, manager's draft book 1868–1923, security registers (3) 1882–1962 inc, deposit receipt books 1905–54, safe custody registers (2) 1921–61, loan ledgers (3) 1942–62
London, Notting Hill Gate: security registers (2) 1825–1920, signature books (7) 1868–1962, information book 1868–1963, safe custody register 1892–1963, letter books (2) 1922–27

London, Strand: letter books (10) 1897–1930, signature books (9) 1897–1950, security registers (2) 1898–1935, safe custody registers (3) 1919–60, staff circular book 1915–60
London, Willesden: signature books (7) 1882–1969, safe custody registers (4) 1890–97, security registers (5) 20 cent, customer instruction books (3) 20 cent, day books (2) 1948–55

Records' Location: Williams & Glyn's Bank Ltd

424   NATIONAL BANK OF LIVERPOOL

Location: Liverpool, Merseyside

History: est 1863; amlg with Parr's Banking Co Ltd 1883

Records: articles of association 1863 1869, daily committee minutes 1864–65, annual report 1870, amlg papers 1883–84

Records' Location: National Westminster Bank Ltd

425   NATIONAL BANK OF SOUTH AFRICA LTD

Location: London

History: overseas bank; est 1891 as National Bank of the South African Republic Ltd; known as above 1902; amlg with Anglo-Egyptian Bank Ltd & Colonial Bank to form Barclays Bank (Dominion, Colonial & Overseas) 1925

Records: London committee minutes c1926–35, agenda book 1920–30

Records' Location: Barclays Bank International Ltd, 54 Lombard St, London EC3P 3AH

426   NATIONAL BANK OF WALES LTD

Location: Manchester (1879), Aberdare (1880), Cardiff (1882)

History: est 1879; acquired by Metropolitan Bank (of England & Wales) Ltd 1893

Records: articles of association 1879, balance sheet 1883, annual reports 1891–92, liquidator's papers 1893

Records' Location: Midland Bank Ltd

427   NATIONAL COMMERCIAL BANK OF SCOTLAND LTD

Location: Edinburgh, Lothian

History: est 1825 as National Bank of Scotland; amlg with Commercial Bank of Scotland to form National Commercial Bank of Scotland Ltd 1959; merged with Royal Bank of Scotland 1969

Records 1: minute books f1825, secret letter book 1825–27, general ledgers f1825, journals f1825, reports to shareholders f1825, cash books (12) 1828–31, private minute book 1828–35, charter & supplements f1828, statement of sums lodged & lent 1829–34, agenda books 1831–35, instructions to agents & accountants 1840, outstanding debt ledger 1845–49, general manager's annual reports 1908–13 inc, annual reports f1864, balance sheets 1867–1901, manager's annual reports 1867–79, circular books (2) 1869–1923, registers of money lent & lodged (6) 1872–80 1893–1949, reports of directors to agms 1877–1925, reports on securities & bookkeeping at London office 1885–90, state of debt book 1903–38, opinion books (2) late 19 cent, registers of life policies held as security (5) nd

Records' 1 Enquiries: National Register of Archives (Scotland), Scottish Record Office, PO Box 36, HM General Register House, Edinburgh EH1 3YY Ref: list 349

Records 2: papers re amlg 1912–19

Records' 2 Location: Lloyds Bank Ltd

Records 3: extracts from directors' minutes & annual reports 1825–1920, extracts from secret letter book 1825–26, balance sheets 1865–1907 inc

Records' 3 Location: Scottish Banking Collection, University of Glasgow Archives, The University, Glasgow G12 8QQ

428   NATIONAL DISCOUNT CO LTD

Location: London

History: discount house; est 1856; acquired by Gerrard & Reid Ltd to form Gerrard & National Discount Co Ltd 1969

Records: deed of settlement 1856, articles of association 1856, board minute books (19) f1856, agm minutes f1856, weekly reports of supervisory committee 1856–63, half yearly reports & balance sheets f1856, general ledgers (20) f1856, journals (4) 1856–87 f1937, manager's cash book 1856–57, correspondence 1856–57, building committee minutes 1856–60, register of shareholders 1864, audited balance sheets f1866, profit & loss statements f1866, reports of proceedings of agms f1886, Bank of England weekly returns record books (2) f1899, papers re trial of clerk 1900, registers of directors (2) f1901, foreign exchange cash book 1908–26, investment ledgers (6) f1916, papers & correspondence re premises (3 files) f1916, pension fund minutes & accounts f1922, treasury bills tender book f1928

Records' Location: Guildhall Library, Aldermanbury, London EC2P 2EJ

429 NATIONAL PROVINCIAL BANK LTD

Location: London

History: est 1833 as National Provincial Bank of England; amlg with Union of London & Smith's Bank to form National Provincial & Union Bank of England Ltd 1918; known as above 1924; combined with Westminster Bank Ltd & District Bank Ltd to form National Westminster Bank Ltd 1968

Records 1: court minute books (19) 1828–78, prospectuses 1829–30, deed of settlement 1833, share registers (3) 1833–64 inc, rotation committee minute books (55) 1833–78, note registers (5) 1833–97 inc, secretary's letter book 1833, annual reports 1834–1968, agm proceedings books (3) 1834–39, extraordinary general meetings proceedings book 1834–99, licences to issue notes (9) 1835–56, information books re branches 1834, list of managers 1836, papers re general manager 1836–43, head office & agents' circular books (50) 1838–1936, assignments re bad debts 1839–53, instructions to local directors & branch managers 1840, branch committee minute books (2) 1843–45 1889–1916, register of cancelled notes 1844–1955, bank note indemnity books (2) 1845–79, manuscript history of bank c1850, balance sheet & profit & loss books 1856–81, legal opinions re shareholders 1859–85, incidental charges book 1859–68, branch balance sheets 1860–

77, scales of staff payments 1860, salaries committee minutes 1862–87, candidates for apprenticeship books (3) 1867–1918, circulars re staff guarantee fund 1869–86, law books (2) 1870–1949, agm attendance lists 1870–89, chairman's books (11) 1873–78, senior staff salary book 1877–1920, correspondence department minutes 1878–1966, finance committee minute books (3) 1879–1915, annual returns 1879–83, staff agreement books (2) 1886–1916, register of outstanding notes f1897, private letter books (2) 1899–1918, register of directors (2) 1901–23, private court minutes 1904–20, branch premises history ledger 1905–20, agm minutes 1908–20, papers re opening of branches 1918, amlg papers 1918, holiday fund committee minutes 1925–51, regulations for admission of staff probationers 1929, papers re regulations for the issue of corporation stocks 1930–31

Bangor: manager's letter book 1861–93
Beaumaris: character book 1878–1906
Birmingham: character books (2) 1887–1914
Bridgend: bill registers (3) 1835–57, character books (2) 1898–1922
Bristol: character books (8) 1876–1921, interview books (3) 1892–1908, letter book 1902–03, loan book 1911–24, analysis of advances & discounted bills 1936–48
Bristol, Corn St: plans of premises 1889–90
Bristol, Redlands: plans of premises 1889–1927
Conway: character book 1878–1929
Dartmouth: drafts issued book 1876–1966
Dolgellau: details of daily payments into branch 1842–63, manager's drafts 1846–52, cash in hand book 1855–59, general ledger & cash book 1861–62
Ledbury: customer ledger 1835–43, deposit ledger 1835–80
Leeds: character book 1878–84
Lichfield; security register 1834–72, character books (3) 1877–1908 inc
Llandudno: character books (2) 1876–1900
London, Dartford: letters with head office 1850–66
London, Hackney: manager's letters 1904–24
London, Lombard St: information book 1908–48
London, Paddington: profit & loss account book 1904–37

March: character books (6) 1875–1952,
interview books (3) 1913–26
Scarborough: manager's letters 1902–26
Sherborne: letter books (2) 1862–1929,
character books (4) 1874–1929 inc,
interview book 1930–35
Totnes: information book 1843–68
Wolverhampton: information book 1899–
1918, branch statistics 1899–1926
Wotton-under-Edge: branch minutes 1834–
74
Records' 1 Location: National Westminster
Bank Ltd
Records 2: personal papers of Llangefni
branch manager 1850–86
Records' 2 Location: Liverpool Record Office,
City Libraries, William Brown St, Liverpool
L3 8EW
Ref: 920 MD
Records 3: Caerphilly: waste books (2) 1839–
41 1875–76, current account ledger
1864–70, deposit ledger 1865–74
Records' 3 Location: Glamorgan Record
Office, County Hall, Cathays Park, Cardiff
CF1 3NE
Ref: D/D Xhs 4/1–4

430   NEVILLE, REID & CO

Location: Windsor, Berks
History: est 1780; amlg with Barclays & Co
Ltd 1914
Records: ledger of account with William
Deacon & Co 1838–41, 'bank journal' 1844–
64, 'bank ledgers' (ie private ledgers) (3)
1844–62
Records' Location: Berkshire Record Office,
Shire Hall, Reading RG1 3EE
Ref: D/ECg B1, 8, 9

431   NEWCASTLE COMMERCIAL JOINT STOCK BANKING CO

Location: Newcastle upon Tyne, Tyne &
Wear
History: est 1836, failed 1856
Records: deed of settlement 1837, mortgage
as security for customer's account 1847
Records' Location: Northumberland County
Record Office, Melton Park, North
Gosforth, Newcastle NE3 5QX
Ref: NRO 530.20/296; ZMD 32/3

432   NEWCASTLE, SHIELDS & SUNDERLAND UNION JOINT STOCK BANK

Location: Newcastle upon Tyne, Tyne &
Wear
History: est 1836; dissolved & business
acquired by Woods, Parker & Co 1853
Records 1: securities for loans c1830s–50s,
bankers' licences 1836–40, signature book
1841–59, list of shareholders 1847
Records' 1 Location: Barclays Bank Ltd
Records 2: report & minutes 1838, list of
shareholders 1849
Records' 2 Location: Durham County Record
Office, County Hall, Durham DH1 5UL
Ref: NCBI/JB/1860; NCBI/TH/54

433   NICHOLLS, BAKER & CRANE

Location: Bewdley, Staffs
History: est c1782 as Roberts, Skey &
Kenrick; known as Pardoe, Nicholls &
Baker c1826; known as above c1830;
acquired by Midland Bank 1862
Records: London remittance books (2)
Forster & Co 1798–1803 1810–13, receipt
books bills payable (2) 1812 1818, general
ledger 1812–13, private ledgers (2) Hoare
Barnett & Co 1818–21, bills discounted
book 1821–34, cash books (2) 1838–42,
acceptance books (2) 1852–55
Records' Location: Midland Bank Ltd

434   JOHN, WILLIAM & GEORGE NIGHTINGALE

Location: London
History: est 1730 as Vere & Asgill; known as
Vere, Asgill & Wickenden 1748; as Asgill,
Nightingale, Ransom & Wickenden 1754; as
above 1788; failed 1796
Records: goldsmith's book c1740s
Records' Location: Williams & Glyn's Bank
Ltd

435   NORFOLK & NORWICH JOINT STOCK BANKING CO

Location: Norwich, Norfolk
History: est 1826; absorbed by East of
England Bank 1836
Records: agreement with East of England
Bank 1836
Records' Location: Barclays Bank Ltd

436 NORTH DEVON BANK

Location: Barnstaple, Devon

History: amlg with National Provincial Bank of England 1835

Records: abstracts from ledgers 1813–34, registers of bad & doubtful debts (2) 1816–36, partners' account with London bank 1821–28, papers re account with Exeter General Bank 1823–30, partnership agreements (2) 1826, letters with customers 1830–39, letters & statements from London agents 1830–42, memoranda book re advances 1832, letters re partners 1835–40, register of joint notes 1835–36, amlg agreement 1835, list of past due bills 1836

Records' Location: National Westminster Bank Ltd

437 NORTH EASTERN BANKING CO LTD

Location: Newcastle upon Tyne, Tyne & Wear

History: est 1872; amlg with Bank of Liverpool Ltd 1914

Records: prospectus 1872, articles of association 1872–1911, letters with Bank of England & agents 1872–1901, circulars 1872–99, staff daily instruction book 1873–1915, list of shareholders 1873–93, annual reports 1873–1914, papers re shares 1873–1910, special letter books (46) 1874–1920, papers & letters re amlgs 1875–1914, security book 1885–89, papers re corporate customers 1880–1920, schedule of branch accounts & other branch statistics 1897–98, letters re staff 1912–19

Records' Location: Barclays Bank Ltd

438 NORTH OF ENGLAND UNION JOINT STOCK BANKING CO

Location: Newcastle upon Tyne, Tyne & Wear

History: est 1832; failed 1847

Records: customer securities for loans 1828–50

Records' Location: Public Record Office, Ruskin Av, Kew, Richmond, Surrey TW9 4DU

Ref: J90/1544–1563

439 NORTH KENT BANK LTD

Location: London; Greenwich

History: est 1864; absorbed by the London & Provincial Bank Ltd 1878

Records: reports & accounts with notes on standing of directors & lists of shareholders 1867–69

Records' Location: Barclays Bank Ltd

440 NORTH OF SCOTLAND BANK LTD

Location: Glasgow, Strathclyde

History: est 1836; known as North of Scotland & Town & County Bank Ltd after amlg with Town & County Bank 1908; known as above 1923; merged with Clydesdale Bank Ltd to form the Clydesdale & North of Scotland Bank Ltd 1950

Records 1: instructions to agents & accountants 1848 1856, declarations of trust 1849–54, circular books (52) 1864–1950, annual reports with press cuttings 1869–1921, descriptions of books in use at branch offices 1872–1909, list of shareholders 1879–1909, contract of co-partnery 1882, note circulation returns books (2) 1882–1918, board minute books (3) 1908–22, list of branches & correspondents 1914 1924, instructions for branch offices 1929

Records' 1 Location: Clydesdale Bank Ltd, Head Office, 30 St Vincent Place, Glasgow G1 2HL

Records 2: balance sheets 1865–1910, annual reports 1897–1926 mostly inc

Records' 2 Location: Scottish Banking Collection, The Archives, University of Glasgow, Glasgow G12 8QQ

441 NORTH & SOUTH WALES BANK LTD

Location: Liverpool, Merseyside

History: est 1836; acquired by Midland Bank Ltd 1908

Records: prospectus 1836, deed of settlement 1836, board minute books (25) 1836–1908, agm minute books (3) 1836–1908, share registers (10) 1836–1905, share ledgers (2) 1836–46, share transfer register 1836–41, security books (3) 1836–70, tellers' cash book 1836, general ledgers (27) 1836–1907, bad debt books (2) 1837–42, annual reports

1839–1907 inc, abstract of balance sheets (21 vols) 1843–1909, staff registers (4) 1845–76, committee minute books (7) 1846–57, branch inspection reports 1848–64, rents book 1849–73, instructions for officers books (7) 1849–1900, memoranda book re banking practice 1851–1907, 'own notes unissuable' books (3) 1861–1908, note registers (7) 1863–1907, loan books (10) 1868–1904, Liverpool managers' letter book 1869–93, customer memoranda book 1874–96, shareholders' registers (3) 1874–89, correspondence re limited liability 1876–79, half yearly balance working papers 1879–1908, chairman's private letter book 1880–96, general manager's memoranda 1891–1901, correspondence re projected amlgs 1893–1907, press cuttings book 1894–1908, articles of association 1901, classification of advances 1907, amlg papers 1908–10
Aberystwyth: general ledgers (9) 1836–80, letter book 1836–44, deposit receipt ledgers (4) 1836–79, security books (2) 1836–61, private ledgers (6) 1840–76 inc, general ledger balance books (5) 1846–78, bills of exchange register 1869–73
Barmouth: general ledger balance book 1874–82
Caernarvon: general ledgers (9) 1836–77, deposit receipt ledger 1836–56
Dolgellau: general ledgers (8) 1878–1914
Ffestiniog: private ledger 1837–39
Knighton: general ledger balance books (4) 1856–1909
Liverpool, North: general ledgers (4) 1863–78
Liverpool, South: signature books (4) 1863–1916
Llanfyllin: accounts opened books (2) 1888–1909
Llangollen: security registers (2) 1863–1909, signature books (2) 1863–1909
Mold: deposit receipt ledger 1834–74, private ledgers (3) 1838–44
Oswestry: general ledgers (10) 1836–81, letter books (4) 1862–1902, reference book 1874–92
Portmadoc: deposit receipt ledger 1839–42, analysis of accounts 1883–89
Pwllheli: deposit receipt ledgers 1836–48
Ruthin: deposit receipt ledger 1838–62
Welshpool: general ledger 1836–39, security register 1836–74
Wrexham: general ledgers (4) 1836–40

1903–12, security books (5) 1836–1902, balance books (12) 1837–1909, character book 1873–85
Records' Location: Midland Bank Ltd

442   NORTH WESTERN BANK LTD
Location: Liverpool, Merseyside
History: est 1807 as Moss & Co; reconstructed as North Western Bank 1864; acquired by Midland Bank 1897
Records: current account ledgers (5) 1838–64 inc, share registers (3) 1864–97, prospectus & annual reports 1864–90, board minute books (2) 1866–97, shareholders' minutes 1866–97, bad debt books (2) 1865–94, general ledger 1882–85, amlg papers 1897
Records' Location: Midland Bank Ltd

443   NORTH WILTS BANKING CO
Location: Melksham, Wilts
History: est 1835; amlg with Hampshire Banking Co to form Hampshire & N Wilts Banking Co 1877
Records: prospectus 1835, board minute books (2) 1835–77, rough minutes 1858–70, fidelity bond 1841, security register 1851–86, deed of settlement 1865, agm minutes 1865–76, balance sheets 1865–76, list of shareholders 1876
Records' Location: Lloyds Bank Ltd

444   NORTHAMPTONSHIRE BANKING CO
Location: Northampton, Northants
History: est 1836 as Northamptonshire Central Banking Co; known as above 1838; amlg with Capital & Counties Bank Ltd 1890
Records: deed of settlement 1836, board minutes 1888–90, amlg papers 1889–90
Daventry: cash book 1836
Records' Location: Lloyds Bank Ltd

445   NORTHAMPTONSHIRE UNION BANK LTD
Location: Northampton, Northants
History: est 1836; amlg with National Provincial Bank of England Ltd 1920
Records: prospectus 1836, deeds of settlement 1836–99, half yearly accounts

books (3) 1836–1920, agm minute books (2) 1837–1920, board minute books (8) 1849–1921, committee minute books (2) 1856–81, statistics book 1866–1920, half yearly reports 1888–1919 inc, manager's information book 1890–1905, security registers 1891–96, manager's letter book 1891–95, salary book 1895–1920, amlg papers 1914–20
Daventry: waste book 1837
Records' Location: National Westminster Bank Ltd

446   SIR S H NORTHCOTE & CO

Records: agreement re establishment of bank 1792
Records' Location: Devon Record Office, Castle St, Exeter EX4 3PQ
Ref: 51/24/29/2

447   NORTHERN & CENTRAL BANK OF ENGLAND

Location: Manchester, Gt Manchester
History: est 1834; failed 1837 & liquidated 1839
Records 1: prospectus 1833, supplementary deed of settlement 1836, agreement for transfer of Bristol branch to National Provincial Bank 1836
Records' 1 Location: National Westminster Bank Ltd
Records 2: notice of establishment 1834, miscellaneous notices & letters 1836, notice re transfer of Colne branch to Craven Bank 1836
Records' 2 Location: Lancashire Record Office, Bow Lane, Preston PR1 8ND

448   NORTHERN COUNTIES BANK LTD

History: est 1871; failed 1881
Records: articles of association 1872
Records' Location: National Westminster Bank Ltd

449   NORTHUMBERLAND & DURHAM DISTRICT BANK

Location: Newcastle upon Tyne, Tyne & Wear
History: est 1836; failed 1857
Records 1: annual reports 1839–42
Records' 1 Location: Barclays Bank Ltd

Records 2: deed of settlement 1836, liquidator's report 1862, liquidation papers 1862–68
Records' 2 Location: Northumberland Record Office, Melton Park, North Gosforth, Newcastle NE3 5QX Ref: ZR1 34 1; NRO 530.20/272; NRO 997/2/14; NRO 606
Records 3: correspondence re liquidation 1857–58
Records' 3 Enquiries: National Register of Archives (Scotland), PO Box 36, HM General Register House, Edinburgh EH1 3YY
Ref: list 945

450   NOTTINGHAM & DISTRICT BANK LTD

Location: Nottingham, Notts
History: est 1889; known as Midland Counties Bank Ltd 1899; amlg with the Birmingham District & Counties Banking Co Ltd 1904
Records: annual reports 1897–1903, register of shareholders 1903–04, amlg papers 1904–05
Records' Location: Barclays Bank Ltd

451   NOTTINGHAM JOINT STOCK BANK LTD

Location: Nottingham, Notts
History: est 1865; acquired by Midland Bank Ltd 1905
Records: provisional committee minutes 1865, prospectus 1865, board minute books (4) 1865–1905, annual reports 1865–1904, share transfer register 1865–1900, general ledgers (11) 1865–1905, security registers (3) 1865–80, list of shareholders 1869 1882, general ledger balance book 1873–1903, board agenda & rough minute books (2) 1881–99, amlg papers 1905
Hucknall: general ledger 1885–95
Records' Location: Midland Bank Ltd

452   NOTTINGHAM & NOTTINGHAMSHIRE BANKING CO

Location: Nottingham, Notts
History: est 1834; amlg 1919 with the London, County, Westminster & Parr's Bank Ltd
Records: deeds of settlement 1834 1873, board minute books (15) 1834–1918, note

register 1834–1918, customer ledger 1834–35, general manager's letter book 1844–61, investment & property ledgers (2) 1858–80, clerks' salary minute book 1872–1901, officers' engagement agreement book 1873–92, summary of share capital 1880, staff rules book 1893, manager's letter book 1897–1909, salary book 1901–18, balance sheets 1907–18, amlg papers 1917–18
Newark: general ledger 1835–42

Records' Location: National Westminster Bank Ltd

453   NUNN & CO

Location: Manningtree, Essex

History: est 1810; absorbed by London & County Bank 1870

Records: amlg papers 1870–74

Records' Location: National Westminster Bank Ltd

454   OAKES, BEVAN, MOORE & BEVAN

Location: Bury St Edmunds, Suffolk

History: est 1795; known also as Oakes, Bevan & Co & Oakes, Bevan, Tollemache & Co; amlg with Capital & Counties Bank Ltd 1900

Records 1: partnership agreements (14) 1827–99, cash book 1856–88, amlg papers 1899–1903
Mildenhall: papers re amlg 1899–1900
Stowmarket: agreement for appointment of agent 1830
Sudbury: security register 1878–82, cashier's book 1883–85

Records' 1 Location: Lloyds Bank Ltd

Records 2: misc papers re audit, securities, assets & liabilities, profits, etc c1800–1916, note register(?) 1837, customer quarterly balance books (19) 1839–43, rough cash books (9) 1848–53, customer overdraft ledger 1894, balance sheet 1899, abstract of balances transferred 1900, list of bad debts nd, 'payments & receipts' ledger nd, papers of Bevan & Oakes families 19 cent
Stowmarket: list of balances 1863, 'debtors ledger' 1892–93, overdraft sheets 1894
Sudbury: overdraft balances 1892–93

Records' 2 Location: Suffolk Record Office, School Hall St, Bury St Edmunds, Suffolk 1P33 1RX

455   OAKES, FINCHAM & CO

Location: Diss, Norfolk

History: est 1802; known as Fincham & Simpson 1856; absorbed by London & Provincial Bank Ltd 1871

Records 1: partnership agreements 1827–29

Records' 1 Location: Lloyds Bank Ltd

Records 2: papers re suspension of business 1871

Records' 2 Location: Barclays Bank Ltd

456   OLDHAM JOINT STOCK BANK LTD

Location: Oldham, Gt Manchester

History: est 1880; acquired by Midland Bank 1898

Records: prospectus 1880, board minute books (4) 1880–98, board agenda 1880–98, reports & balance sheets 1880–98, share registers (2) 1880–98, investment register 1880–86, security registers (3) 1881–98, investment ledger 1883–98, general ledger 1882–92, building society account ledger 1883–98, summary of capital & shareholders 1898

Records' Location: Midland Bank Ltd

457   OLIVER, OLIVER, LANGHORN & HARRISON

Location: Stony Stratford, Bucks

History: est 1797; failed 1843; known also as Stony Stratford & Buckinghamshire Bank

Records: letters, notebooks & papers of M D Mansell agent at Newport Pagnell 1798–1822

Records' Location: Buckinghamshire Record Office, County Hall, Aylesbury HP20 1VA
Ref: D/U/9

458   ORIENTAL BANK CORPORATION

Location: London

History: overseas bank; est 1851; known as New Oriental Bank Corp 1884; failed 1893

Records: customers' securities for loans 1851–84

Records' Location: Public Record Office, Ruskin Av, Kew, Richmond, Surrey TW9 4DU
Ref: J90/1770–1774

459 ORIENTAL COMMERCIAL BANK

Location: London

History: liquidated 1878

Records: papers re liquidation 1878

Records' Location: Williams & Glyn's Bank Ltd

460 OVEREND, GURNEY & CO

Location: London

History: est 1802; failed 1867

Records 1: papers re failure 1866–67

Records' 1 Location: Durham County Record Office, County Hall, Durham DH1 5UL Ref: D/HO/F65

Records 2: papers re failure 1866–93

Records' 2 Location: Williams & Glyn's Bank Ltd

461 OWEN & GRIFFITHS

Location: Welshpool, Powys

History: est c1800; failed 1816; known also as Montgomeryshire Old Bank

Records 1: correspondence re partnership matters, banking practice & failure 1807–31

Records' 1 Location: National Library of Wales, Aberystwyth SY23 3BU

Ref: Glansevenn Collection

Records 2: partnership agreement 1807

Records' 2 Location: Lloyds Bank Ltd

462 P & O BANKING CORPORATION LTD

Location: London

History: est 1920; acquired by Chartered Bank of India, Australia & China 1938

Records: board minute books (6) 1920–37, articles of association 1920, staff declarations of secrecy 1920–38, share registers (14) 1920–28, annual reports 1921–38, 'office arrangements' for men & women 1921–37, correspondence re legal matters 1924–41, directors' committee minute books (9) 1928–37, analysis of branch results 1928–33, journal 1932–39, papers re premises at Shanghai 1935–38, papers re acquisition by Chartered Bank 1938–39

Records' Location: Standard Chartered Bank Ltd, Head Office, 10 Clements Lane, London EC4N 7AB

At the time of publishing this guide researchers can be given very little access to the records

463 PAGET & CO

Location: Leicester, Leics

History: est 1825; taken over by Lloyds Bank Ltd 1895

Records: partnership agreements (6) 1838–92, private memoranda book 1888–1900, amlg papers 1895

Records' Location: Lloyds Bank Ltd

464 PAISLEY BANKING CO

Location: Paisley, Strathclyde

History: est 1783; absorbed by British Linen Co 1837

Records 1: papers re opening branch at Dundee 1789–91

Records' 1 Enquiries: National Register of Archives (Scotland), HM General Register House, Edinburgh EH1 3YY Ref: list 1964

Records 2: note register 1783–1838

Records' 2 Enquiries: as above.

Ref: list 945

465 PAISLEY UNION BANK CO

Location: Paisley, Strathclyde

History: est 1788; absorbed by Glasgow Union Banking Co 1838

Records: journal 1795–96, ledger 1836–39, list of debts owing 1838

Records' Enquiries: National Register of Archives (Scotland), PO Box 36, HM General Register House, Edinburgh EH1 3YY

Ref: list 1110

466 PALATINE BANK LTD

Location: Liverpool, Merseyside

History: est 1899; amlg with Bank of Liverpool & Martin's Ltd 1919

Records: amlg papers 1919–21

Records' Location: Barclays Bank Ltd

467 PARES LEICESTERSHIRE BANKING CO

Location: Leicester & London

History: est 1800 as Pares & Heygate; a joint stock bank 1836; amlg with Parr's Bank Ltd 1902; London agency wound up 1832

Records 1: customer ledger 1800–06, deed of settlement 1836, board minute books (5) 1836–1902, agm minutes 1837–1902, annual reports 1836–1902, private ledgers (9) 1836–1902, monthly balance book 1844–1902, stock register 1860–83, private cash books (2) 1880–1902, share transfer notice book 1889–1902, rough board minutes 1890–1902, balance sheets 1897–1901, schedule of bad & doubtful debts 1902, amlg papers 1902

Hinckley: customer ledger 1826–27

Records' 1 Location: National Westminster Bank Ltd

Records 2: Pares family papers (extensive) 18–19 cents

Records' 2 Location: Derby Local Studies Library, Derby Central Library, The Wardwick, Derby DE1 1HS

Ref: Pares Collection

Records 3: memorandum re foundation and development 1864

Records' 3 Location: Leicestershire County Record Office, 57 New Walk, Leicester LE1 7JB

Ref: DE 365/298

468   PARKER, SHORE & CO

Location: Sheffield, S Yorks

History: est 1774; premises & part of business (?) acquired by Sheffield Union Bank 1843

Records: papers re estates of J Parker, H Parker & H Blakelock c1840–60

Records' Location: Midland Bank Ltd

469   PARR, LYON & CO

Location: Warrington, Cheshire

History: est 1782; became Parr's Banking Co on conversion to joint stock bank 1865

Records 1: partnership agreements (6) 1804–57, correspondence with customers 1823–26, list of debts owed to bank 1851, salary books (3) 1856–63, counsel's opinion re distribution of profits 1860, papers re Parr family 19 cent

Records' 1 Location: National Westminster Bank Ltd

Records 2: papers, deeds & accounts re Lyon family estates (72 boxes) 1566–1860, ditto re Parr family estates (c40 boxes) 1600–1900

Records' 2 Location: Warrington Local Studies Library & Local Record Office, Warrington Library, Museum St, Warrington, Cheshire WA1 1JB

470   PARR'S BANK LTD

Location: London

History: est 1865 as Parr's Banking Co Ltd by reconstruction of Parr, Lyon & Co; amlg with Alliance Bank Ltd to form Parr's Banking Co & the Alliance Bank Ltd 1892; known as above 1896; amlg with London, County & Westminster Bank Ltd to form London, County, Westminster & Parr's Bank Ltd 1918

Records: circular re formation 1865, articles of association 1865–1909, share ledger 1865–90, annual reports 1865–1917, board minute books (7) 1865–1918, select committee minutes 1865–66, agm minutes 1866–1918, letters re securities 1891–1909, notebook of J Rae 1890–1905, circulars re Association of English Country Bankers 1888–1910, weekly committee minutes 1892–95, list of shareholders 1897, general manager's reports 1897–1901, branch & premises committee minutes 1898–1902, papers re transfer of head office to London 1899–1903, directors' correspondence 1897, lists of officers (8 vols) 1897–1922, papers re projected amlg with Union Bank of Manchester 1900, register of directors 1901–16, correspondence re bad debts 1902, staff instruction book 1903, statistics of branches & staff 1904, general purpose committee minutes 1908–29, salary book 1908–31, daily committee minutes 1909–13, 'A','B' & 'C' committee minutes 1910–23, branch results 1913, scheme of charges 1912, memoranda book re comparative performances with other banks & papers re projected amlgs 1917, amlg papers 1917–18

Chester: salary book 1914–54

Clifton: bill ledger f1909

Leicester: list of overdrawn accounts 1904

Loughborough: branch minute book 1903–07

London, Cavendish Sq: branch minute book 1901–06

London, Charing Cross: comparative statements & analysis of profits 1896–1903

Matlock: branch minute book 1915

Northwich: branch minute books (3) 1888–1901

Runcorn: branch minutes f1860, premises expenditure book f1892
Sandbach: discount ledger f1873, branch minute book f1883
Teddington: deposit ledger 1899–1917, general ledgers (3) 1899–1918, returns book 1899–1918, minute book 1900–18, loan ledgers 1901–18

Records' Location: National Westminster Bank Ltd

471   PARSONS, THOMSON, PARSONS & CO

Location: Oxford, Oxon

History: est 1771; amlg with Barclay & Co Ltd 1900

Records: customer ledgers (2) c1810–15, ditto (c200) 1800–1910, sundry ledgers (c23) f1775

Records' Location: Barclays Bank Ltd

472   PAYNE & CO

Location: Crewkerne, Wilts

History: est 1810; amlg with Stuckeys Banking Co 1829

Records: customer ledgers (2) 1810–21

Records' National Westminster Bank Ltd

473   PAYNE, HOPE & CO

Location: Wells, Somerset

History: est 1800; failed 1831

Records: partnership agreement & papers re failure 1809–31

Records' Location: Somerset Record Office, Obridge Rd, Taunton, Somerset TA2 7PU
Ref: DD/WM 435, 438–441

474   PEACOCK, WILLSON & CO

Location: Sleaford, Lincs

History: est c1792 as Peacock, Handley & Co; known as above 1861; taken over by Lloyds Bank Ltd 1912

Records 1: wills & papers re Handley family 1719–1866, customer ledgers (2) 1792–1812, profit & loss accounts 1815–21, waste books (3) 1802–04, memoranda book 1805–27, note registers (2) 1816–77, ledger of estate of A Peacock c1830s, partnership agreement 1869, private ledgers (4) 1888–1924, stock exchange loan book 1895–1909, staff books

(2) 1900–10, amlg papers 1912
Bourne: security book 1897–1906
Lincoln: security book 1899–1906
Newark: bill book 1807–09, day books (6) 1809, correspondence 1809–1921, customer balances 1814–16, account with Sleaford office 1844–46, security books (2) 1875–1904

Records' 1 Location: Lloyds Bank Ltd

Records 2: papers re partnership matters 1819–1908, customer balances & memoranda 1841, correspondence re a customer's account 1841, papers re mortgages & law suits 1880–1918, papers re proposed new partner 1900–02, amlg papers 1912

Records' 2 Location: Lincolnshire Archives Office, The Castle, Lincoln LN1 3AB
Ref: PSJ 7/26

475   J & J W PEASE

Location: Darlington, Co Durham

History: est 1820 as Pease & Co; known as above 1870; failed & taken over by Barclay & Co Ltd 1902

Records 1: correspondence of Pease family 1793–1902, notebooks & diaries of John Pease (11) 1817–45, extracts from diaries of Edward Pease 1841–57, papers re failure 1900–06

Records' 1 Location: Durham County Record Office, County Hall, Durham DH1 5UL
Ref: D/HO/C; D/HO/F93, 96–106; D/Pe 3/130–149

Records 2: papers re failure 1902

Records' 2 Location: Barclays Bank Ltd

476   JOSEPH PEASE & CO

Location: Hull, Humberside

History: est 1754; amlg with York Union Banking Co Ltd 1894; known also as Pease, Knowsley & Co; Pease, Liddell & Co; & Pease's Old Bank

Records 1: customer ledgers (3) 1757–66, partnership agreement 1890

Records' 1 Location: Barclays Bank Ltd

Records 2: passbooks of Pease family c1754–1818, correspondence re personal, family & banking matters c1795–1850, journals of J R Pease (2) 1822–65, partnership papers 19 cent, ledger 1809–49

Records' 2 Location: Kingston upon Hull City Record Office, 79 Lowgate, Kingston upon Hull HU1 2AA
Ref: DEP 338–43, 897, 1801–4, 1821, 2937, 3002

477   PERCIVAL & CO
Location: Northampton, Northants
History: est c1800; amlg with Northamptonshire Union Bank 1836
Records: papers re infringement of Bank of England's monopoly 1836
Records' Location: National Westminster Bank Ltd

478   PEDDERS & CO
Location: Preston, Lancs
History: est 1776; wound up 1861
Records 1: notes, booklet, cheque book etc 1776–1861, agreement for winding up 1861
Records' 1 Location: Lancashire Record Office, Bow Lane, Preston PR1 8ND
Ref: DDX 103, 842
Records 2: deed of dissolution 1827
Records' 2 Location: Yorkshire Archaeological Society, Claremont, Clarendon Rd, Leeds LS2 9NZ
Ref: MD 290 bx 9

479   PERFECT & CO
Location: Pontefract, W Yorks
History: est c1800; amlg with Yorkshire District Bank 1834
Records: business & family papers of Perfect family 1772–1848, amlg papers 1835
Records' Location: Leeds Archives Dept, Chapeltown Rd, Sheepscar, Leeds LS7 3AP
Ref: Acc 1744

480   PERTH BANKING CO
Location: Perth, Tayside
History: est 1763; absorbed by Union Bank of Scotland 1857
Records 1: 'progressive ledgers' (20) 1768–89, sederunt book 1785–1811, bill book 1787–88, teller's cash book 1787–88, bills discounted book 1788–92, stock journals (4) 1787–1857, dividends paid books (5) 1788–1882, cashier's cash books (3) 1795–1831, stock ledgers (2) 1804–57, board minute books (3) 1807–72, contracts of co-partnery 1808 1828, bankrupt ledger 1811–25, interest receipt books (4) 1821–57, note

circulation registers (3) 1843–67
Dunkeld: ledger 1809–17
Records' 1 Enquiries: National Register of Archives (Scotland), PO Box 36, HM General Register House, Edinburgh EH1 3YY
Ref: list 1110
Records 2: minute book, ledgers & partnership papers 1786–1857
Records' 2 Enquiries: as Records 1
Ref: list 945

481   PERTH PARISH BANK
Location: Perth, Tayside
Records: cash book 1815–20
Records' Enquiries: National Register of Archives (Scotland), PO Box 36, HM General Register House, Edinburgh EH1 3YY
Ref: list 1110

482   PERTH UNITED BANKING CO
Location: Perth, Tayside
History: est 1766; absorbed by Perth Banking Co 1787
Records: stock ledger 1766–90, transfer journal 1766–90, dividend book 1771–90
Records' Enquiries: National Register of Archives (Scotland), PO Box 36, HM General Register House, Edinburgh EH1 3YY
Ref: list 1110

483   PERTH UNITED CO
Location: Perth, Tayside
History: est 1766; absorbed by Perth Banking Co 1787
Records 1: share transfer journal 1766–90, stock ledger 1766–90, dividend book 1771–90
Records' 1 Enquiries: National Register of Archives (Scotland), PO Box 36, HM General Register House, Edinburgh EH1 3YY
Ref: list 1110
Records 2: general ledger 1766–67
Records' 2 Enquiries: as Records 1
Ref: list 945

484   PIERSON & SON
Location: Hitchin, Herts
History: est c1759; failed 1841; otherwise known as Hitchin & Hertfordshire Bank

Records: private ledgers (2) 1815–1834, partnership agreement 1789, partner's passbooks (2) 1789–1808, account books (3) 1804–24, partner's executors' accounts (3) 1825–36

Records' Location: Hertfordshire Record Office, County Hall, Hertford SG13 8DE
Ref: Wilshere Family Archives 61507–15, 61544, 67367

485 PINKNEY BROTHERS

Location: Salisbury, Hants
History: est 1811 as Everett & Co; known as above 1859; amlg with Wilts & Dorset Banking Co Ltd 1897
Records: dividend ledgers (7) 1799–1804 1811–17 1837–72 1895–97, security registers 19 cent, interest ledgers (4) 1811–42 1871–97, signature books 1864–97, amlg agreement 1896
Records' Location: Lloyds Bank Ltd

486 POCKLINGTON, RASTELL, OLIVER & RAY

Location: Newark, Notts
History: est c1797; wound up 1809
Records: deed of dissolution 1799–1800
Records' Location: Nottingham Record Office, County House, High Pavement, Nottingham NG1 1HR
Ref: DDSK 191/31–32; CP5/7/128

487 POLE, THORNTON, FREE, DOWN & SCOTT

Location: London
History: est 1773 as Down, Thornton & Free; known as above 1815; failed 1825
Records: profit & loss ledger 1789–1831, personal papers of H Thornton (also re his sugar refinery) 1800–22, private ledger of H Thornton 1810–27
Records' Location: Williams & Glyn's Bank Ltd

488 POMFRET, BURRA & CO

Location: Ashford, Kent
History: est 1875; taken over by Lloyds Bank Ltd 1902
Records: partnership agreements 1833 1848, amlg papers 1902
Records' Location: Lloyds Bank Ltd

489 PRAEDS & CO

Location: London; Fleet St
History: est 1802; amlg with Lloyds Bank Ltd 1891
Records: security ledgers & registers (6) 1806–60s, customer list 1831, deed registers (3) 1840s-60s, safe custody register 1850s, general ledger 1840s, signature books 1854–91, coupon registers 1860s, standing order book 1870s, amlg papers 1891
Records' Location: Lloyds Bank Ltd

490 PRESCOTT'S BANK LTD

Location: London, Cornhill
History: est 1766 as Prescott, Grote, Culverden & Hollingsworth; operated under several titles until 1891 when known as Prescott, Dimsdale, Cave, Tugwell & Co Ltd; known as above 1903; amlg with Union of London & Smiths Bank Ltd 1903
Records: customer ledger 1766, partnership agreements (13) 1776–1888, partners' expenses book 1779–85, papers re bad debts, bankruptcies etc 1787–1888, weekly balance sheets & profit & loss accounts 1780–1864, income & expenditure books of W W Prescott (6) 1799–1863, signature books (8) 1794–1891, partners' passbooks (3) 1801–38, salary book 1807–89, fidelity bonds 1809–65, partner's letter book 1815–36, stock register 1818–31, papers re partners' interests in shipbuilding firms 1825–95, standing orders register 1834–44, partners' minute books (11) 1839–90, security register 1852–92, salary lists 1859–1901, bad debts register 1860–1918, salary registers 1865–1932, statements of final balances 1871, half yearly balance sheets 1871–90, assignment of shares in firm 1872–75, advances registers (3) 1876–1911, staff register 1889–1966, agreement for formation of limited company 1890, articles of association 1890, board minute books (2) 1891–1903, agenda books (3) 1891–1903, committee minute books (2) 1891–1904, papers re proposed amlgs 1891–97, secretary's memoranda book f1891, investment & premises register 1891–1903, letters from branches 1891–1903, central ledger with details of mergers 1891–1902, papers re legal case against Bank of England 1892, law book 1892–1905, profit & loss

accounts & balance sheets 1900–03, amlg
papers 1903
Bath: agreement for appointment of agent
1891
Bristol: correspondence re overdrafts 1900
Winchester: agreement for appointment of
agent 1891, inspectors' reports 1891–93,
report on overdrawn accounts 1894
Records' Location: National Westminster
Bank Ltd

491   PRESTON BANKING CO LTD

Location: Preston, Lancs

History: est 1844; acquired by Midland Bank
Ltd 1894

Records: provisional committee minutes &
report 1844, list of shareholders 1844, board
minute books (4) 1844–72, annual reports &
balance sheets 1844–94, shareholders'
minute book 1844–60, weekly balance book
1844–65, salary books ('expenses') (2)
1844–66, balance sheets 1845–65, deed of
settlement 1845, royal charter 1845, share
transfer register 1845–65, report of
shareholders' meeting 1866, applications for
advances books (6) 1866–67, liquidation
papers 1867, customers' balance sheets
1868–69, specimen staff contracts (7 items)
1871–88, security deposit ledger 1878–94,
letter book 1883–85, investment ledger
1883–84, annual summaries of capital &
shareholders 1884–92, applications for
advances 1884, amlg papers 1894

Records' Location: Midland Bank Ltd

492   PRETOR & CO

Location: Sherborne, Dorset

History: est 1740; amlg with National
Provincial Bank of England 1843

Records: partner's private cash book 1763–
76, partner's private ledger 1793–1824,
letter book 1794–1805

Records' Location: Dorset Record Office,
County Hall, Dorchester DT1 1XJ
Ref: D33/1–3

493   PRITCHARD, GORDON & CO

Location: Brosley, Salop

History: est as Vickers, Son & Co 1799;
known as above 1884; taken over by Lloyds,
Barnett & Bosanquet Bank Ltd 1888

Records: partnership agreement 1801,
minute of admission to partnership 1820,
amlg papers 1888
Records' Location: Lloyds Bank Ltd

494   PUGH, JONES & CO

Location: Pwllheli, Gwynedd

History: est 1848; acquired by National Bank
of Wales 1891; known also as Pwllheli
District Bank

Records: amlg agreement 1890–91

Records' Location: Midland Bank Ltd

495   THOMAS & ROBERT RAIKES

Location: Hull, Humberside

History: est c1790 as Sykes, Creyke,
Broadley & Lockwood; known as Broadley
& Raikes 1801; as Robert Raikes, Williams
& Isaac Currie 1808; as above 1821; failed
1861; known otherwise as East Riding Bank

Records: Raikes family papers 18 cent,
balance books (2) 1808–13, note registers
1810–50, profit & loss accounts 1813–14

Records' Location: Williams & Glyn's Bank
Ltd

496   RANSOM, BOUVERIE & CO

Location: London; Pall Mall

History: est 1782 as Ransom, Morland &
Hammersley; known as Ransom, Morland
& Co 1795; Morland, Ransom & Co 1813;
Ransom & Co 1818; as above 1856; amlg
with Barclay, Bevan, Tritton & Co to form
Barclay, Bevan, Tritton, Ransom, Bouverie
& Co 1888

Records: letters of administration (G
Ransom) 1784, papers re failure of Charles
Rashfield & Son c1795, papers re Surtees,
Burdon & Co 1801–02, customer ledgers
(18) 1802 1806–08 1887–88, liquidation
ledger 1818, liquidation letter book 1819,
dividend authority registers c1820–40,
papers re estate of P P Bouverie 1823–48,
memoranda book re customers & staff
c1825–76, private ledgers (2) 1841–56, amlg
papers 1896

Records' Location: Barclays Bank Ltd

497   RANSOM, MORLAND & CO

Location: Dundee, Tayside

History: est 1802; absorbed by Dundee Banking Co 1838; known also as Dundee New Bank

Records 1: partners' minutes 1802–04 & accounts book 1802–37, 'state of circulation' books (2) & papers 1804–05, statements of specie in safe books (3) 1806–38 inc, papers re winding up of first co-partnery 1804–09, balance books of cash accounts (3) 1806–36 inc, journal sheets 1809–13, small long standing balance list 1812–38, papers re merger c1820–40, petty cash book 1827–41, current account ledger 1836–38, waste book 1846–47, papers re merger c1820–40, petty cash book 1827–41, current account ledgers 1836–38, waste book 1846–47

Arbroath: balance sheets 1802–17

Brechin: balance sheets 1803–16

Forfar: progressive ledger 1802–38

Records' 1 Enquiries: National Register of Archives (Scotland), PO Box 36, HM General Register House, Edinburgh EH1 3YY

Ref: 1964

Records 2: extracts from partners' minutes 1802–03 & private letter book 1802–04

Records' 2 Location: Scottish Banking Collection, Glasgow University Archives, The University, Glasgow G12 8QQ

498   R RAPHAEL & SONS LTD

Location: London

History: est 1787 as R Raphael & Sons; known as Raphael, Robinson & Glyn 1967 & as above 1977

Records: partnership ledger f1876, private ledgers f1909, partnership agreements 1928, balance sheets f1940s, extensive notes on Raphael family

Records' Location: R Raphael & Sons Ltd, 10 Throgmorton Av, London EC2N 2DP

499   RAWDON, BRIGGS & SONS

Location: Halifax, W Yorks

History: est 1811 as Rhodes, Briggs & Garlick; known as Rhodes & Briggs 1815; as above 1816; converted to a joint stock bank, Halifax Commercial Banking Co 1836

Records: particulars of insolvent estates 1812–16, general balances 1818–24, securities for loans 1820–34

Records' Location: Barclays Bank Ltd

500   REEVES & PORCH

Location: Glastonbury, Somerset

History: est 1812; amlg with Stuckey's Banking Co 1835

Records: assignment of property for debt 1825–28

Records' Location: Somerset Record Office, Obridge Rd, Taunton, Somerset TA2 7PU

Ref: DD/BR nw/8

501   RICHARDS & CO

Location: Llangollen, Clwyd

History: est 1854; amlg with National Provincial & Union Bank of England Ltd 1920

Records: balance sheets & profit & loss accounts 1910–19, amlg papers 1920

Records' Location: National Westminster Bank Ltd

502   SIR M RIDLEY BART, CHAS WM BIGGE & CO

Location: Newcastle upon Tyne, Tyne & Wear

History: est 1755 as Bell, Cookson, Carr & Airey; known under a number of titles until 1791 when called Ridley, Cookson, Widdrington, Bell & Co; known as Ridley, Bell, Wilkinson & Gibson 1796; Ridley, Bell & Gibson 1802; Ridley, Bigge, Gibson & Co 1806; Sir M Ridley Bart, Chas Wm Bigge & Co 1832; merged in the Northumberland & Durham District Bank 1839

Records 1: letter books (2) 1807–35, profit & loss accounts 1825–31

Records' 1 Location: Lloyds Bank Ltd

Records 2: partnership agreements 1756–1836, papers re legal dispute 1804–08, letters to Sir M W Ridley re banking matters 1820s, papers re proposed extension of business to Berwick 1827, statements re assets & liabilities 1836 1844, papers re investigation of bank affairs 1836, 'ledger balances' 1836, amlg papers 1839, division & final accounts of assets 1868

Records' 2 Location: Northumberland Record Office, Melton Park, North Gosforth, Newcastle upon Tyne NE3 5QX
Ref: ZR1 34/1–2, ZCE 8/23, ZCK 10

503   ROBARTS, CURTIS & CO

Location: London

History: est 1791 as Robarts, Curtis, Were, Hornyold & Berwick; known as Robarts, Curtis, Robarts & Curtis 1804; as Sir William Curtis, Robarts & Curtis 1818; as above 1833; amlg with Sir John William Lubbock & Co 1860

Records: signature books 1805–60, staff book 1810–28, safe deposit books 1835–62

Records' Location: Coutts & Co, 440 The Strand, London WC2R 0QS
All enquiries must be made in writing to the Archivist

504   ROBERTS & GREGORY

Location: Newport, Isle of Wight

History: est c1780s; failed c1790s

Records: papers re failure 1790–92

Records' Location: Isle of Wight County Record Office, 26 Hillside, Newport PO3 2EB
Ref: M3/4,5,9,23,105,107; WhP 965

505   ROBIN BROTHERS

Location: Jersey, Channel Islands

History: est 1808 as Janvrin & Durell; known as Robin Brothers 1879; taken over by Parr's Bank Ltd 1908; known otherwise as Jersey Commercial Bank

Records: extracts from partnership agreements 1808–1908, letter book 1870–71, receipts for securities 1888–1908, balance sheets 1896–1907, amlg notice 1908

Records' Location: National Westminster Bank Ltd

506   ROBINS, FOSTER, COODE & BOLITHO

Location: St Austell, Cornwall

History: est 1867; amlg with Bolitho Sons & Co to form Bolitho, Foster, Coode & Co 1889; known also as East Cornwall Bank

Records: private ledgers (2) 1873–85, bond register f1882

Records' Location: Barclays Bank Ltd

507   JAMES & GEORGE ROBINSON & CO

Location: Mansfield, Notts

History: est 1804; purchased by Samuel Smith & Co 1871

Records: agreement for sale of business 1870

Records' Location: National Westminster Bank Ltd

508   ROCHDALE JOINT STOCK BANK LTD

Location: Rochdale, Lancs

History: est as Rochdale Commercial Loan & Discount Co 1856; renamed Rochdale Joint Stock Bank Ltd 1872; acquired by Oldham Joint Stock Bank 1882

Records: prospectus 1856, reports & balance sheets 1861–81, papers re transfer of business 1881–82, statements of customer accounts 1882

Records' Location: Midland Bank Ltd

509   ROSKELL, ARROWSMITH & CO

Location: Preston, Lancs

History: est 1825 as Lawe, Roskell, Arrowsmith & Co; known as above 1833; failed 1868

Records: partnership agreement 1825, ledger abstracts & re correspondence 1833–50, character book (of this bank ?) 1834–57, legal papers (3 boxes) c1850s, press cuttings re failure 1868

Records' Location: Lancashire Record Office, Bow Lane, Preston PR1 8ND
Ref: DDTs ·

510   N M ROTHSCHILD & SONS LTD

Location: London

History: merchant bank; formed by N M Rothschild who was a textile merchant at Manchester f1798; est London c1803; known as above 1836

Records: early account ledgers (Manchester & London) (49) 1743–1831, private & business correspondence with Rothschild partners & cousins (c560,000 items) 1802–1914, general in-correspondence (c616,000 items) 1802–1914, home & foreign account ledgers (124) 1809–1914, cash books (Jones, Loyd & Co) (16) 1810–23, balance book (Jones, Loyd & Co) 1810–15, cash books

(Masterman, Peters & Co) (28) 1813–56, bill book 1813–14, general business copy letter books (512) 1814–1914, loans payments & receipts copy letter books (74) 1815–1914, balance book (Masterman, Peters & Co) 1816–23, bullion account books (180) 1816–1912, journals (113) 1817–65, bills discounted books (3) 1817–23, specimen bonds 1818–1911, Prussian loan cash book 1818, legal documents re loans 1818–1914, general current account ledgers (418) 1819–1914, cash books (Smith, Payne & Smith) (197) 1820–1914, dividends receivable books (22) 1821–1914, private account ledgers (32) 1822–1914, discounting account ledgers (21) 1823–1912, international correspondence (c8,600 items) 1824–1914, foreign governments correspondence (c4,000 items) 1823–1914, Brazilian government invoices and account ledgers (13) 1827–1914, Rothschild family copy letter books (20) 1825–1914, American accounts & credit books (94) 1831–1914, American copy letter books (112) 1834–1914, American stock ledgers (13) 1834–1914, American Government current account ledgers (3) 1835–43, American coupons purchased copy books (3) 1835–43, foreign ledgers (74) 1836–1909, foreign banks correspondence (c50,000 items) 1837–1914, American tobacco invoices and account sales books (8) 1844–91, United States Bank debenture books (3) 1846–51, corn consignment ledger 1847–48, Brazilian agency account balance & cargo books (13) 1855–1914, Californian journal 1856–78, loan prospectuses 1858–1914, stock account books & sheets (17) 1869–1914, American stock account books (12) 1869–1914, Bank of England balance books (2) 1873–1914, United States 1875 funded loan account books (4) 1875–76, information books (2) 1876–1914, American railway dividend account books (20) 1876–1914, account books (August Belmont & Co) (13) 1877–1904, Chilean government accounts ledgers (4) 1878–1914, Russian dividend account ledgers (4) 1878–1914, dividends posting books Brazilian loans (169) 1879–1914, Bank of California account & credit books (66) 1880–1911, American & Indian paper accounts book 1881–82, American discount books (2) 1882–1903, bills of lading ledgers (5) 1882–1907, consol accounts 1884–1913,

Brazilian railway account books (6) 1885–1914, loans accounts books (2) 1891–1914, stock ledgers (22) 1892–1914, Brazil telegramme books 1898–1914, credit books & ledgers (Austrian Credit Anstalt) (43) 1901–14, foreign stock books (3) 1902–14, cash books (University of London) (46) 1903–14, stock deposit books (4) 1903–14, property ledgers (3) 1906–14, American prices books (2) 1908–09, bills cash books (3) 1909–13

Records' Location: N M Rothschild & Sons Ltd, New Court, St Swithin's Lane, London EC4P 4DU

511   THE ROYAL BANK

Location: London

History: projected 1830

Records: prospectus & papers re proposed formation 1830

Records' Location: National Westminster Bank Ltd

512   ROYAL BANK OF AUSTRALIA

Location: London & Sydney

History: overseas bank; est 1840; ceased business 1850

Records 1: deed of settlement 1840, share application & transfer proforma 1840, shareholders' ledger 1840–65, share transfer register 1840–48, debenture book 1840–48, share sale book 1840–48, minute books (3) 1840–50, cash book 1840–49, journal 1840–49, shareholders' cash book 1840–48, directors' attendance book 1840–45, 'deposit notes' books (2) 1840–43, current account ledger 1840–41, letters of credit book 1840–48, drafts on colonies book 1840–48, sundry letters & vouchers f1840, deposit ledger 1841–56, dividend books (2) 1841–47, bills receivable book 1841–49, bills payable book 1843–52, passbooks Union Bank of London (4) 1844–50, agm minute book 1845–49, letter books (2) 1845–50, cash book 1850–65, liquidator's cash account with Royal Bank of Australia 1850–65, liquidator's ledger 1850–54, liquidator's cash book 1850–65, letters to liquidator etc, list of creditors 1855

Australia Records:

Adelaide: note books (2)

Boyd Town: note book, consignment books

(London) (2) 1840–49, order book for goods 1844–45, saddler's book 1844, ledger 1844–48, store waste book 1847–48, cash book (B Boyd & other) 1847–48, day book (B Boyd & other) 1847–48, ledger (B Boyd & Co & other)1847–48, invoice & stock book 1847–48, letter book 1847–48, loose papers & accounts
Hobart Town: note books (3), journal 1842–48
Launceston: note books (4)
Melbourne: note book
Sydney: note books (2), journal 1840–43
Unspecified: bank ledgers (2) 1840–43, branch account book 1840–47, R Boyd's letters f1840, letters from W S Boyd 1840–49, cash books (13) 1840–48, letter books (7) 1840–50, general ledgers (3) 1840–50, invoice book 1841–43, journals (7) 1841–50, rough journals (2) 1841–45, register of cargo manifests 1841–44, produce received & forwarded book 1841–47, discount bill register 1842–50, letter book (G H Wray) 1842–45, stock books (2) 1842–50, diaries (9) 1842–50, agenda books (2) 1842–49, 'general' letter books 1842–43 1847, petty cash books (4) 1842–48, voucher books (7) 1843–44, dividend receipt books (4) 1843–47, current account ledger 1843–49 London wool sales book 1843–48, agreement with employees books (2) 1844–45, remarks on flocks & herds 1844–47, 'ledgers' (5) 1843–65 inc, accountant's book 1845–49, journals (B Boyd) (3) 1845–48, drafts on Sydney books (2) 1845–48, manifest book 1845–50, Geo Rust's cash book with B Boyd 1845–47, invoice books (2) 1845–46, promissory note book 1845–46, station stores return books (2) 1846–48, livestock book 1846–47, advance notes 1847, accounts with employees book 1847–48, bonded stores book 1847, 'accounts of ships etc' 1847, cash book (B Boyd) 1848, journal (B Boyd) 1848, ledgers (B Boyd) (2) 1848, station returns (7) 1848–50, discount bill diaries (2) 1848, cash book (B Boyd) 1848, letter book (Eumarella) 1848–50, cash abstract book 1849–50, sheep & cattle returns 1848–50, account of debentures outstanding 1849, accounts of merchandise shipped books (2) 1860–61, register of merchants' rents (3) 1858–60, indexes of proprietors (2) application for shares book, bills receivable registers (3)

Records' 1 Location: Public Record Office, Ruskin Av, Kew, Richmond, Surrey TW9 4DU
Ref: J90.1328–1473
Records 2: papers re winding up 1841–58
Records' 2 Location: National Westminster Bank Ltd

513   ROYAL BANK OF LIVERPOOL
Location: Liverpool, Merseyside
History: est 1836; failed 1870
Records: deed of settlement 1861
Records' Location: Barclays Bank Ltd

514   ROYAL BANK OF SCOTLAND LTD
Location: Edinburgh, Lothian
History: est 1727as Royal Bank of Scotland; merged with National Commercial Bank of Scotland Ltd to form The Royal Bank of Scotland Ltd 1969

Records 1: court minutes f1727, minute books of court of proprietors 1727–1879, share registers (2) 1727–1817, stock journal 1727–90, 'charges of management' record 1727–32, dividend books (3) 1727–75, note registers 1728–42 f1874, tellers' cash books (21) 1728–53, cash ledgers (13) 1728–50, journals (9) 1728–54, general ledgers (8) 1728–60 f1913, committee minute books 1728–85, share transfer books 1731–1862 f1900, bank interest (cash credit) books (13) 1739–52, subscription list for capital increase f1788, 'black book' being copies of demands to debtors 1796–1832, additions of general ledgers (4) 1797–1858, sederunt book f1816, 'state of affairs...' reports 1817–65, account book re acquisition of property in St Andrew's Sq 1819–30, bills for negotiation books (4) 1836–71, weekly abstract of accounts 1836–39, deposit receipt ledgers (21) 1839–56, papers re proposed amlg 1845–50, draft balance sheets 1848 1851 1858, committee sederunt books (7) 1857–81, general balance sheets (21) 1858–78, statistical analysis of business of Scottish banks 1865–91, statistics of bank affairs–assets, profit & loss, rates of interest, etc 1872–81, record of advances on City of Glasgow deposits 1878–79, statistics of Royal Bank Guarantee Fund 1881–90, general letter books f1901, chief

accountant's letter book 1912–19
Dundee: letter book 1839–44

Records' 1 Enquiries: National Register of Archives (Scotland), HM General Register House, PO Box 36, Edinburgh EH1 3YY
Ref: list 0266

Records 2: papers re application for charter

Records' 2 Location: Public Record Office, Ruskin Av, Kew, Richmond, Surrey TW9 4DU
Ref: T1/3472

Records 3: extracts from court minutes (4) 1727–1918, extracts from letters of Glasgow joint agent 1801–07, computed balance sheets 1817–64 inc, balance sheets 1866–1907 inc, governor's speeches to agms 1930–39

Records' 3 Location: Scottish Banking Collection, Glasgow University Archives, The University, Glasgow G12 8QQ

515 ROYAL BRITISH BANK

Location: London
History: est 1900; failed 1904
Records: prospectus 1903
Records' Location: Lloyds Bank Ltd

516 ROYAL EXCHANGE BANK LTD

Location: London
History: est 1861 as Metropolitan & Provincial Bank; reconstructed as Metropolitan Bank 1867; reconstructed as Royal Exchange Bank 1879; amlg with Birmingham Banking Co to form Metropolitan & Birmingham Bank 1889
Records: signature books (2) 1862–89, deposit account signature book 1864–92, security books (2) 1883–94, share dividend summary books (6) 1884–89
Records' Location: Midland Bank Ltd

517 RUFFORD & WRAGGE

Location: Stourbridge, W Midlands & Bromsgrove, Hereford & Worcester
History: est 1792; failed 1851
Records: records re salt trade & banking 1838–59
Records' Location: Staffordshire Record Office, Eastgate St, Stafford ST16 2LZ
Ref: D695/1/32/2–3

518 RUSSELL, ALAN & MALING

Location: Sunderland, County Durham
History: est 1787; liquidated 1803
Records: petty account book 1798–1801
Records' Location: North Yorkshire County Record Office, County Hall, Northallerton DL7 8SG
Ref: Acc ZGD

519 SADDLEWORTH BANKING CO

Location: Saddleworth, Greater Manchester
History: est 1833; absorbed by Manchester & County Bank Ltd 1866
Records: deed of settlement 1833, shareholders' journal 1833–36, list of eligible candidates for directorships 1839–63, monthly abstracts from general ledgers 1842–52, list of shareholders 1865
Dobcross: customer ledger 1833–34, day book 1833–34, general ledgers (2) 1834–36, note register 1836–57, deposit ledger 1849–74, half yearly balances 1856–64
Oldham: customer ledger 1836–38, deposit ledger 1835–39, general ledgers (4) 1836–51
Records' Location: National Westminster Bank Ltd

520 ST BARBE, DANIELL & CO

Location: Lymington, Hants
History: est 1788; amlg with Capital & Counties Bank Ltd 1896
Records: amlg papers 1896
Records' Location: Lloyds Bank Ltd

521 ST VINCENT COMMERCIAL BANK

History: overseas bank; believed not to have been formed
Records: papers re charter 1838
Records' Location: Public Record Office, Ruskin Ave, Kew, Surrey TW9 4DU
Ref: TI/3473

522 SANDEMAN, SONS & CO

Location: London
Records: letter book (Spain, Portugal, S America) 1795–97, cash book 1799–1806, ledger 1800–06, journal 1806–09, waste books (2) 1809–12 1838–39, banker's ledger 1817–19, inland letterbooks (2) 1885–87
Records' Location: Guildhall Library, Aldermanbury, London EC2 2EJ

523 SANDERS, SNOW & CO

Location: Exeter, Devon

History: est 1769 as Sanders & Co; known as above 1901; otherwise known as Exeter Bank; amlg with Prescott, Dimsdale, Cave, Tugwell & Co Ltd 1902

Records: partnership agreements 1784–1877, staff surety bonds (2) 1796 1832, bankers' licences 1815–1900, probates of partners' wills 1819–40, papers re premises 1835–70, general balance books (3) 1845–1901, private ledgers (3) 1864–1917, papers re partners' indemnity fund 1878–1900, balance sheets 1892–1901, profit & loss accounts 1895–99, amlg papers 1901–02

Records' Location: National Westminster Bank Ltd

524 SAPTE, MUSPRATT, BANBURY, NIX & CO

Location: London, Lombard Street

History: est c1787 as Vere, Lucadon, Troughton, Lucadon & Smart; then under a succession of names drawing members also from the Baron, Hawkins, Sapte, Muspratt, Nix & Banbury families; amlg with Fullers & Co to form Fuller, Banbury, Nix & Mathieson & subsequently Fuller, Banbury & Co 1859

Records: fidelity bonds 1788–1837, diary of payments 1788–95, correspondence with bankers 1793–1827, correspondence re staff securities 1807–28, papers re clerk's fraud 1809, papers re partner's fraud 1809–14, papers re liquidation of A Sheath & Son 1814, customer balance books (3) 1815, memoranda books re Christmas gifts to staff (2) 1818–19, correspondence re loans & securities 1826–57, statements of partnership & liquidation accounts 1833–44, customer balance books (5) 1853

Records' Location: National Westminster Bank Ltd

525 SAXTON BROTHERS

Location: Market Drayton, Salop

History: est 1851; amlg with Midland Banking Co Ltd 1872

Records: schedule of accounts taken over 1873

Records' Location: Barclays Bank Ltd

526 SCHOLFIELD, CLARKSON & CLOUGH

Location: Howden, Humberside

History: est 1809; business acquired by York City & County Bank 1832; known otherwise as Howden Bank

Records: private ledger 1830–31

Records' Location: Midland Bank Ltd

527 SIR SAMUEL SCOTT, BART & CO

Location: London; Cavendish Sq

History: est 1824; amlg with Parr's Banking Co & the Alliance Bank Ltd 1894

Records: private ledger 1824–32

Records' Location: National Westminster Bank Ltd

528 SCOTT, BURTON & CO.

Location: Shrewsbury, Salop

History: est 1808; amlg with Eyton, Reynolds & Bishop 1884; known otherwise as Burton, Lloyd & Co

Records: resolutions of partners' meetings 1848–84, partnership agreements (2) 1863–79, papers re G B Lloyd 1867–91

Records' Location: Lloyds Bank Ltd

529 SCOTT, PALMER, BIRD & GREENE

Location: Lichfield, Staffs

History: est 1765; failed 1855; known also as Lichfield Bank

Records: partnership agreements (4) 1814–46, papers re failure 1855

Records' Location: Staffordshire Record Office, Eastgate St, Stafford ST16 2LZ

Ref: D(W)1851/8/57(a)

530 SCOTTISH & UNIVERSAL FINANCE BANK LTD

History: est 1864; wound up 1866

Records: analysis of Scottish banks' balance sheets 1865–66

Records' Location: Manchester Central Library Archives Dept, St Peter's Sq, Manchester M2 5PD

Ref: MS f310.5.M5

531 SEATON, BROOK & CO

Location: Huddersfield, W Yorks

History: est c1797 as Joseph Brook; known as above 1806; failed 1810

Records: papers re failure 1810–18

Records' Location: Nottinghamshire Record Office, County House, High Pavement, Nottingham N91 1HR
Ref: CP 5/8/85–135

532 SECCOMBE, MARSHALL & CAMPION LTD

Location: London

History: discount house; est 1860 as W Marshall & Son; known as M W Marshall & Co 1922; as above 1922

Records: tenders for treasury bills 1919–22 1927–28, notice of change in partnership 1920, statements of account 1920–21, balance sheets f1920, articles of partnership (4) 1922–43, diaries with details of state of market & treasury bills 1922–25, journals (3) 1933–41, general ledgers 1934–47, statements of profits 1936–47

Records' Location: Seccombe, Marshall & Campion Ltd, 7 Birchin Lane, London EC3U 9DE

533 SELIGMAN BROTHERS LTD

Location: London

History: merchant bank; est 1864; acquired by S G Warburg & Co Ltd 1957

Records: private current account ledgers (19) 1906–21, general ledgers (16) 1906–20, bills payable registers (5) 1907–11 1921–23, 'impersonal & liquidation ledgers' (20) 1920–48

Records' Location: S.G. Warburg & Co Ltd, 30 Gresham St, London EC2P 2EB

534 SHARPLES, TUKE, LUCAS & SEEBOHM

Location: est 1820 as Sharples & Exton; known as Sharples, Exton & Lucas 1836; as Sharples, Tuke, Lucas & Lucas 1855; as above 1859; incorporated with Barclay & Co Ltd 1896

Records: letter of confidence 1825, proprietors' ledgers (4) 1852–96, note register 1882–1905, amlg papers 1896

Records' Location: Barclays Bank Ltd

535 SHEFFIELD BANKING CO LTD

Location: Sheffield, S Yorks

History: est 1831; amlg with National Provincial & Union Bank of England Ltd 1919

Records: board minutes 1831, private ledger 1831–38, deed of settlement 1832, salary books (3) 1851–1922 inc, note register 1874–1907, annual reports 1884–1914 inc, balance sheet 1906, amlg papers 1919
Rotherham: minute book 1834–38

Records' Location: National Westminister Bank Ltd

536 SHEFFIELD & HALLAMSHIRE BANK LTD

Location: Sheffield, S Yorks

History: est 1836; acquired by Midland Bank 1913

Records: board minute books (19) 1836–1913, shareholders' minute books (2) 1836–1913, share transfer registers 1836–1913, deed of settlement 1837, annual reports 1837–1911, declarations of secrecy 1837–99, petition re staff holidays 1846, staff private minute book 1861–68, proposals re adoption of limited liability 1872, staff rules etc 1875, managers' minute books (3) 1882–1913, private ledger 1893–1906, share registers (5) 1893–1912, board rough minute books (4) 1894–1913, half yearly returns 1897–1900, papers re alterations to articles of association 1897–99, dividend books (3) 1898–1913, board agenda books (5) 1901–13, managers' notebook re customers 1909–13, acceptances book 1912–40

Records' Location: Midland Bank Ltd

537 SHEFFIELD & RETFORD BANK

Location: Sheffield, S Yorks & Retford, Notts

History: est 1839 as Borough Bank of Sheffield; renamed 1842 on acquiring Retford branch of Nottingham & Nottinghamshire Banking Co; 1846 Retford business acquired by Sheffield Union Bank; failed 1846 & business absorbed by Sheffield Banking Co

Records: list of shareholders 1839, deed of settlement 1839, board minutes 1839–42, schedule of promissory notes & bills of exchange 1840–48, liquidation papers 1849

Records' Location: Midland Bank Ltd

538   SHEFFIELD & ROTHERHAM JOINT STOCK BANK

Location: Sheffield, S Yorks

History: est 1791 as Walker, Eyre, Stanley & Co; reconstructed as above 1836; amlg with Williams Deacons Bank Ltd 1907

Records: partnership agreement 1829, general meeting book 1829–35, customer ledger 1793–97, deeds of settlement 1836–1900, board minute books (21) 1836–1907, agm minutes 1837–1907, annual reports 1836–1907, bills accepted register 1838–50, notes on manager's visits to branches 1865–72, premises rebuilding contracts 1866, customer addresses & occupations book 1898, papers re increase of share capital 1900, papers re note issue 1907, staff indemnity bonds 1907

Records' Location: Williams & Glyn's Bank Ltd

539   SHEFFIELD UNION BANKING CO LTD

Location: Sheffield, S Yorks

History: est 1843; acquired by Midland Bank 1901

Records: deed of settlement 1843, board minute books (8) & index books (4) 1843–1901, summary of balance sheets 1845–46, list of current account balances 1846, reports & balance sheets 1862–1901, tabulated balance sheets 1862–1900, list of investments 1884–97, summary of history of bank 1891, weekly balance sheets 1893–1901, advisory board minute book 1901–16, press cuttings re amlg 1899, circulars re liquidator's appointment 1901 1917

Records' Location: Midland Bank Ltd

540   SHILSON, COODE & CO

Location: St Austell, Cornwall

History: est 1793; amlg with National Provincial & Union Bank of England Ltd 1920; known otherwise as The St Austell Bank

Records: report on development of business since 1910 1920, amlg papers 1920

Records' Location: National Westminister Bank Ltd

541   SHIP BANK

Location: Glasgow, Strathclyde

History: est 1749; absorbed by the Glasgow Bank Co to form Glasgow & Ship Bank 1837

Records 1: daily entry books (3) 1728–1830 inc, deposit receipt ledger 1785–1831, customer ledgers (49) 1788–1837, bond register 1796–1835, loan books (2) 1819–28 deposit ledger 1824, private ledger 1824–25

Records' 1 Enquiries: National Register of Archives (Scotland), PO Box 36, HM General Register House, Edinburgh EH1 3YY Ref: list 1110

Records 2: partners' balances 1752–61, ledger 1769–72, journal 1778–79

Records' 2 Location: Strathclyde Regional Archives, City Chambers, Glasgow G2 1DU

Records 3: correspondence re routine transactions 1834–37

Records' 3 Location: Scottish Banking Collection, University of Glasgow Archives, The University, Glasgow G12 8QQ

542   SHROPSHIRE BANKING CO

Location: Shrewsbury, Salop

History: est 1836; absorbed by Lloyds Banking Co 1874

Records: deed of settlement 1836, shareholders' register 1837–75, annual reports 1837–73, shareholders' minutes 1855, letter book 1856–58, minute book 1871–75, list of shareholders 1871–74, record of customer accounts 1873, amlg papers 1874–84

Records' Location: Lloyds Bank Ltd

543   J & C SIMONDS & CO

Location: Reading, Berks

History: est 1814; amlg with Barclay & Co Ltd 1913

Records: partnership agreements 1791–1906, customer ledgers 1814–1933 mostly inc, note registers (6) 1814–1908, deposit ledgers (4) 1817–82 mostly inc, cash book 1825, general balance books (11) 1830–80, private ledger c1830s, securities books (6) 1836–73 inc, profit & loss account book 1838–40, consolidated balance sheet book 1870s, diary of standing orders 1871, salary books (2) 1876–1914, letter book 1896–1900,

balance sheets 1902–13, branch statistics
1900–12, amlg papers 1913
Basingstoke: security book 1906
High Wycombe: customer ledger 1888–89
Wokingham: customer ledger (2) 1900

Records' Location: Barclays Bank Ltd

544 SIMPSON, CHAPMAN & CO

Location: Whitby, N Yorks

History: est 1785; acquired by York Union
Banking Co Ltd 1892; otherwise known as
Whitby Old Bank

Records: declaration of confidence 1797

Records' Location: Barclays Bank Ltd

545 SKINNER & CO

Location: Stockton, Cleveland

History: est c1815; amlg with National
Provincial Bank of England 1836

Records: legal opinion re amlg 1836

Records' Location: National Westminster
Bank Ltd

546 SLOCOCK, MATTHEWS, SOUTHBY & SLOCOCK

Location: Newbury, Berks

History: est 1791; amlg with Capital &
Counties Bank Ltd 1895

Records 1: partnership agreement 1881, amlg
papers 1895–97

Records' 1 Location: Lloyds Bank Ltd

Records 2: H Bunny's account (1851–55)
1864

Records' 2 Location: Berkshire Record Office,
Shire Hall, Shinfield Park, Reading RG2
9DX
Ref: D/EX 198 L1

547 SAMUEL SMITH, BROTHERS & CO LTD

Location: Hull, Humberside

History: est 1784; merged into Union of
London & Smiths Bank Ltd 1902

Records: general ledgers (8) 1784–1845 inc,
partnership agreements (7) 1787–1862,
ledger balances 1802–15, D R Smith's letter
books/ dossiers (6) 1866–81, details of
general accounts 1870–99, information
books (2) 1891–1901

Records' Location: National Westminster
Bank Ltd

548 SAMUEL SMITH & CO

Location: Derby, Derbys

History: est 1806; merged into Union of
London & Smiths Bank Ltd 1902

Records: general ledger 1806–10, letters to
London agent 1806–09, customer list 1816,
note register 1816–43, private ledgers 1816–
1902, petty expenditure book 1817–82, note
circulation monthly returns book 1844–49,
balance sheets 1845–54, information book
1864–72, partner's diaries (3) 1876–1902
inc, loans memoranda book 1876–79,
opinion book 1878–84, bad debts accounts
1888–1902, general balance book 1888–
1902, partners' letter books (3) 1889–1902,
liquidation accounts 1902–03

Records' Location: National Westminster
Bank Ltd

549 SAMUEL SMITH & CO

Location: Nottingham, Notts

History: est 1688; merged with Union Bank
of London & Smiths' Banks at London,
Derby, Hull & Lincoln to form Union of
London & Smiths Bank Ltd 1902

Records 1: receivership accounts 1741–58,
partnership agreements (7) 1765–98, A
Smith's private ledger 1757–74, account
with London agent 1756–59, A Smith's
letter book 1760–84, interest & discount
return books (4) 1774–1878 inc, general
balance books (8) 1780–1808 inc, monthly
totals of discounts 1783, list of bad &
doubtful debts 1799, private ledgers (5)
1810–82, customer ledger 1814–22, security
register 1824–67, letters re bad debts 1858–
60, character book 1859–77, unclaimed
balances 1876–98, partners' household
account book 1894–1904
Ripley: private ledger 1875–1900

Records' 1 Location: National Westminster
Bank Ltd

Records 2: papers & accounts re A Smith
1788–94, balance sheets with lists of debtors
& creditors 1796–98, annual accounts of
income in cash, bills & rent 1838–47

Records' 2 Location: Nottinghamshire Record
Office, County House, High Pavement,
Nottingham N91 1HR

Records 3: correspondence of Abel Smith
family (39 items) 1733–1839

Records' 3 Location: Nottinghamshire Record Office, County House, High Pavement, Nottingham N91 1HR

550   SMITH, ELLISON & CO

Location: Lincoln, Lincs

History: est 1775; merged into Union of London & Smiths Bank Ltd 1902

Records 1: partnership agreement 1775, notes on loan contracting 1802, summary of assets 1902
Grimsby: general ledger 1846–57, manager's diaries & interview notes (22) 1878–1920

Records' 1 Location: National Westminster Bank Ltd

Records 2: partnership agreement 1800, list of debtors & creditors 1799–1800

Records' 2 Location: Nottinghamshire Record Office, County House, High Pavement, Nottingham N91 1HR

Records 3: papers re staff & premises 1851–1904

Records' 3 Location: Lincolnshire Archives Office, The Castle, Lincoln LN1 3AB
Ref: SE/32/2

551   SMITH, OSBORN & CO

Location: Northampton, Northants

History: est 1810; failed 1825; known otherwise as Northamptonshire Town & County Bank

Records: papers re failure 1828, private & business papers of partner 1828–53

Records' Location: Northamptonshire Record Office, Delapre Abbey, Northampton NN4 9AW
Ref: O(N) 94–489

552   SMITH, PAYNE & SMITHS

Location: London; Lombard St
History: merged with Smiths Banks at Derby, Hull, Lincoln & Nottingham and Union of London Bank to form Union of London & Smiths Bank Ltd 1902

Records 1: partnership agreements (15) 1782–1857, customer list 1762–65, private ledgers (16) 1776–1854, out clearing book 1777, partners' miscellaneous correspondence 1777–1873, register of clerks 1783–1918, profit & loss ledgers (13) 1793–1849, order book 1795–1800, balance sheet

1797, private ledger of J H Smith 1829–86, investment ledger of O Smith 1830–63, rules for admission of partners 1836, private diaries of J H Smith 1840–58, investment ledger of E Carrington 1852–1905, investment ledger of J Smith 1856–83, letter books (2) 1858–90, weekly statistics of note circulation 1884–1904, minute book of M R Smith 1889–1901, half yearly reports 1891–1902, details of profits 1892–1902, list of bad debts 1892–1901, salary register 1895–1913, amlg papers 1902, private papers of Smith family 19 cent

Records' 1 Location: National Westminster Bank Ltd

Records 2: partnership agreement 1785, general papers & accounts 1777–1847

Records' 2 Location: Nottinghamshire Record Office, County House, High Pavement, Nottingham N91 1HR
Ref: SMT/144–169

553   SMITH ST AUBYN & CO LTD

Location: London

History: discount house; est 1891

Records: diaries with notes on business transacted, money market interest rates etc (63) 1891–1959 inc, ledgers with clients (1891–1922) & general accounts (20) 1891–1954, cash books (20) 1891–1960 inc, day books (135) 1891–1958, bills balance book 1891–92, trade acceptors ledgers (2) 1927–55, ledger of partners' & trustee accounts 1930–39, private accounts loan book 1931–38, loans ledger 1932–39, 'average rate bills No 1' with details of bills bought, sold & due, & discounting operations 1933–56, loans books (4) 1944–52, journals (4) 1946–56, private accounts interest book 1948–52, rough loan book 1949–52, rough day books (8) 1949 1955–58

Records' Location: Guildhall Library, Aldermanbury, London EC2P 2EJ

554   SOUTH WALES UNION BANK LTD

Location: Swansea & Cardiff, Glamorgan

History: est 1873 as Swansea Bank; renamed as above 1888; acquired by Metropolitan Bank (of England & Wales) Ltd 1892

Records: prospectus 1872, board minute book 1872–92, shareholders' minute book 1873–92, memoranda of deposit 1873–1905, manager's memoranda book 1876–92, board committee minutes books (3) 1876–85, letter books (3) 1878–91, board rough minute book 1888–92, amlg papers 1892–93

Records' Location: Midland Bank Ltd

555 SPARROW, TUFNELL & CO

Location: Chelmsford, Essex

History: est 1801 as Sparrow, Brown, Hanbury & Savill 1801; known as Sparrow, Brown, Hanbury, Savill & Simpson 1814; known as above 1826, incorporated with Barclay & Co Ltd 1896

Records 1: customer ledgers (6) 1807–25, ledger of account with London agent 1807–44, partnership agreements (10) f1817, private ledgers (5) 1833–96 inc, safe custody register 1830s, memoranda re partner's debts 1844, balance sheets 1855–80 1891–96, partners' minutes 1874–96, partners' out-letter book 1887–97, amlg papers 1896
Billericay: customer ledgers (3) 1818–44
Maldon: customer ledger 1826–29

Records' 1 Location: Barclay Bank Ltd

Records 2: partnership agreements (10) 1817–70, premises deeds 1854–1909, papers re legal proceedings against debtors 1823–96, agreement with manager 1892

Records' 2 Location: Essex Record Office, County Hall, Chelmsford CM1 1LX

Refs: D/DDW B4/1–17, D/DDW B8/1–10, D/DDW T180/1–10

556 STAFFORDSHIRE JOINT STOCK BANK

Location: Bilston, Staffs

History: est 1864; acquired by Birmingham Banking Co 1889

Records: prospectus 1864, security register 1876–89, general ledger 1884–91, reports on shareholders' meetings 1888–91, investigation committee report 1890, liquidator's reports 1890, liquidator's pass book 1890–91, amlg papers 1890–91

Records' Location: Midland Bank Ltd

557 STAFFORDSHIRE UNION BANK

History: unknown

Records: prospectus 1881

Records' Location: Lloyds Bank Ltd

558 STAMFORD, SPALDING & BOSTON BANKING CO

Location: Stamford, Lincs

History: est 1831 as Stamford & Spalding Joint Stock Banking Co; known as above 1836; acquired by Barclay & Co Ltd 1911

Records 1: board minutes 1831–33, annual reports 1852–1910, miscellaneous staff papers 1866–1917, deed of settlement 1870, profit & loss analysis by branches 1858, agm report 1911
Desborough: memoranda book 1887–95
Grimsby: security book 1890–1900
Northampton: signature book f1878, manager's letter book 1901–27
Oakham: signature books f1886, letter book f1888, head office circulars f1895
Uppingham: customer ledgers (7) 1845–68, letter books 1846–73, security books (3) 1858–96

Records' 1 Location: Barclays Bank Ltd

Records 2: deed of settlement 1832

Records' 2 Location: Spalding Gentlemen's Society, The Museum, Broad St, Spalding, Lincs PE11 1TB

559 STANDARD BANK LTD

Location: London

History: overseas bank; est as Standard Bank of British South Africa Ltd 1862; known as Standard Bank of South Africa Ltd 1883; as above 1962

Records: prospectus 1862, articles of association f1862, board minute books (40) f1862, board agenda (19) 1863–66 1938–59, general ledgers (68) f1862, registers of members f1862, premises plans, photographs & papers f1862, agm attendance books f1863, annual reports f1863, dividend registers f1863, balance sheets f1863, secretary's letter book Capetown–London 1864–66, out-letters London – general managers in S Africa (c600 vols & files) 1865–1954, lists of shareholders f1867, customer ledgers (c40) 1875–1927 inc, investment ledgers (7) 1879–1955, share allotment books f1880, secretary's letters to other banks 1880–90, letters from Port Elizabeth to general manager (1 parcel) 1882, bad debts written off books c1886–1973, quarterly statements of liabilities & assets for Cape & S African governments 1891–1960s, directors' remuneration books (2) 1893–1965, abstract of weekly balances (14 vols & 4 parcels) 1893–1960, papers re Army Pay Dept at Natal 1895–1908, private board correspondence 1896–1902, letter books chairman to general manager (3), 1897–1955, branch inspection reports 1897, profit & loss accounts 1897–1911, general manager's routine letters (120) 1898–1959, sports club minutes, rules & other papers 1903–58, weekly balances Africa & London 1903–44, power of attorney registers (c27) f1904, analysis of administration expenses books (30) 1907–59, chairman's speeches to agms 1909–54, register of directors f1919, executorship account books (18) 1922–39, seal registers (9) f1922, statements of exchange transactions (6) 1925–32, London committee minutes 1937–56

Durban: letter book 1863

London Wall: safe custody registers (2) 1914–36, general ledgers (11) 1918–58

New York Agency: profit & loss statements 1917–49

Records' Location: Standard Chartered Bank Ltd, Head Office, 10 Clements Lane, London EC4N 7AB

At the time of publishing this guide only very limited access to the records can be given

560   STEPHENS, BLANDY & CO

Location: Reading, Berks

History: est 1790 as Micklem, Stephens, Simonds & Harris; known as above 1841 & as Stephens, Blandy, Barnett, Butler & Co 1892; taken over by Lloyds Bank 1899

Records: partnership agreements 1791–1892, stock day books (2) 1795–1807, profit and loss books (9) 1797–1887 inc, stock ledgers (4) 1810–56, bad debt ledger 1814, unclaimed balances book 1814–96, balance sheets 1815–76, cash book 1817–19, exchequer bill accounts (2) 1841–89, customer accounts balance books (2) 1845–55, papers re bankruptcies & securities 1847–98, solicitor's accounts 1849–88, solicitor's opinions 1851–74, petty expenses books (2) 1858–81 inc, correspondence with Maidenhead branch 1878–87, papers re Maidenhead premises 1882–91, amlg papers 1899

Records' Location: Lloyds Bank Ltd

561   STEVENSON, SALT & CO

Location: Stafford, Staffs

History: est 1737 as John Stevenson; known as above c1777; taken over by Lloyds Banking Co Ltd 1866

Records 1: memoranda book 1764–1853, general ledgers (3) 1777–88 inc, cash book 1777–78, discount ledgers (4) 1781–87, bankers' licence 1809, salary book 1847–66, amlg papers 1865–66

Records' 1 Location: Lloyds Bank Ltd

Records 2: partnership agreements 1777–1856, wills of Stevenson & Salt families f1777, correspondence of Salt family re legal & financial matters 1815–57

Records' 2 Location: William Salt Library, Eastgate St, Stafford, Staffs ST16 2LZ

Ref: D1716 bdls 1, 3, 5; M597

562   STEVENSON, SALT & SONS

Location: London

History: est c1766 as Thomas & John Stevenson; known as above c1787; amlg with Bosanquet, Salt, Whatman & Harman 1867

Records: partnership deeds 1766–75

Records' Location: William Salt Library, Eastgate St, Stafford, Staffs ST16 2LZ

Ref: 1716 bdl 4

563   STILWELL & SONS

Location: London; Pall Mall

History: est 1774; absorbed by Westminster Bank Ltd 1923

Records: deeds re partners and partners' families 1815–1920, papers re estate of T Stilwell 1846

Records' Location: National Westminster Bank Ltd

564   STOCKTON & DURHAM COUNTY BANK

Location: Stockton, County Durham

History: est 1838; dissolved & business acquired by National Provincial Bank of England 1846

Records: prospectus 1838, board minutes 1838–53, agm minutes 1838–53, deed of settlement 1839

Records' Location: National Westminster Bank Ltd

565   STOREY & THOMAS

Location: Shaftesbury, Wilts

History: est 1816; business acquired by Wilts & Dorset Banking Co 1855

Records: agreement for purchase of goodwill by Wilts & Dorset Banking Co 1855

Records' Location: Lloyds Bank Ltd

566   STOURBRIDGE & KIDDERMINSTER BANKING CO

Location: Stourbridge, Hereford & Worcester

History: est 1834; acquired by Birmingham Banking Co 1880

Records: resolutions of inaugural meeting 1834, deed of settlement 1834, board minute books (5) 1834–80, general ledgers (9) 1834–77, shareholders' minute books (2) 1835–80, weekly balance sheets 1838–62, manager's notebook c1840–60, monthly balance sheet books (7) 1862–71, half yearly statements 1865–79, manager's interview diary 1867–80, amlg agreement 1880
Chipping Norton: balance statements 1857–65
Moreton-in-Marsh: balance statements 1857–65
Shipston-on-Stour: balance statements 1857–65
Stratford-upon-Avon: balance statements 1859–60

Records' Location: Midland Bank Ltd

567   T & R STRANGE

Location: Swindon, Wilts

History: est 1807; amlg with Capital & Counties Bank Ltd 1842

Records: amlg agreement 1842

Records' Location: Lloyds Bank Ltd

568   STUCKEY'S BANKING CO LTD

Location: Bristol, Avon

History: est 1826 by a union of Stuckey, Lean & Co of Bristol, Stuckey, Woodland & Co of Bridgwater & Stuckey & Co of Langport; amlg with Parr's Bank Ltd 1909

Records 1: board minute books (5) 1827–1909 inc, deed of settlement 1831, accounts of transactions between Bristol and Somerton branch 1838–41, balance sheets 1848–1909, proprietors' minute books (2) 1858–1909, committee minute books (6)

1861–1900, manager's notebook 1876–84, correspondence book 1778–1809, amlg agreement 1909
Clifton, Queen's Rd: branch minutes 1874–96
Yeovil: security register 1878–85, managers' information books (5) 1879–1925

Records' 1 Location: National Westminster Bank Ltd

Records 2: accounts of assets & liabilities c1830–40, papers re building of bank 1823

Records' 2 Location: Somerset Record Office, Obridge Rd, Taunton TA4 7PU
Ref: DD/FS Bx3; DD/DP Bxs 91–92

569   SURTEES, BURDON & CO

Location: Berwick & Newcastle

History: est 1768; failed 1803; known otherwise as Exchange Bank

Records: out letters 1773–1806

Records' Location: Northumberland Record Office, Melton Park, North Gosforth, Newcastle NE3 5QX
Ref: 2/OE/35/15

570   SWALEDALE & WENSLEYDALE BANKING CO LTD

Location: Richmond, N Yorks

History: est 1836; taken over by Barclay & Co Ltd 1899

Records 1: deed of settlement 1837, directors' reports 1837–48, shareholders' register 1839–70, balance sheets 1839–41 1851–68, list of shareholders 1862
Hawes: diary 1843

Records' 1 Location: Barclays Bank Ltd

Records 2: deed of settlement 1837

Records' 2 Location: Durham County Record Office, County Hall, Durham DH1 5UL
Ref: NCB1/D/78

571   SWANN, CLOUGH & CO

Location: York, N Yorks

History: est 1771; failed 1879 & business acquired by East Riding Bank

Records: opening notice 1771, liquidation report 1879

Records' Location: National Westminster Bank Ltd

572   JAMES TAYLOR & SONS

Location: Bakewell, Derbys

History: est c1800; amlg with Crompton & Evans' Union Bank Ltd 1879

Records: cash account ledger 1797–1809; bill book 1808–13

Records' Location: National Westminster Bank Ltd

573   THISTLE BANK CO

Location: Glasgow, Strathclyde

History: est 1761; absorbed by Glasgow Union Banking Co 1836

Records 1: customer ledgers (21) 1769–1836 inc, debts due book 1786–92, private ledger 1827–29, transfer ledger 1827–29, teller's cash book 1835–36

Records' 1 Enquiries: National Register of Archives (Scotland), HM General Register House, PO Box 36, Edinburgh EH1 3YY
Ref: list 1110

Records 2: postage accounts 1795–1834, receipts & accounts for expenditure on premises, administration, etc (27) 1795–1836, bankers' licences (6) 1813–34

Records' 2 Location: Scottish Banking Collection, Archives Department, University of Glasgow, Glasgow G12 8QQ

574   TOMES, CHATTAWAY & FORD

Location: Stratford-upon-Avon, Warws

History: est 1810 as Oldaker, Tomes & Chattaway; known as above 1833; acquired by Stourbridge & Kidderminster Banking Co 1834

Records: partnership agreements 1813 1833

Records' Location: Midland Bank Ltd

575   TOMKINS & CO

Location: Abingdon, Berks

History: est c1782; wound up 1812

Records: papers re J Tomkins (1 bdl) 1808–38

Records' Location: Berkshire Record Office, Shire Hall, Reading RG1 3EE
Ref: D/EP 4 B1

576   TOWN & COUNTY BANKING CO

Location: Aberdeen, Grampian

History: est 1825 as Aberdeen Town & County Banking Co; title changed to Town & County Bank Ltd 1882; amlg with North of Scotland Bank Ltd to form North of Scotland & Town & County Bank Ltd 1908

Records 1: board minutes (13) 1824–1922, sub-committee minutes (2) 1825–85, lists of partners 1828–72, instructions to agents and accountants 1842–73, agm minutes (3) 1843–1908, salary books (3) 1878–1908

Records' 1 Location: Clydesdale Bank Ltd, 30 St Vincent Pl, Glasgow G1 2HL

Records 2: extracts from sederunt books of sub-committee 1825–35 and directors' court 1825–1908, balance sheets 1860–1908, annual reports 1876–1908

Records' 2 Location: Scottish Bank Collection, The Archives, University of Glasgow G12 8QQ

577   TUBB & CO

Location: Bicester, Oxon

History: est 1793 as G & H Tubb; known as above 1885; absorbed by Barclays Bank Ltd 1920; otherwise known as Bicester & Oxfordshire Bank

Records: note registers f1847, private ledgers f1860, customer address book 1878

Records' Location: Barclays Bank Ltd

578   TUFNELL, FALKNER & FALKNER

Location: Bath, Avon

History: est c1775; amlg with Stuckey's Banking Co 1841

Records 1: papers re bad debts 1822–36, private ledger 1825–34, cash books (2) 1826–44, balance sheets 1826–43, statistics re note circulation & drafts 1834–41, papers re note circulation 1841, lists of drafts, notes & debts outstanding 1842, amlg papers 1838–41

Records' 1 Location: National Westminster Bank Ltd

Records 2: partnership agreements 1812–25

Records' 2 Location: Somerset Record Office, Obridge Rd, Taunton TA2 7PU
Ref: DD/WM 435, 438–441

579 TURNER & MORRIS

Location: Gloucester, Gloucs

History: est c1793; failed 1825

Records: resolutions of creditors 1827

Records' Location: Gloucestershire Collection, Public Library, Brunswick Rd, Gloucester, GL1 1HT

Ref: 4610 NR 15.2

580 RICHARD TWINING & CO

Location: London; Strand

History: est 1824; amlg with Lloyds Bank Ltd 1892

Records: customer ledger 1834–38, standing order book 1850s, loan books (3) 1851–92, security registers (6) 1851–92, safe custody registers (2) f1857, ledgers of account with Bank of England 1871–92, signature book 1876–88, cash book 1884–87, amlg papers 1892

Records' Location: Lloyds Bank Ltd

581 UNION BANK OF BIRMINGHAM

Location: Birmingham, W Midlands

History: est 1878; acquired by Midland Bank Ltd 1883

Records: share ledger A-H 1878–79, letter book 1878–83, staff salary list 1878–83, board minutes 1880–81, report & balance sheet 1882, declarations of secrecy 1883, amlg papers 1883, share transfer register 1883–84

Records' Location: Midland Bank Ltd

582 UNION BANK OF MANCHESTER LTD

Location: Manchester, Gt Manchester

History: est 1836; absorbed by Barclays Bank Ltd 1940

Records: deed of settlement 1836, board minute books (20) 1836–1935, private minutes 1836–41, agreement with Glyn's Bank 1836, shareholders' journal 1836–56, applications for clerkships 1836–41, dividend register 1837–59, agm minutes 1837–1907, bad and doubtful debt ledgers (2) 1830s, papers re purchase of premises 1846, memoranda book re bad debts 1840s, register of bill drawers 1850s, annual reports 1864–1939 inc, regulations 1897, circulars 1897–1904, premises ledgers (4) 1908–33,

consultative committee minute books (2) 1908–14, directors' committee minutes 1914–21, profit and loss accounts and balance sheets 1913–39, signature book 1917–25, registers of shareholders (5) 1918–19, papers re affiliation with Barclays Bank 1919, amlg papers (2 boxes) 1939

Accrington: balance sheet & memoranda book f1884, probate register 1897–1916

Records' Location: Barclays Bank Ltd

583 UNION BANK OF SCOTLAND

Location: Glasgow, Strathclyde

History: est 1830 as Glasgow Union Banking Co; known as above 1843; share capital acquired by Bank of Scotland 1952 & complete fusion achieved 1955

Records 1: board minutes (13) 1830–31 1879–1943, stock transfer registers (3) 1830–50, list of partners 1830, stock ledgers (9) 1830–90, private ledgers (6) 1830–1910, abstracts general ledgers (6) 1830–31 1923–55, deposit account ledgers (3) 1830–32, private journals (7) 1830–1946, bills discounted books (3) 1831–35 1896–1909, check ledger 1832–33, bonds for credit accounts 1835–66, partnership ledger 1836–43, cash book 1836–38, abstract quarterly balances (3) 1838–64, head office deposit book 1836–39, protested bills book 1847–69, claims books (9) 1847–1951, stock register indexes (3) 1850 1862–71, record of transfers registered 1850–62, secretary's private letter books (8) 1852–1905, printed discount & interest rates (3) 1854–1919, properties account books (3) 1854–1904, abstract annual balances 1857–65, head office circular books (14) 1860–1948, protested bills ledger 1861–1909, general quarterly balances (8) 1862–65 1913–54, records of documents under seal (6) 1863–1901, abstract profit & loss accounts Edinburgh & London offices (3) 1863–1900, register of directors 1863–1915, estimated losses on bad & doubtful debts books (5) 1864–1955 inc, profit & loss accounts 1865–1912, general circular books (15) 1870–1935, mandates record 1873–1923, heritable properties books (branches) (5) 1875–1943, press cutting books (4) 1875–1902, large loans minute books (5) 1879–90 1898–1947, accountant's minute book 1879–96, investments journal 1879–90, reports on

Scottish banks 1884–93, salary notes (1 envelope) 1884–1910, deposit money interest on loans & profit & loss accounts 1884–86, cashier's notebooks 1890–1921, banking investment sinking fund book 1889–1926, board business letter books (16) 1892–1914, agency ledger balance books (3) 1899–1928, Institute of Bankers in Scotland letterbook 1902–31, circulars Scottish banks 1904–21, private letter books (28) 1905–57, bills recall letterbooks 1914–27, abstract weekly balance books (12) 1914–55, advertisement cost book 1919–48

Branch records covering the twentieth century are extremely extensive. The list below describes nineteenth century records. A full list of twentieth century records is available in the Scottish Record Office (list 1110).

Anderston: progressive ledger 1855–56, opinion books (2) 1880–1909, letter books (65) f1882, half yearly balance books (12) 1883–1959, securities ledgers (2) 1893–1944, bill book 1889–98, securities registers (3) 1896–1902, bill register 1897–1902

Ardrossan: letter books (18) 1864–1953, half yearly account book 1891–1920

Ayr, High St: current account ledgers (2) 1876–78

Barrhill: bill book 1878–1952

Beith: progressive ledger 1847–54

Bridgeton Cross: branch ledger 1844, current account ledger 1860–61

Broxburn: clean cash book 1866–67, general ledger 1872

Buchlyvie: past due bills register 1880–1916, discount ledger 1894–1921, reserve book 1895–99

Clydebank: current account ledger 1897–1901

Coatbridge: general ledger 1851–53, teller's cash book 1851–54

Cowcaddens: general ledger 1856–60

Dumfries, Irish St: opinion books (2) 1891–1924, half yearly balance books (13) 1898–1954, current account ledger 1899–1910

Eglinton St: teller's cash book 1898–1900, current account ledger 1899–1901

Fairlie: deposit receipt ledger 1880–1954

Gatehouse: deposit receipt ledger 1858–1954, past due bills book 1865–1915

Girvan: letter books (2) 1830–34, current account ledger 1875–85

Glasgow, Hope St: current account ledger 1897–99, teller's cash book 1897–98

Grangemouth: letter books (5) 1893–1950

Hamilton: past due bills book 1863–85, half yearly balance books (8) 1885–1943

Hutchestown: past due bills register 1865–1919, deposit account book 1875–79, bills dishonoured register 1879–1945

Innerleithen: deposit account ledger 1856–62, teller's cash book 1858

Irvine: letter book 1821–22, deposit account ledger 1855–59

Kelvinbridge: weekly statement of bills book 1878–91, securities lodged registers (2) 1884–1905

Kilmarnock: general ledger 1843–48, bill book 1846–50, deposit receipt register 1849–79, securities lodged register 1876–1936

Kirkcaldy: current account ledger 1831–40, general ledger 1843, index to ledger c1846

Largs: teller's cash book 1878–79, current account ledger 1878–81, deposit receipt register 1879–86

Maryhill: deposit account ledger 1855–60

Millport: savings bank ledger 1879

Moffat: bond book 1860–86, bills sent for acceptance 1865–1915, past due bills book 1872–99

Montrose: deposit account ledger 1856–61

Neilston: progressive ledger 1836–45, teller's cash book 1836–39, deposit account ledger 1856–58

Partick: current account ledger 1873–78

Peebles: deposit account ledger 1855–62, teller's cash book 1855–57

Perth: protested bill book 1834–42, record of credit accounts 1885–1907, opinion book 1890–1953

Pitlochry: general ledger 1853–59

Pollock St: teller's cash book 1853–57

Pollockshields: current account ledgers (9) 1891–99

Port Glasgow: deposit account ledger 1853–56, bill registers (2) 1887–1935, protest register 1895–1916, letter book 1890–98

St Briax: current account ledgers (2) 1873–94

Selkirk: deposit account ledger 1853–60

Shettleston: letter books (2) 1898–99

Springburn: current account ledger 1895–1900, teller's cash book 1895–97

Stobcross: current account ledger 1853–55

Stockwell: general branch ledger 1845–46

Stranraer: general ledger 1837–41

Strathaven: current account ledger 1831–44

Thornhill: bills discounted book 1836–37
Tollcross: current account ledger 1898–1902
Tradeston: deposit account ledger 1858–61,
teller's cash book 1872–73
Trongate: letter books (28) 1862–1953,
security receipt book 1878–1908
Troon: interest receipt book 1843–54, bill
book 1843–54, general ledger 1848–53, letter
book 1881–82, monthly statements &
reports 1887–91
Records' 1 Enquiries: National Register of
Archives (Scotland), PO Box 36, HM
General Register House, Edinburgh EH1
3YY
Ref: list 1110
Records 2: cash balance books 1830–32, local
& Edinburgh committee minutes books
1836–1942, private letter book 1838–59,
'memoranda, notes, instructions' 1839–94,
'annual balances, profit & loss accounts,
etc' 1854–1955, architectural drawings
1857–1912, securities held for safekeeping
register 1884–1955, large notes register
1887–1953, large notes destroyed register
1888–1954, journals of securities held
against advances (2) 1898–1960
Records' 2 Enquiries: National Register of
Archives (Scotland), PO Box 36, HM
General Register House, Edinburgh EH1
3YY
Ref: list 945
Records 3 extracts from court minutes 1830–
1919, papers re routine transactions 1832–
43, papers of general manager 1836–92,
balance sheets & profit & loss accounts
1867–78 1896–1907, letters to general
manager 1853 1876–77 1910–11
Records' 3 Location: Scottish Banking
Collection, University of Glasgow Archives,
The University, Glasgow G12 8QQ

584 UNION OF LONDON & SMITHS BANK LTD
Location: London
History: est 1839 as Union Bank of London;
amlg with Smith, Payne & Smiths
(London), Smith, Ellison & Co (Lincoln),
Samuel Smith Bros & Co (Hull), & Samuel
Smith & Co (Derby) to form Union of
London & Smiths Bank Ltd 1902; amlg
with the National Provincial Bank of
England to form National Provincial &
Union Bank of England Ltd 1918

Records: prospectus 1839, deed of settlement
1839, board minute books (c59) 1839–1920,
annual reports 1839–1918, profit & loss
books (6) 1839–1920, general ledger 1840–
42, investment ledgers (2) 1853–1918, list of
proprietors 1858, monthly statements of
accounts 1891–1918, amlg papers 1902–05,
directors' attendance book 1903–19, profit
& loss & average balances register 1904–52,
information book 1908–18, list of unclaimed
balances 1910, amlg papers 1918–19
Bristol: law book 1892–1905, loans book
1911–24
Derby: manager's diaries 1902–09
London, Chancery Lane: list of promissory
notes 1870
London, Prince's St: manager's information
books (2) 1873–1925
London, Regent St: half yearly profit & loss
statements 1841–1929
Records' Location: National Westminster
Bank Ltd

585 UNITED COUNTIES BANK LTD
Location: Birmingham, W Midlands
History: est 1836 as Birmingham, Town &
District Banking Co; amlg with Dudley &
West Bromwich Banking Co to form
Birmingham, Dudley & District Banking
Co 1874; amlg with the Wolverhampton &
Staffordshire Banking Co 1889 to form
Birmingham, District & Counties Banking
Co Ltd; amlg with Bradford Old Bank to
form United Counties Bank Ltd 1907; amlg
with Barclay & Co Ltd 1916

Records 1: deeds of settlement (4) 1836–84,
board minute books (c11) 1836–1916,
annual reports 1836–1916, private ledgers
(5) 1836–1915 inc, agm minutes f1837, lists
of shareholders (5) 1866–1915, papers re
projected takeover 1879, statistics of credits
and overdrafts 1864–65, statements of losses
1866–68, details of profits 1868–1904,
investment register 1874–1900, rules and
regulations for staff 1875, salary books (2)
1870–89, quarterly statements books (5)
1875–1915, analysis of branch profits and
losses 1877–78 1902–25, premises register
1880s, staff register 1879–81, shareholders'
register 1881–1907, papers re incorporation
1881, managers of branches minute book
1881, staff lists 1882–85, superannuation
fund rules 1884, general managers' letter
books (c6) c1883–1923, papers re bad debts

1886, half yearly balance sheets & profit & loss accounts 1894–1915, instructions to cashiers 1888–1916, salary board sanctions 1890–94, papers re brokers' loans 1901–16, premises ledger 1901–12, weekly balances customer accounts (17) 1904, stock exchange commission allowed branches 1905–10, analysis of profit & loss accounts 1913–15, term book 1909
Birmingham, Colmore Row: probate register 1874–75
Cradley Heath: probate register 1877–1923
Dudley, High St: probate register 1883–1920s, general authorities f1905
Tipton: probate register 1877–1929, security registers (2) f1899, note register f1906, letters to customers 1908–38
Records' 1 Location: Barclay Bank Ltd
Records 2: deed of settlement 1836, annual reports 1862–66
Records' 2 Location: Birmingham Reference Library, Birmingham B3 3HQ

586   VEASEY, DESBOROUGH & CO
Location: Huntingdon, Cambs
History: est 1804 as Rust, Sweeting & Veasey; known as Veaseys, Desborough & Veasey 1853; known as above 1855; incorporated with Barclay & Co Ltd 1896
Records: private ledger f1808, partnership agreements 1853–76, papers re partnership matters 1859–95, amlg papers 1896
Records' Location: Barclays Bank Ltd

587   VINCENT, BAILEY & VINCENT
Location: Newbury, Berks
History: est 1782; failed 1816; known also as Newbury Old Bank
Records: partnership agreements & re papers 1788–1815, memoranda books (2) 1788–1808, goldsmith book 1788–92, money books (7 boxes) 1788–1806, daily cash balance books (5) 1788–1806, out letter books (8) 1789–1809, customer ledgers (2) 1800–02, note registers (4) 1794–1812, day books (3) 1800–02
Records' Location: Public Record Office, Ruskin Ave, Kew, Richmond, Surrey
Ref: C171.20–47; J90.321

588   VIVIAN, KITSON & CO
Location: Torquay, Devon
History: est 1832; taken over by Lloyds Bank Ltd 1900
Records: declaration of confidence 1841, amlg papers 1899
Records' Location: Lloyds Bank Ltd

589   VIZARD & CO
Location: Dursley, Gloucs
History: est 1803; amlg with County of Gloucester Bank 1836
Records: amlg agreement 1836
Records' Location: Lloyds Bank Ltd

590   VYE & HARRIS
Location: Ilfracombe, Devon
History: est 1807; amlg with National Provincial Bank 1836
Records: amlg papers 1836
Records' Location: National Westminster Bank Ltd

591   VYNER
Location: London
History: goldsmith bankers
Records: papers re financial & banking transactions 1655–1705
Records' Location: Leeds Archives Dept, Chapeltown Rd, Sheepscar, Leeds LS7 3AP
Ref: Newby Hall MSS

592   WAKEFIELD & BARNSLEY UNION BANK
Location: Wakefield, W Yorks
History: est 1832 as Wakefield Banking Co; known as above 1840; amlg with Birmingham District & Counties Banking Co Ltd 1906
Records: board minutes 1832–1906, articles of association 1897, list of shareholders 1906, amlg papers 1906
Barnsley: half yearly statements 1903–06
Horbury: manager's minute book 1898–1906
Records' Location: Barclays Bank Ltd

593 WAKEFIELD, CREWDSON & CO
Location: Kendal, Cumbria
History: est 1788 as Maude, Wilson & Crewdsons Bank; amlg with Bank of Liverpool 1893; known also as Kendal Bank
Records 1: private ledger of W D Crewdson 1820–68, diaries of W D Crewdson 1823–29 inc, partnership ledgers 1826–92, security books (2) 1840–92, customer address book 1847, day books (3) 1867–79, cash books with details of account with London agent (2) 1869–81, balances of certain customer accounts 1867–83, staff book 1870–81, letter book of W D Crewdson 1880–95, overdraft memoranda book 1875–83, branch balance sheets 1883–95, agreement with Bank of Liverpool 1885, minute book 1885–97, partnership agreements 1890–93, amlg papers 1893–95
Ambleside: deeds book 1864–81, overdraft memoranda books (2) 1871–81
Barrow: security notebook 1859–75, overdraft memoranda books 1873–81, security book 1873–81, notes on customers 1875–80
Kirkby Stephen: overdraft notebook 1869–71
Milnthorpe: guarantees notebook 1851–70
Ulverston: security books 1864–81, overdraft notebooks (3) 1869–77, customer accounts balance books 1873–82, deeds book 1874–75, details of guarantees 1881–82
Records' 1 Location: Barclays Bank Ltd
Records 2: letter & bill books of J Maude (2) 1761–1803, cash book of J Maude 1777–88, letter book of J Maude 1794–1801, Crewdson family papers 18–19 cents, account book re loans to S Parrat 1826–27
Records' 2 Location: Cumbria Record Office, County Offices, Kendal LA9 4RQ
Ref: WD/K; WD/Cr; WDX/314

594 WARWICK & LEAMINGTON BANKING CO
Location: Warwick, Warws
History: est 1834; absorbed by Lloyds Banking Co 1866
Records: deed of settlement 1834, lists of shareholders 1834 1866, amlg agreement 1866
Records' Location: Lloyds Bank Ltd

595 WATKINS & CO
Location: Daventry, Northants
History: est 1783; formed into Northamptonshire Bank 1836
Records: partner's will 1810, agreement with clerk 1810, misc papers inc banknotes, receipts, letters etc (65 items) 1794–1835
Records' Location: Northamptonshire Record Office, Delapre Abbey, Northampton NN4 9AW
Ref: Acc 1967/174 Watkins & Daventry papers

596 WATTS & CO
Location: Teignmouth, Devon
History: est 1840; taken over by Capital & Counties Bank Ltd 1891
Records: amlg papers 1891
Records' Location: Lloyds Bank Ltd

597 WEBB & CO
Location: Ledbury, Hereford & Worcester
History: est 1815; taken over by Gloucestershire Banking Co Ltd 1883
Records: amlg papers 1883
Records' Location: Lloyds Bank Ltd

598 WELLS, HOGGE & LINDSELL
Location: Baldock, Herts
History: est 1830; amlg with Capital & Counties Bank Ltd 1893
Records: letter book 1849–98, general ledger 1862–1908, overdraft book 1877–1907, journal 1895–1908
Records' Location: Lloyds Bank Ltd

599 WENTWORTH, CHALONER & RISHWORTH
Location: London & Yorkshire
History: est 1812 in Yorkshire and 1813 in London; failed 1825
Records 1: papers re failure 1826
Records' 1 Location: Nottinghamshire Record Office, County House, High Pavement, Nottingham NG1 1HR
Ref: M 11781–3
Records 2: statement of failure 1825
Records' 2 Location: Lloyds Bank Ltd

600   WEST OF ENGLAND & SOUTH WALES BANK

Location: Bristol, Avon

History: est 1834; failed 1878

Records 1: board minute books (2) 1834–42, teller's cash book 1835, deed of settlement 1837, committee minute book 1837–38, security registers 1870s

Records' 1 Location: Lloyds Bank Ltd

Records 2: papers re failure (6 folders) 1878–80

Records' 2 Location: Bristol Record Office, Council House, College Green, Bristol BS1 5TR

Ref: Veale, Benson & Co collection

601   WEST RIDING UNION BANKING CO

Location: Huddersfield, W Yorks

History: est as Mirfield & Huddersfield District Banking Co 1832; known as above 1836; amlg with Lancashire & Yorkshire Bank Ltd 1902

Records: deeds of settlement 1832–83, board minute books (8) 1833–1902, applications for staff appointments 1832, agreements with clerks 1833–34, balance books with branch accounts 1833–77, private ledgers 1840–1902, annual reports 1863–1902, monthly record of general & customer accounts 1864–1902, salary book 1866–1939, securities for loans 1880–97, general manager's agenda books (5) 1890–1914, amlg papers 1902
Batley: deed book 1861–85, profit and loss ledger 1863–98, inquiry book 1877–86, security book 1883–1913

Records' Location: Barclays Bank Ltd

602   WEST YORKSHIRE BANK LTD

Location: Halifax, W Yorks

History: et 1829 as Halifax Joint Stock Banking Co; known as above 1911; amlg with Lloyds Bank Ltd 1919

Records: deed of settlement with supplements 1829–89, chairman's minute books (11) 1887–1921, agm minutes 1887–1919, directors' minute books (3) 1888–1920, board agenda (2) 1900–15, board minutes 1915–22, amlg papers (4) 1919
Huddersfield: private memoranda book f1884

Halifax: customer registers & ledgers fc1900

Records' Location: Lloyds Bank Ltd

603   WESTERN BANK OF SCOTLAND

Location: Glasgow, Strathclyde

History: est 1832; failed 1857

Records 1: deeds of co-partnery (3) 1832–57, plans & elevations of premises 1845–58, papers re failure 1858–63

Records' 1 Location: Glasgow University Archives, The University, Glasgow G12 8QQ

Ref: UGD 84.1–4

Records 2: letters, accounts, press cuttings 1850–60

Records' 2 Location: National Library of Scotland, George IV Bridge, Edinburgh EH1 1EW

Records 3: returns 1832–34, misc papers 1842–57 1865–69, list of partners 1858

Records' 3 Enquiries: National Register of Archives (Scotland), PO Box 36, HM General Register House, Edinburgh EH1 3YY

Ref: list 349

Records 4: instructions to agents & accountants 1848–56

Records' 4 Location: Clydesdale Bank Ltd, Head Office, 30 St Vincent Place, Glasgow G1 2HL

Records 5: pass book 1830–56, correspondence & papers re failure 1851–70

Records' 5 Enquiries: As Records 3

Ref: list 2408

Records 6: miscellaneous papers 1842–57

Records' 6 Enquiries: As Records 3

Ref: list 349

Records 7: records of bills received, negotiations 1857–58

Records' 7 Enquiries: As Records 3

Ref: list 945

Records 8: co-partnership contract 1832

Records' 8 Enquiries: As Records 3

Ref: list 452

Records 9: correspondence with Dundee Banking Co 1847

Records' 9 Enquiries: As Records 3

Ref: list 1964

604 WESTERN COUNTIES BANK LTD

Location: Liskeard, Cornwall

History: est 1885; taken over by Capital & Counties Bank Ltd 1890

Records: papers re takeover 1890

Records' Location: Lloyds Bank Ltd

605 WESTMINSTER BANK LTD

Location: London

History: formed by amlg of London & County Banking Co Ltd with London & Westminster Bank Ltd to form London, County & Westminster Bank Ltd 1909; amlg with Parr's Bank Ltd to form London, County, Westminster & Parr's Bank Ltd 1918; name changed to Westminster Bank Ltd 1923; formed National Westminster Bank Ltd 1968

Records: articles of association f1909, board minutes f1909, register of directors f1909, annual reports f1909, amlg papers 1909–23, head office circulars 1909–29, standing orders of board 1911, salary book 1914–54, staff register 1917–47, statistics re staff 1937, foreign business committee minute books (2) 1918–39, foreign discount committee minutes 1918
Aylesbury: minute books (3) 1900–31, information book 1878–1932
Bakewell: profit & loss statements 1918–33
Brentford: information books (2) 1885–1936
Brighton: minute book 1909–26
Buxted: papers re purchase of premises 1921–22
Cambridge: profit & loss statements (2) 1910–31
Chesham: profit & loss statements 1923–35
Chester: salary book 1914–54, profit & loss statements 1918–37
Dorking: half yearly returns 1909–18
London, Bloomsbury: minute books (2) 1910–20
London, Chancery Lane: minute books (8) 1911–29
London, Finsbury Park: half yearly returns 1920
London, Hammersmith: profit & loss statements (2) 1910–36
London, Harley St: profit & loss statements 1910–27
London, Lombard St: minutes 1910
London, Marylebone: minute books (5) 1910–22
London, Regent St: profit and loss statements 1910–27
London, Southwark: bad & doubtful debt returns 1910
Milborne Port: letter book with head office 1910–29
Peterborough: press cutting book re new premises 1933
Salisbury: half yearly returns 1922–59
Sherborne: letter book with head office 1916–31
Teddington: minute book 1922–26, returns book 1923–28, letter book 1925–27
Uckfield: papers re fall in business 1923–30, papers re redecoration of premises 1925–30
Weston-super-Mare: profit & loss statements 1918–30

Records' Location: National Westminster Bank Ltd

606 WESTMINSTER FOREIGN BANK LTD

Location: London

History: overseas bank; est 1913 as London, County & Westminster Bank (Paris) Ltd; known as London, County, Westminster & Parr's Foreign Bank Ltd 1920; known as Westminster Foreign Bank Ltd 1923

Records: articles of association 1913 1923, board minutes f1913, annual reports f1913, foreign business committee minutes (20) f1913, staff committee minutes (4) 1914–39, papers re share capital 1919–20, sanction books (2) 1936–40, 'war books' (2) 1939–45

Records' Location: National Westminster Bank Ltd

607 THOMAS WHEELER & CO

Location: High Wycombe, Bucks

History: est 1812; amlg with Capital & Counties Bank Ltd 1896

Records: amlg papers 1896

Records' Location: Lloyds Bank Ltd

608   WHITCHURCH & ELLESMERE BANKING CO

Location: Whitchurch, Salop

History: est 1840; acquired by Lloyds Bank Ltd 1881

Records: amlg papers 1881

Records' Location: Lloyds Bank Ltd

609   WHITEHAVEN JOINT STOCK BANKING CO LTD

Location: Whitehaven, Cumbria

History: est 1829; amlg with Parr's Bank Ltd 1908

Records: deeds of settlement 1829–73, papers re transfer of shares 1837–88, statement of money lent & securities 1842, correspondence with customers 1834–1901, annual reports 1846–76 inc, papers re bank's investments (3 dossiers) 1847–1907, balance sheets 1848–60 inc, statement of correspondents' accounts 1848–49, rough board minutes 1857–63, weekly statements of London remittances 1858–59, letters re recruitment of staff 1862–83, general manager's correspondence with his family 1869–83, regulations & provisions 1888, amlg papers 1908

Records' Location: National Westminster Bank Ltd

610   WIGAN, MERCER, TASKER & CO

Location: Maidstone, Kent

History: est 1818; amlg with Union of London & Smiths Bank Ltd 1903

Records: premises rental agreement 1818, partnership agreement 1821, declaration of confidence 1826, amlg papers 1903–05

Records' Location: National Westminster Bank Ltd

611   WILKINS & CO

Location: Brecon, Powys

History: est 1778; taken over by Lloyds Bank 1890

Records: fidelity bond 1889, amlg papers 1889–90

Carmarthen: security register 1834–67

Records' Location: Lloyds Bank Ltd

612   P & H WILLIAMS

Location: Wednesbury, Staffs

History: est 1851; taken over by Lloyds Bank 1865

Records: amlg papers 1865

Records' Location: Lloyds Bank Ltd

613   WILLIAMS & CO LTD

Location: Chester, Cheshire

History: est 1792; taken over by Lloyds Bank 1897

Records 1: cash book re new premises 1796–98, balance sheets 1821–30, profit & loss accounts 1823–25, staff book c1850–95, private memoranda books (8) 1881–1922, amlg papers 1897
Bangor: private memoranda book 1874
Caernarvon: day book 1792–96

Records' 1 Location: Lloyds Bank Ltd

Records 2: papers re partnership 1817–90, half yearly balance book 1877–97, profit & loss account book 1885–96, papers & accounts re rebuilding of premises 1892–97, amlg papers 1895–97, papers re accounts of certain clients late 19 cent

Records' 2 Location: City of Chester Record Office, Town Hall, Chester CH1 2HJ
Ref: CR 4

614   WILLIAMS DEACON'S BANK LTD

Location: London & Manchester

History: est 1770 as Williams, Son, Moffat, Burgess & Lane; known as Williams, Burgess & Williams 1822; as Williams, Deacon, Labouchere & Co 1827; as Williams Deacon, Labouchere, Thornton & Co 1841; as Williams, Deacon, Thornton & Co 1876; as Williams, Deacon & Manchester & Salford Bank Ltd following amlg with Manchester & Salford Bank Ltd 1890; as Williams Deacon's Bank Ltd 1901; merged with Glyn, Mills & Co & the National Bank Ltd to form Williams & Glyn's Bank Ltd 1970

Records 1: private ledgers (2) 1801–23 1878–88, credit information book 1825–40, 'private letter books' (19) 1828–1900, staff salary papers (2 boxes) 1845–1920, private papers of W S Deacon c1857–1900, sundry debtors journal 1873–94, head office

circulars 1888–1970, interview book 1889–1901, profit & loss accounts (2) 1890–1916, information books (3) 1890–1922, board minutes f1890, proceedings of agms f1890, annual reports f1890, 'general correspondence' (extensive) 1900–62, branch progress reports 1899–1929, manager's customer record books (2) 1894–1920, balance sheet working papers f1900, salary ledger & record book 1900–25, staff indemnity bonds (2 boxes) 19 cent, papers of general managers, joint general managers & assistant general managers (extensive) 19 cent, articles of association f1901, 'London letter books' 1902–40, 'general manager's sundry out letters' 1902–04, 'general London letters' 1902–05, 'general manager's dept private letter books (55) 1908–68, reserves ledgers (8) 1917–33, staff bonus papers 1919–25, 'West End Office Correspondence'1925–46, 'London Office Correspondence' 1925–50, London Office rebuilding papers 1932–35, London directors' minutes f1933
Manchester, Heywood's Branch: profit & loss accounts 1890–1913
Rochdale: information book 1890–1913, private letter book 1914–34
Sheffield: manager's record books of customer accounts (3) 1907–23
Records' 1 Location: Williams & Glyn's Bank Ltd
Records 2: private papers of partner (R Lowe) c1771–85
Records' 2 Location: University of Nottingham Library, University Park, Nottingham N97 2RD
Ref: Drury Lowe Collection

615   WILLIAMS & ROWLAND

Location: Neath, W Glamorgan
History: est 1821; combined with Eaton & Co to form Glamorganshire Banking Co 1836
Records: customer ledger 1821–29
Records' Location: Lloyds Bank Ltd

616   WILLIAMS & SONS

Location: Dolgellau & Barmouth, Gwynedd
History: est c1803; acquired by North & South Wales Bank 1873

Records: list of partners 1873, agreement & correspondence re sale of business 1873
Records' Location: Midland Bank Ltd

617   R & R WILLIAMS, THORNTON, SYKES & CO

Location: Dorchester, Dorset
History: est 1786 as William Cox & Co; known as above 1878; amlg with Wilts & Dorset Banking Co 1897
Records 1: private ledgers (2) 1876–97, balance sheets 1839–97, amlg paper 1897
Records' 1 Location: Lloyds Bank Ltd
Records 2: agreement to rent banking room 1832–39
Records' 2 Location: Dorset Record Office, County Hall, Dorchester DT1 1XJ
Ref: D141/B1–2

618   WILLIAMS, WILLIAMS, BROWN & CO

Location: Leeds, W Yorks
History: est 1813; amlg with Lloyds Bank Ltd 1900
Records: profit & loss ledger 1844–57
Records' Location: Lloyds Bank Ltd

619   WILLIS, PERCIVAL & CO

Location: London
History: est 1670 as Willis & Reade; known as Reade, Moorhouse & Co 1774; as Moorhouse, Willis & Reade 1778; as Willis, Wood & Co 1787; as Willis, Wood, Percival & Co 1792; as above 1814; failed & business acquired by Capital & Counties Bank Ltd 1878
Records: partnership agreement 1812, correspondence with customers 1825–68, fidelity bonds 19 cent
Records' Location: Lloyds Bank Ltd

620   WILLYAMS, WILLYAMS & CO

Location: Truro, Cornwall
History: est 1771; amlg with Bolitho, Williams, Foster, Coode, Grylls & Co 1890; otherwise known as The Miners' Bank
Records: partnership agreements (3) 1771–78, minute book 1794–1806, correspondence re partnership matters 1808 1827, accounts 1806–08

Records' Location: Cornwall County Record Office, County Hall, Truro TR1 3AY
Ref: DDBU 431; DDW 78; DDW 79/1–2; ADD 59(3)/2

621   WILTS & DORSET BANKING CO LTD

Location: Salisbury, Wilts

History: est 1835; amlg with Lloyds Bank Ltd 1914

Records: provisional committee minute book 1835, deed of settlement & supplements 1835–64, shareholders' register 1835–53, note registers (8) 1835–1914, annual reports 1837–1914, balance sheets 1841–72 inc, seal registers 1874–1914, memoranda re branches 1874–92, amlg papers including letter books (7) 1914
Bath: profit & loss account book 1892–1914
Blandford: probate register 1865–1914, security registers 1887–1914
Bridgwater: probate registers f1875, security registers (3) 1888–1912
Exeter: security registers (2) 1873–1906
Frome: security registers f1836, signature books 1860–1900
Gillingham: security register 1860s
Lyme Regis: probate registers f1897, security registers f1897
Malmesbury: security books c1830s-1910
Marlborough: safe custody registers f1840s, security registers 1880s
Mere: security registers 1838–83
Poole: salary records 1885–1914
Ringwood: security registers f1861, probate registers f1866
Sherborne: salary book 1885–1914, security registers f1890
Southampton: security register 1869–90, salary book 1885–1914
Swindon: manager's diaries (4) 1882–85
Warminster: salary book 1885–1935
Wimborne: general correspondence (41 files) 1879–90

Records' Location: Lloyds Bank Ltd

622   WISE, FARNWELL & BENTALL and WISE, FARNWELL, BAKER & BENTALL

Location: Totnes & Newton Abbot, Devon

History: Wise, Farnwell & Bentall est 1792 & failed 1841; Wise, Farnwell, Baker & Bentall est 1815 & failed 1841

Records: partnership agreement 1792, half yearly balances (Newton Abbot) 1834–41, papers re failure 1841

Records' Location: Devon Record Office, Castle St, Exeter EX4 3PQ
Ref: 872 A/PZ 154; 924 B/E2/18; 924/B4/1

623   WOLVERHAMPTON & STAFFORDSHIRE BANKING CO

Location: Wolverhampton, W Midlands

History: est 1831; amlg with Birmingham, Dudley & District Banking Co to form Birmingham, District & Counties Banking Co 1889

Records 1: deed of settlement 1842, customer ledgers 1832–35, deposit ledger 1832–47, cash book 1831–34, provisions for government 1860, annual reports 1887–88, amlg papers 1889

Records' 1 Location: Barclays Bank Ltd

Records 2: papers re proposed amlg with Lloyds Bank Ltd 1866

Records' 2 Location: Lloyds Bank Ltd

624   WOOD, PITT & CO

Location: Tetbury, Gloucs

History: est c1800; formed into County of Gloucester Banking Co 1836

Records: correspondence re Dursley Agency 1817–25

Records' Location: Gloucestershire Collection, Public Library, Brunswick Road, Gloucester GL1 1HT
Ref: 8439 RF 115.103

625   WOOD, WOOD & CO

Location: Cardiff, S Glamorgan

History: est 1804; failed 1823

Records: legal & other papers re John Wood (8 bdls) c1785–1845

Records' Location: Glamorgan Archive Service, County Hall, Cathcays Park, Cardiff CF1 3NE
Ref: MS3.639,644; MSS.135

626   WOODALL, HEBDEN & CO

Location: Scarborough, N Yorks

History: est in 1788; known as Woodall, Tindall & Co 1792; as Woodall, Hebden &

Co 1863; incorporated with Barclay & Co Ltd 1896

Records: general ledger 1788–91, customer ledgers 1798–1800, note registers 1853–1916, safe register 1860–90, amlg papers 1896

Records' Location: Barclays Bank Ltd

627 WOODBRIDGE, LACY, HARTLAND, HIBBERT & CO

Location: Uxbridge, Middlesex

History: est 1791; amlg with Barclays & Co Ltd 1900

Records 1: partnership agreement 1881

Records' 1 Location: Barclays Bank Ltd

Records 2: papers re amlg 1900–01

Records' 2 Location: Greater London Record Office, 40 Northampton Rd, London EC1 0HB

Ref: Acc 538/2nd dep/1058

628 THOMAS WOODCOCK, SONS & ECKERSLEY

Location: Wigan, Greater Manchester

History: est as Thicknesse & Woodcocks 1792; known as above 1833; amlg with Parr's Bank Ltd 1874

Records: customer ledger 1792, correspondence with London agents 1800–03, amlg agreement 1874

Records' Location: National Westminster Bank Ltd

629 WOODHEAD & CO

Location: London

History: est 1809; taken over by Holt & Co 1915

Records: procedure manual 1801, loan book 1811–37, 'prize' ship ledger 1842–67, circulars 'Admiralty' 1870–1904, signature book 1886–1910

Records' Location: Williams & Glyn's Bank Ltd

630 WOODS & CO

Location: Newcastle upon Tyne, Tyne & Wear

History: est 1853; amlg with Barclay & Co Ltd 1897

Records: 'monthly statements' 1860–70, private ledgers (3) 1860–1903, licence to

issue notes at Sunderland 1861, signature books (2) 1863–1907, architect's drawings 1874, rules for managers & clerks 1890s, private journal 1897–1903, amlg papers 1897

Seaham: Seaham Harbour Infirmary account ledger 1843–49, security register 1863–1905, arrangement book 1894–1906

Records' Location: Barclays Bank Ltd

631 WORCESTER CITY & COUNTY BANKING CO

Location: Worcester, Hereford & Worcester

History: est 1840; amlg with Lloyds Bank Ltd 1889

Records: staff agreements 1864–74, agm minutes 1866–89, board minutes 1879–89, amlg papers 1889–95

Birmingham, Colmore Row: private memoranda books f1870s, signature books f1870s, standing order books f1870s, safe custody registers f1870, security registers f1870

Bridgnorth: status enquiry book 1868–89

Gloucester: letter book 1886–92

Kidderminster: expenses book 1857–89

Leominster: private memoranda books (4) 1880–89

Records' Location: Lloyds Bank Ltd

632 THOMAS WORSWICK, SONS & CO

Location: Lancaster, Lancs

History: est c1780; failed 1822

Records: papers re failure 1822, valuation of partners' estate 1822

Records' Location: Lancashire Record Office, Bow Lane, Preston PR1 8ND

Ref: DDPa/2,7,8,19

633 J & J C WRIGHT & CO

Location: Nottingham, Notts

History: est 1760; amlg with Capital & Counties Bank Ltd 1898

Records 1: private ledgers 1836–97, agreement for sale of Burton branch 1877, signature books 1880s, weekly balance book 1887–92, amlg papers 1898

Records' 1 Location: Lloyds Bank Ltd

Records 2: private diaries of I Wright c1815–62

Records' 2 Location: Nottinghamshire Record Office, County House, High Pavement, Nottingham N91 1HR
Ref: M5586–8

634   WYLDE & CO
Location: Southwell, Notts
History: est 1806; wound up 1875
Records: partner's will 1853
Records' Location: Nottinghamshire Record Office, County House, High Pavement, Nottingham N91 1HR
Ref: M3691

635   YATES & CO
Location: Liverpool, Merseyside
History: amlg with Union Bank of Manchester Ltd 1904
Records: apprenticeship agreement 1890
Records' Location: Barclays Bank Ltd

636   YORK CITY & COUNTY BANKING CO LTD
Location: York, N Yorks
History: est 1830 as York City & County Bank; renamed York City & County Banking Co Ltd 1893; amlg with London Joint Stock Bank 1909
Records: prospectus 1830, deed of settlement 1830, board minute books (42) 1830–1916, general ledgers (2) 1830–74, security books (branches) (71) 1833–1902, annual reports 1839–1909, branch memoranda book 1841–51, branch reports & balance sheets 1874–1910, reports of agms 1883–1900, shareholders' minutes 1894–1909, comparison of profits 1896–1900, quarterly balances 1898–1908, branch managers' instruction book 1902
Bridlington: general ledgers (2) 1879–81
Howden: memoranda book 1842–70
Ripon: memoranda book 1850–75
Scarborough: general ledger 1861–71
Selby: cash books (2) 1832–83
Records' Location: Midland Bank Ltd

637   YORK UNION BANKING CO LTD
Location: York, N Yorks
History: est 1833; amlg with Barclays & Co Ltd 1902

Records: board minute books (12) 1833–1902, customer ledgers (2) 1833–36, interest paid on deposits 1851–68, chairman's memoranda book 1866–81, balance sheets 1883–1901, register of members & annual list 1886–91
Hull: daily agenda book 1900–05
Driffild & York: note registers 19 cent
Records' Location: Barclays Bank Ltd

638   YORKSHIRE BANK LTD
Location: Leeds, W Yorks
History: est 1911 as Yorkshire Penny Bank Ltd to acquire Yorkshire Penny Savings Bank est in 1859; known as above 1959
Records: prospectus 1856, minutes of provisional committee 1856–59, list of subscribers to guarantee 1858–59, board minutes f1858, annual reports f1859, investment register 1859–68, reports on branches 1863–64, rough minutes 1864–1903 inc, reports of central committee 1870–99, articles of association 1871–97, minutes of trustees and managers (Triangle Penny Bank) 1882–98, reports of school transfer committee 1890–1911, papers re loan repayments of local authorities (3 vols) 1890–1911, chairman's memoranda book 1891–1906, resolutions of branch sub committees 1898–1912, profit & loss accounts 1899–1910, list of branches with details of general accounts 1899–1913, rules for staff 1894, general manager's address to Sheffield branch staff 1900, local board minutes 1911–14, chairman's minutes f1911, reorganisation agreement 1911, register of directors 1911–24, staff committee notes 1921–23, head office circulars f1930
Records' Location: Yorkshire Bank Ltd, 2 Infirmary St, Leeds L51 1QT

639   YORKSHIRE BANKING CO LTD
Location: Leeds, W Yorks
History: est 1834 as Yorkshire District Banking Co; reconstructed as Yorkshire Banking Co 1843; acquired by Midland Bank 1901
Records 1: deeds of settlement 1834 1843, board minute books (20) & indexes (14) 1834–1901, shareholders' minute books 1835–50 1898–1901, prospectus 1843,

committee of investigations notebook 1843,
half yearly reports 1843–1901, profit & loss
accounts (2) 1843–1902, half yearly
balances 1843–88, auditors' reports on
branches (5) 1844–1901, supplemental deed
of settlement 1865, letter books (8) 1878–95,
half yearly statements 1880–86, head office
circulars 1880–98, board meeting agenda
(8) 1891–1901, share registers (2) 1892–
1901, register of directors 1901, amlg papers
1901, liquidators' papers 1901–02
Beverley: general ledgers (4) 1838–52
Doncaster: declarations of secrecy 1835–
1914
Goole: general ledgers 1838–73
Guiseley: letter book 1899–1912
Huddersfield: general ledger 1860–71
Leeds: general ledgers (3) 1866–76
Pontefract: deposit receipt ledgers (3) 1843–
82
Ripon: general ledgers (3) 1843–69
Thirsk: declarations of secrecy 1835–1922,
general ledgers (2) 1861–73
Wetherby: reference book 1870
Records' 1 Location: Midland Bank Ltd
Records 2: deed of settlement & papers re
formation 1834, security registers (2) 1834–
51, legal papers re claims of bank 1833–48,
securities for loans 1844–1901
Records' 2 Location: Leeds Archives Dept,
Chapeltown Rd, Sheepscar, Leeds L57 3AP
Ref: DB 255; DW 911, 916; Brooke, North
& Goodwin MSS

Select Bibliography

General Works

Baster, A S J — *The Imperial Banks*, London, 1929, pp.vii and 275. Reprinted 1977

Baster, A S J — *The International Banks*, London, 1935, pp.vii and 269. Reprinted 1977

Boase, C W — *A Century of Banking in Dundee*, Edinburgh, 1867, pp.xxxi and 379

Butlin, S J — *Australia and New Zealand Bank*, London, 1961, pp.xiv and 459

Butlin, S J — *Foundations of the Australian Monetary System 1788–1851*, Melbourne, 1953. Reprinted Sydney, 1968, pp.xvi and 727

Cameron, R (ed) — *Banking in the Early Stages of Industrialisation*, Oxford, 1967, pp.xiv and 349

Cave, C H — *A History of Banking in Bristol from 1750 to 1899*, Bristol, 1899, pp.xvii and 292

Chapman, S D — 'British Marketing Enterprise. The Changing Roles of Merchants, Manufacturers and Financiers 1700–1860', *Business History Review*, LIII, 1979

Chapman, S D — 'The International Houses. The Continental Contribution to British Commerce 1800–1860', *Journal of European Economic History*, 6, 1977

Checkland, S G — *Scottish Banking. A History 1695–1973*, Collins, 1975, pp.736

Cottrell, P L and Anderson, B L — *Money and Banking in England. The Development of the Banking System 1694–1914*, David & Charles, 1974, pp.351

Davies, A S — *The Early Banks of Mid Wales*, Welshpool, 1935, pp.14

Feaveryear, A E — *The Pound Sterling*, Oxford, 1931. Revised by E V Morgan, Oxford, 1963, pp.xi and 466

Gibson, J C — *The Old Private Banks of Stirling*, Stirling, 1930

Goodhart, C A E — *The Business of Banking 1891–1914*, London, 1972

Gregory, T E (ed) — *Select Statutes. Documents and Reports Relating to British Banking*, 2 vols, Oxford, 1929. Reprinted 1964

Grindon, L H — *Manchester Banks and Bankers*, Simpkin Marshall, 1877, pp.333

Hughes, J — *Liverpool Banks and Bankers*, Liverpool, 1906, pp.xvi and 243

Joslin, D M — 'London Private Bankers 1720–1785', *Economic History Review* 1954. Reprinted in E M Carus-Wilson, *Essays in Economic History*, Vol.II, London, 1962

Kerr, A W — *History of Banking in Scotland*, Glasgow, 1884, pp.vii and 255

King, W T C — *History of the London Discount Market*, London, 1936, pp.xix and 355. Reprinted London, 1972

Munn, C W — *The Scottish Provincial Banking Companies 1747–1864*, John Donald, 1981, pp.xi and 306

Perkins, M — *Dudley Tradesmen's Tokens and History of Dudley Banks, Bankers and Bank Notes,* Dudley, 1905, pp.202

Phillips, M — *Banks, Bankers and Banking in Northumberland, Durham and North Yorkshire,* London, 1894, pp.xxx and 432

Pressnell, L S — *Country Banking in the Industrial Revolution,* Oxford, 1956, pp.xvi and 591

Price, F G H — *A Handbook of London Bankers,* London, 1890–91

Rae, G — *The Country Banker. His Clients, Cares and Work,* John Murray, 1885, pp.viii and 320. Reprinted 1976

Richards, R D — *The Early History of Banking in England,* London, 1929, pp.xx and 319

Roth, H L — *The Genesis of Banking in Halifax,* Halifax, 1914

Sayers, R S — *Central Banking after Bagehot,* Oxford, 1957, pp.149

Somers, R — *The Scotch Banks and the System of Issue,* Edinburgh, 1873

Thomas, S E — *The Rise and Growth of Joint Stock Banking. Britain to 1860,* London, 1934, pp.viii and 689

Wadsworth, J E — *The Banks and the Monetary System in the UK 1959–71,* London, 1973, pp.x and 527

Whittlesey, C R and Wilson, J S G (eds) — *Essays in Money and Banking in Honour of R S Sayers,* Clarendon Press, 1968, pp.x and 327

Bank Histories

Acres, W M — *The Bank of England from Within,* Oxford, 1931, 2 vols, pp.xvi and 328 and vii and 606

Andreades, A — *History of the Bank of England,* London, 1909, pp.xxxix and 455. Reprinted 1966

Anon. — *Antony Gibbs & Sons Ltd. Merchant Bankers 1808–1958,* privately printed, c1958, pp.136

Anon. — *The Arms Granted to the Union Bank of Scotland Ltd,* privately printed, pp.39

Anon. — *Arthur Heywood, Sons & Co, 1773–1883,* privately printed, 1949, pp.15

Anon. — *A Bank in Battledress being the Story of Barclays Bank (Dominion, Colonial and Overseas) during the Second World War 1939–45,* privately printed, 1948, pp.viii and 212

Anon. — *Bank of London and South America. A Short History 1862–1970,* privately printed, 1970, pp.28

Anon. — *A Banking Centenary. Barclays Bank (Dominion, Colonial and Overseas) 1836–1936,* privately printed, 1936, pp.270

Anon. — *Cater Ryder. Discount Bankers 1816–1966,* privately printed, 1966, pp.16

Anon. — *Decades of the Ulster Bank 1836–1964,* Belfast, 1965, pp.xiii and 274

Anon. — *Gosling's Branch 1650–1950,* privately printed, (Barclays Bank Ltd), c1950, pp.16

Anon. — *Hambro's Bank Ltd 1839–1939,* privately printed, 1939, pp.iii and 43

Anon. — *History of Knowles and Foster 1828–1948,* privately printed, 1948, pp.92

Anon. — *Hoare's Bank. A Record 1672–1955,* privately printed, 1932 (revised edition 1955), pp.x and 116

Anon. — *Manchester Exchange and Investment Bank Ltd 1876–1976,* privately printed, 1976, pp.6

Anon. — *Morgan, Grenfell & Co 1838–1958,* privately printed, pp.xiii and 30

Anon. — *Prescott's Bank 1766–1966,* privately printed, c1966, pp.16

Anon. — *Reliance Bank Ltd,* privately printed, 1951, pp.28

Anon. — *A Short History of the London and South Western Bank Ltd,* London, 1913, pp.32

Anon. — *Standard Chartered Bank. A Story Brought up to Date,* privately printed, 1980, pp.65

Anon. — *Story of the Lancashire and Yorkshire Bank Ltd 1872–1922,* 1922, pp.102

Anon. — *Williams Deacon's 1771–1970,* privately printed, 1971, pp.xi and 180

[Bareau, P] — *Ionian Bank Ltd. A History,* privately printed, 1953, pp.47

Bidwell, W H — *Annals of an East Anglian Bank* (Gurney & Co), Norwich, 1900, pp.vii and 411

Blainey, G — *Gold and Paper. A History of the National Bank of Australasia Ltd*, Melbourne, 1958, pp.xiii and 430

Bolitho, H and **Peel, D** — *The Drummonds of Charing Cross*, London, 1967, pp.232

Bramsen, B and **Wain, K** — *The Hambros 1799–1979*, London, 1979, pp.457

Broomhead, L J — *The Great Oak: a Story of the Yorkshire Bank*, 1981, pp.100

Brown, J C — *Hundred Years of Merchant Banking. A History of Brown Brothers & Co, Brown Shipley & Co and the Allied Firms*, New York, 1909

Chandler, G — *Four Centuries of Banking as Illustrated by the Banks, Customers and Staff Associated with the Constituent Banks of Martins Bank Ltd*, London, 2 vols: vol 1, 1964, pp.572; vol 2, 1968, pp.608

Chapman, S D — 'The Foundation of the English Rothschilds: N M Rothschild as a Textile Merchant', *Textile History*, 8, 1977

Chappell, N M — *New Zealand Banker's Hundred. A History of the Bank of New Zealand 1861–1961*, Wellington, 1961, pp.408

Clapham, Sir John — *The Bank of England. A History 1694–1944*, 2 vols, Cambridge, 1944. Reprinted 1970, pp.x and 305 and 7 and 460

Clarke, P — *The First House in the City. An Excursion into the History of Child and Co to Mark its 300th Year of Banking at the Same Address*, London, 1973, pp.67

Collis, M — *Wayfoong. The Hongkong and Shanghai Banking Corporation*, London, 1965, pp.xx and 269

Corti, Count E C — *The Rise of the House of Rothschild* and *The Reign of the House of Rothschild*, London, 1928, pp.463 and pp.xii and 511

Cottrell, P L — 'London Financiers and Austria 1863–1875. The Anglo Austrian Bank', *Business History*, xi, 2, 1969

Crick, W F and **Wadsworth, J E** — *A Hundred Years of Joint Stock Banking*, London, 1936, pp.vii and 464

Crossley, Sir J and **Blandford, J** — *The DCO Story. A History of Banking in Many Countries 1925–71*, privately printed, 1975, pp.xxvii and 339

Dennett, L M — *The Charterhouse Group 1925–1979*, London, 1979, pp.175

Dixon, K F — *The Story of Alexanders Discount Co Ltd 1810–1960*, privately printed, c1960, pp.8

Easton, H T — *The History of a Banking House. Smith, Payne & Smiths*, London, 1903, pp.xvi and 127

Ellis, A — *Bold Adventure*, privately printed (National Provincial Bank Ltd), c1960s, pp.26

Ellis, A — *Heir of Adventure. The Story of Brown, Shipley & Co. Merchant Bankers 1810–1960*, privately printed, 1960, pp.vi and 165

Forbes, Sir W — *Memoirs of a Banking House* (Sir William Forbes, James Hunter & Co), Edinburgh, 1860, pp.ix and 92

Fry, R — *Bankers in West Africa. The Story of the Bank of British West Africa Ltd*, London, 1976, pp.xiii and 270

Fulford, R — *Glyn's 1753–1953. Six Generations in Lombard St*, London, 1953, pp.xvi and 267

Gibbs, J A — *The History of Antony and Dorothea Gibbs*, privately printed, 1922, pp.xvi and 509

Giuseppi, J — *The Bank of England*, London, 1966, pp.xii and 224

Gladstone, J S — *History of Gillanders, Arbuthnot & Co and Ogilvy, Gillanders & Co*, 1910

Gore-Brown, E — *Glyn Mills & Co*, privately printed, 1933, pp.200

Green, E — *The Making of a Modern Banking Group. A History of the Midland Bank since 1900*, privately printed, 1979, pp.xii and 116

Gregory, T E — *Westminster Bank Ltd through a Century*, Oxford, 1936, 2 vols, pp.xii and 396 and viii and 355

Henry, J A and **Siepmann, H A** (eds)
The First Hundred Years of the Standard Bank, Oxford, 1963, pp.ix and 371

Hidy, R W
The House of Baring in American Trade and Finance 1763–1861, Harvard, 1949 (reprinted 1970), pp.xxiv and 631

Hunt, W
Heirs of Great Adventure. The History of Balfour, Williamson & Co Ltd 1851–1951, privately printed, 1951, pp.216

Isaac, A W
The Worcester Old Bank, privately printed, 1908

Jones, G
'Lombard St on the Riviera. The British Clearing Bank and Europe 1900–1960', *Business History*, xxiv, 1982

Joslin, D M
A Century of Banking in Latin America to Commemorate the Centenary in 1962 of The Bank of London and South America Ltd, Oxford, 1963, pp.xi and 307

Keith, A
The North of Scotland Bank Ltd 1836–1936, Aberdeen, 1936, pp.viii and 188

Leader, R E
The Sheffield Banking Co Ltd, Sheffield, 1916, pp.vii and 137

Leighton-Boyce, J A S L
Smiths the Bankers, privately printed, 1958, pp.xiii and 337

Lloyd, H
The Quaker Lloyds in the Industrial Revolution, London, 1975, pp.xiv and 322

Lloyd, S
The Lloyds of Birmingham, Birmingham, 1907, pp.xvi and 246

Mackenzie, C
Realms of Silver. One Hundred Years of Banking in the East, London, 1954, pp.xiv and 338

Malcolm, C A
British Linen Bank. A History, privately printed, 1950, pp.xii and 251

Marriner, S
Rathbones of Liverpool 1845–73, 1961, pp.xi and 246

Martin, J B
The Grasshopper in Lombard St, London, 1892, pp.xx and 328

Matthews, P W and **Tuke, A W**
History of Barclays Bank Ltd, London, 1926, pp.xiv and 441

Mottram, R H
The Westminster Bank 1836–1936, 1936, pp.28

Munro, N
The Royal Bank of Scotland 1727–1927, privately printed, 1928, pp.xviii and 416

Price, F G H
The Marygold by Temple Bar being a History of the Site now occupied by . . . the Banking House of Child & Co, London, 1902, pp.xliii and 202

Rait, R S
The Union Bank of Scotland. A History, privately printed, 1930, pp.xviii and 392

Reid, J M
History of the Clydesdale Bank 1836–1938, Blackie, 1938, pp.ix and 299

Robinson, R M
Coutts Bank, London, 1929, pp.xii and 189

Roth, C
The Sassoon Dynasty, London, 1941, pp.280

Sayers, R S
The Bank of England 1891–1944, Cambridge, 1976, 3 vols, vol.1, xxiv and 385, vol.2, vi and 385–680, vol.3, viii and 403

Sayers, R S
Gilletts in the London Money Market 1867–1967, Oxford, 1968, pp.viii and 204

Sayers, R S
Lloyds Bank in the History of English Banking, Oxford, 1957, pp.xiv and 381

Saunders, P T
Stuckey's Bank, Taunton, 1928, pp.viii and 116

Taylor, A M
Gilletts. Bankers at Banbury and Oxford, Oxford, 1964, pp.xiii and 247

Tuke, A W and **Gillman, R J H**
Barclays Bank Ltd 1926–69. Some Recollections, privately printed, 1972, pp.viii and 167

Turner, B B
Chronicles of the Bank of England, 1897, pp.xii and 296

Tyson, G
100 Years of Banking in Asia and Africa 1863–1963 (National & Grindlays Bank Ltd), privately printed, 1963, pp.xii and 246

Wadsworth, J
Counter Defensive. The Story of a Bank in Battle, London, 1946, pp.106

Winton, J R
Lloyds Bank 1918–1969, Oxford, 1982, pp.xi and 210

Withers, H
National Provincial Bank 1833 to 1933, privately printed, 1933, pp.xi and 90

Biographies of Bankers

Amburger, C   *William Brandt and the Story of His Enterprises,* unpublished typescript, 1937, University of Nottingham Archives Dept

Boyle, A   *Montagu Norman. A Biography,* London, 1967, pp.xi and 349

Clay, Sir H   *Lord Norman,* London, 1957, pp.xi and 495

Coleridge, E H   *The Life of Thomas Coutts, Banker.* London, 1920, 2 vols, pp.xii and 305 and ix and 459

Currie, C L (ed)   *Bertram Wodehouse Currie 1827–96. Recollections. Letters and Journals,* privately printed, 1901, 2 vols

de Fraine, H G   *Servant of this House. Life in the old Bank of England.* London, 1960, pp.x and 200

Japhet, S   *Recollection from My Business Life,* privately printed, 1931, pp.159

Murray, A J   *Home from the Hill. A Biography of Frederick Huth. Napoleon of the City.* London, 1970, pp.xiii and 242

Rathbone, W   *William Rathbone. A Memoir,* privately printed, 1905

Index to Lists of Bank Records

Bank Title	List Number	Bank Title	List Number	Bank Title	List Number
Gotch (John C) & Sons	252	Hammond & Co	275	Hodgkin, Barnett, Pease,	
Grant, Gillman & Long	253	Hammond, Plumptre, Hilton,		Spence & Co	306
Grant & Maddison's Union		McMaster & Furley	276	Hollings, Dallaway & Co	307
Banking Co Ltd	253	Hampshire Banking Co	277	Holsworthy Bank	308
Greenock Banking Co	204	Hampshire & North Wilts		Holt & Co	309
Greenway, Smith & Greenway	254	Banking Co	119	Holt, King & Co	339
Greenwood, Cox & Co	166	Hanbury, Lloyd & Co	278	Holt, Lawrie & Co	309
Gregson (W), Sons, Park &		Hanbury, Taylor & Lloyd	278	Hongkong & Shanghai Banking	
Morland	255	Hankey & Co	279	Corp	310
Grindlay, Brandts Ltd	256	Hankey (Sir Joseph) & Co	279	Hoskins & Co	311
Guernsey Banking Co	257	Hankey (Joseph) Esq & Co	279	Huddersfield Banking Co Ltd	312
Guernsey Commercial		Hankey, Hall, Hankey &		Huddleston & Co	313
Banking Co Ltd	258	Alers	279	Hull Banking Co Ltd	314
Guinness, Mahon & Co	259	Hardcastle, Cross & Co	280	Hunt, Trim & Co	331
Gundry & Co	260	Harding & Co	281	Huth (Frederick) & Co	315
Gunner & Co	261	Hardy & Co	282		
Gurneys, Alexanders & Co	6	Harris & Co	284	Ideal Bank	316
Gurneys, Alexanders, Birkbeck,		Harris (Charles, Henry &		Imperial Bank of Iran	89
Barclay, Buxton & Kerrison	6	Alfred) & Co	284	Imperial Bank Ltd	317
Gurneys, Birkbeck, Barclay &		Harris, Butleel & Co	283	Imperial Bank of Persia	89
Buxton (Fakenham)	262	Harris, H A & W M	284	Innes & Clerk	318
Gurneys, Birkbeck, Barclay &		Hart, Fellows & Co	285	International Bank of London	
Buxton (Wisbech)	263	Hartsinck, Hutchinson &		Ltd	319
Gurneys, Birkbeck, Barclay,		Playfair	286	Ionian Bank Ltd	320
Buxton & Cresswell	264	Harvey & Hudsons	287	Isle of Man Joint Stock Bank	321
Gurneys, Birkbeck, Barclay,		Harwood & Co	288	Isle of Wight Joint Stock	
Buxton & Orde		Head (J M) & Co	289	Banking Co	322
(Gt Yarmouth)	265	Hector, Lacy & Co	290		
Gurneys, Birkbeck, Barclay,		Hedges, Wells & Co	291	Janvrin & Durell	505
Buxtons & Orde		Helston Banking Co	292	Jenner & Co	323
(Halesworth)	266	Hemming, Needham & Co	293	Jennings, F W	324
Gurneys, Round, Green & Co	267	Henley, Clarke, Wheadon &		Jersey Banking Co Ltd	325
Gurneys & Turner	266	Hallett	294	Jessel Toynbee & Co Ltd	326
Guthrie, James	268	Henty & Co	295	Jones & Blewitt	327
		Herefordshire Banking Co	296	Jones (David) & Co	328
Hack, Dendy, Hack &		Herries (Sir Robert) & Co	297	Jones & Davis	329
Farenden	408	Herries (Robert) & Co	297	Jones (William) & Son	330
Halifax Commercial Banking		Herries, Farquhar & Co	297	Jones, Wright & Co	304
Co Ltd	269	Heywood Brothers & Co	298		
Halifax Equitable Bank Ltd	215	Heywood (Arthur) Sons & Co	299	Kellow & Co	331
Halifax & Huddersfield Union		Heywoods, Kennard & Co	300	Kensingtons & Co	332
Banking Co	270	Higginson & Co	301	Kent, Surrey & Sussex Bank	374
Halifax Joint Stock Banking		Hill (Philip), Higginson,		Keyser (A) & Co Ltd	333
Co	602	Erlangers Ltd	301	King (Henry S) & Co	334
Hall, Bevan, West & Bevans	271	Hill Samuel & Co Ltd	302	Kinnersley & Sons	335
Hall & Morgan	272	Hill & Sons	303	Kleinwort, Benson Ltd	336
Hallifax, Glyn, Mills &		Hilton, Ridgen & Co	304	Kleinwort Sons & Co	336
Mitton	246	Hoare (C) & Co	305	Knapp (Henry) & John	
Halstead, Woodbridge,		Hoare (Henry) & Co	305	Tomkins	337
Gruggen & Gauntlett	408	Hoare (Henry Hugh) & Co	305	Knaresborough & Claro	
Hambro (C J) & Son	273	Hoare, Henry & Benjamin	305	Banking Co Ltd	338
Hambros Bank Ltd	273	Hoare, Henry & Richard	305	Knewney & King	339
Hambros Bank of Northern		Hoare (Benjamin) & Partners	305	Knight, Jenner & Co	340
Commerce Ltd	273	Hoare (Sir Richard) &			
Hammersley, Greenwood &		Partners	305	Lacons, Youell & Kemp	341
Brooksbank	274	Hoare (Richard) & Partners	305	Lacy, Hartland, Woodbridge	
Hammersley, Montolieu,		Hoare, Richard	305	& Co	342
Brooksbank, Greenwood &		Hodge & Co	243	Lacy & Son	342
Drewe	274			Lambton & Co	343

Bank Title	List Number
National Bank of South African Republic Ltd	425
National Bank of Wales Ltd	426
National Commercial Bank of Scotland	427
National Discount Co Ltd	428
National Provincial Bank of England	429
National Provincial Bank Ltd	429
National Provincial & Union Bank of England	429
Neville Reid & Co	430
New Oriental Bank Corp	458
Newcastle Commercial Joint Stock Banking Co	431
Newcastle, Shields & Sunderland Union Joint Stock Bank	432
Nicholls, Baker & Crane	433
Nightingale, John, William & George	434
Norfolk & Norwich Joint Stock Banking Co	435
North Devon Bank	436
North Eastern Banking Co Ltd	437
North of England Union Joint Stock Banking Co	438
North Kent Bank Ltd	439
North of Scotland Bank Ltd	440
North of Scotland & Town & County Bank Ltd	440
North & South Wales Bank Ltd	441
North Western Bank Ltd	442
North Wilts Banking Co	443
Northamptonshire Banking Co	444
Northamptonshire Central Banking Co	444
Northamptonshire Union Bank Ltd	445
Northcote (Sir S H) & Co	446
Northern & Central Bank of England	447
Northern Counties Bank Ltd	448
Northumberland & Durham District Bank	449
Nottingham & District Bank Ltd	450
Nottingham Joint Stock Bank Ltd	451
Nottingham & Nottinghamshire Banking Co	452
Nunn & Co	453
Oakes, Bevan & Co	454
Oakes, Bevan, Moore & Bevan	454

Bank Title	List Number
Oakes, Bevan, Tollemache & Co	454
Oakes, Fincham & Co	455
Oldaker, Tomes & Chattaway	574
Oldham Joint Stock Bank Ltd	456
Oliver, Oliver, Langhorn & Harrison	457
Oriental Bank Corp	458
Oriental Commercial Bank	459
Overend, Gurney & Co	460
Owen & Griffiths	461
P & O Banking Corporation Ltd	462
Paget & Co	463
Paisley Banking Co	464
Paisley Union Bank Co	465
Palatine Bank Ltd	466
Pardoe, Nicholls & Baker	433
Pares & Heygate	467
Pares Leicestershire Banking Co	467
Parker Shore & Co	468
Parr, Lyon & Co	469
Parr's Bank Ltd	470
Parr's Banking Co & the Alliance Bank Ltd	470
Parr's Banking Co Ltd	470
Parsons, Thompson, Parsons & Co	471
Payler, Hammond, Simmons & Gipps	276
Payne & Co	472
Payne, Hope & Co	473
Peabody (George) & Co	420
Peacock, Handley & Co	474
Peacock, Willson & Co	474
Peckover, Harris & Co	284
Pease & Co	475
Pease (Joseph) & Co	476
Pease, J & J W	475
Pease, Knowsley & Co	476
Pease, Liddell & Co	476
Pedders & Co	478
Percival & Co	477
Perfect & Co	479
Perth Banking Co	480
Perth Parish Bank	481
Perth United Banking Co	482
Perth United Co	483
Pierson & Son	484
Pinkney Brothers	485
Plymouth & Devon Banking Co	187
Pocklington & Lacy	342
Pocklington, Rastell, Oliver & Ray	486
Pole, Thornton, Free, Down & Scott	487

Bank Title	List Number
Pomfret, Burra & Co	488
Praeds & Co (London)	489
Praeds & Co (Truro)	159
Prescott, Dimsdale, Cave, Tugwell & Co Ltd	490
Prescott, Grote, Culverden & Hollingsworth	490
Prescott's Bank Ltd	490
Preston Banking Co Ltd	491
Pretor & Co	492
Priaulx le Marchant & Co	257
Pritchard, Gordon & Co	493
ProvincialBanking Corp Ltd	379
Pugh, Jones & Co	494
Pybus, Dorset & Cockell	394
Raikes, Thomas & Robert	495
Raikes (Robert), Williams & Isaac Currie	495
Ransom, Bouverie & Co	496
Ransom & Co	496
Ransom, Morland & Co	497
Ransom, Morland & Hammersley	496
Raphael, Robinson & Glyn	498
Raphael (R) & Sons Ltd	498
Rawdon, Briggs & Sons	499
Reade, Moorhouse & Co	619
Reeves & Porch	500
Rhodes, Briggs & Garlick	499
Richards & Co	501
Riches & Co	97
Ridley (Sir M) Bart., Chas Wm Bigge & Co	502
Ridley, Bell, Wilkinson & Gibson	502
Ridley, Bigge, Gibson & Co	502
Ridley, Cookson, Widdrington, Bell & Co	502
Robarts, Curtis & Co	503
Roberts & Gregory	504
Roberts, Skey & Kenrick	433
Robertson, Fraser & Co	390
Robin Brothers	505
Robins, Foster, Coode & Bolitho	506
Robinson (James & George) & Co	507
Rochdale Commercial Loan & Discount Co Ltd	508
Rochdale Joint Stock Bank Ltd	508
Rocke, Eyton & Co	221
Roskell, Arrowsmith & Co	509
Rothschild (N M) & Sons Ltd	510
Round, Green & Co	267
Round, Green & Hoare & Co	267
Royal Bank	511
Royal Bank of Australia	512